D0021766

FATTY
FATTY
BOOM
BOOM

FATTY
FATTY
BOOM
BOOM

A Memoir of Food, Fat, and Family

RABIA CHAUDRY

ALGONQUIN BOOKS OF CHAPEL HILL   2022

Published by
ALGONQUIN BOOKS OF CHAPEL HILL
an imprint of WORKMAN PUBLISHING CO., INC., a subsidiary of
HACHETTE BOOK GROUP, INC.
1290 Avenue of the Americas
New York, New York 10104

Library of Congress Cataloging-in-Publication Data

Names: Chaudry, Rabia, author.
Title: Fatty fatty boom boom / Rabia Chaudry.
Description: Chapel Hill, North Carolina : Algonquin Books of Chapel Hill, [2022] |
Summary: "A memoir about food, body image, and growing up in
a loving but sometimes oppressively concerned Pakistani immigrant family"
—Provided by publisher.
Identifiers: LCCN 2022025653 | ISBN 9781643750385 (hardcover) |
ISBN 9781643753430 (ebook)
Subjects: LCSH: Chaudry, Rabia. | Pakistani American women—Biography.
| Pakistani Americans—Biography. | Pakistani Americans—Food. | Pakistani
Americans—Social life and customs. | Body image—United States—Psychological
aspects. | Overweight persons—United States—Social conditions. Classification:
LCC E184.P28 C53 2022 | DDC 305.8914/122073092 [B]—dc23/eng/20220615
LC record available at https://lccn.loc.gov/2022025653

10 9 8 7 6 5 4 3 2 1
First Edition

This book is dedicated to all the mothers who taught me their ways in the kitchen: Ami, Zuby Aunty, Nani Amma, Lilly, and my mothers-in-law, both current and, yes, even the ex.

It is also dedicated to Abu, my rock through literally thick and thin, and to Irfan, my partner in fatty and fitness pursuits for the past sixteen years.

Finally, it is dedicated to all those who have spent their lives being judged—and judging themselves—for their weight, who have struggled between deprivation and depravity, and who deserve like anyone else to live an abundant life full of great food.

Damned if you do, damned if you don't.

CONTENTS

ONE

Doodh, Dhai, Makhan: Milk, Yogurt, Butter

She swears the first time she saw him was on their wedding night. Her family had tried to show her his picture, but she turned away from it, resigned to her inescapable future. What was the point when she had no choice but to marry him?

That's how the legend goes, legend precisely because while everyone who knows my mother has heard the story hundreds of times, it could be completely made up. She's like that, and if it makes for a good story, it gets repeated until it's canon.

Back to the wedding though.

Khalida Khanum Ghauri, intimidating in name and presence, my Ami, was a singularly independent woman in 1970s Lahore, Pakistan. At the age of twenty-six, when the marriage proposal came to her, she was the headmistress of the Lahore Girls College, a position she had held for half a decade at that point. No one becomes a headmistress at the tender age of twenty, in charge of overseeing much more senior staff and faculty, unless they're a force to be reckoned with.

Few were as formidable as Ami. She was tall and slender, but big-boned like her father and his sisters: broad shoulders, large hands and feet, a frame just begging to be filled out. Her jet-black hair hung straight down to her waist in a tightly knit braid. She had large almond eyes over a delicate, sharp nose, and perfect bow lips that were almost permanently pressed into a sober, and sobering, line.

She was not one for nonsense. All six of her younger siblings knew it, and so did her parents. She barely mixed with the family, claiming the sole bedroom on the second floor for herself. Every morning her bird-like mother delivered a tray of breakfast before the headmistress left for work in a horse-drawn tanga, a covered buggy reserved for her commute. Every morning she got an egg fried in pure ghee, a luxury no other sibling was afforded.

In the evening, when she returned home, she retired to her room, where a dinner tray was brought to her—usually a choice piece of meat in a rich, brown broth, with rice saved from that night's supper and covered with a lace doily. Meat that, again, not everyone in the large family was given.

Still, she felt suffocated, not just by the six siblings who were constantly present, but by the countless other relatives who rotated through their home in a continuous stream, including distant relations who would camp out for months in the already cramped quarters.

Ami both valued her independence and had developed a distaste for the institution of marriage itself, seeing women she knew—aunts, cousins, friends, and even her own mother—lose their identity and freedom in a morass of in-laws and squealing babies.

And for that reason, Khalida had rejected every marriage proposal sent her way since she had come of marriageable age.

Her stubborn refusals filled her parents with trepidation, as they considered how to approach her with my father's proposal.

But this time, things were different.

Nana Abu, my maternal grandfather, a towering, barrel-chested deputy superintendent of police, was sick. Years of indulging in syrupy sweets had done a number on him, but even raging diabetes wasn't enough to convince him to clean up his eating habits. He had lived pleasing his palate, and would die doing so, too.

Nana Abu had been recently released from the hospital and was convalescing at home, but the writing was on the wall. If his eldest daughter didn't accept this marriage proposal, he would likely die without seeing any of his children married.

He called Khalida to his bedside. She listened as he told her she couldn't say no to this proposal, not this time. At twenty-six, she was virtually a spinster. The proposals, which once came fast and frequent, had nearly sputtered out. She had run out of time because he had run out of time. There were pictures of the prospective groom, he said, if she wanted to see. She quietly walked away, but this time without refusing the proposal.

That was her grudging acquiescence.

There was little to celebrate as far as Ami was concerned. What she knew didn't fill her with any excitement or joy. Her groom-to-be was thirty-two years old, a widower, and he came from a large middle-class Punjabi family on the other side of town.

Punjabis, she sniffed. She couldn't believe she was going to be married into Punjabis.

Sure, she had been born and raised in Lahore, the heart of Punjab province, but that was only because in 1946 her family, like many other Muslims, had left Delhi after rumblings of the Partition of India were beginning to grow. They made it into what would become Pakistan right before Ami was born, in January 1947, eight months before the border was drawn.

By that point, the British imperial project in India had lasted nearly two hundred years, beginning with the British East India Company, a trading company, seizing massive parts of the subcontinent thanks to its own private army. The company competed with the Dutch and

Portuguese to strip India of natural resources, harvesting and selling her spices, cotton, silk, tea, indigo dye, and other goods, and grew so prosperous they eventually controlled half of the entire world's trade.

After a hundred years, and in the face of an uprising by Indian soldiers in that private army, control of the company was transferred to the Crown, thus beginning the era of the British Raj in the subcontinent. In 1876 Queen Victoria was declared the Empress of India, and a decade later the Indian National Congress emerged, in opposition to the colonial rulers.

The call for independence grew over the next six decades, and under the leadership of inspirational political leaders such as Mahatma Gandhi, Jawaharlal Nehru, and Muhammad Ali Jinnah, it eventually became reality. But another call ran parallel to the call for independence from Great Britain: a demand for partition and thus the creation of a sovereign nation for Muslims, who comprised 20 percent of the Indian population. In 1940 Jinnah, the leader of the Muslim League party, delivered a resounding two-hour speech that came to be known as the "Pakistan Resolution." It eventually became clear to the British that a transition to independence for India couldn't be achieved without the creation of Pakistan as well.

And so the last British viceroy of India, Lord Louis Mountbatten, a highly celebrated and decorated navy commander, was tasked with splitting the motherland in two and overseeing the transition to independence by June of 1948.

But he didn't want to take that long.

Mountbatten, fearful of rising violence, accelerated the independence plan, calling for it to be executed within six months. Three months after he landed in India, a proposed border, the Radcliffe Line, was drawn between what would be the two new nations, initiating what became historically known as the Partition.

The line cut through existing provinces, towns, and villages, and triggered horrifying violence among Hindus, Sikhs, and Muslims, and when independence was declared for both nations in August of that year, the largest cross-border migration in history took place.

Over 14 million people moved from one side of the new border to the other, and at least a million died during the migration, casualties of horrific communal violence across the region. All hands were bloody—Muslim, Hindu, and Sikh—as Hindus and Sikhs left Pakistan for India, replaced by Muslims who emigrated from cities across mostly northern India.

My mother's family had seen the inevitable and decided not to wait until the two nations officially parted ways to leave Delhi. Before the bloody riots began, they moved to the ancient city of Lahore, in the province of Punjab, which was eventually split between India and Pakistan. They were already settled in their new home when, in August of 1947, independence was declared, and consequently none of the family fell victim to the ensuing violence.

Lahore was an unusual choice for Delhiites to move to; many had crossed right through Punjab and chosen urbane Karachi as their new home. But Ami's family had to settle where her father was now stationed.

Lahore was their new, permanent home, but they were muhajir: immigrants from cosmopolitan centers of culture, now in the land of agricultural, folksy Punjabis. The two didn't even sound remotely alike. The muhajir proudly identified as "Urdu-speaking," Urdu being the polite, refined language of Mughal cities like Delhi and Lucknow, of classical literature and poetry, of intellectuals and royalty, of etiquette and formality. Urdu was rich, complex, and sophisticated.

Punjabi, on the other hand, sounded to my mother's ears as unrefined as she believed the Punjabi people, whether Hindu, Sikh, or Muslim, themselves were. Punjabi was guttural and bouncy, with pointed, yelpy inflections. It was the language of the farmer, of the villager, of rabble-rousers and milk sellers and sleazy young men catcalling on the street. There was no shaking the tonality of it, and even when Punjabis spoke Urdu, they mangled the pronunciation with that unmistakable accent. There was, maybe, some sweetness to the informality of it, to how it made even strangers feel familiar; nonetheless, it was low-class. To her, that is.

When the Partition took place, these two cultures collided. Those new Urdu-speaking Muslim arrivals were, and would always be, outsiders, muhajirs.

Urdu-speaking muhajirs.

This culture clash hasn't smoothed over with the passage of time. From media to politics to entertainment to communal affairs to neighborhoods and families, the divide and sometimes outright distrust, disdain, and dislike, remains.

As do the stereotypes.

Punjabis—rural, uneducated, loud, and uncouth.

Muhajirs—stingy, elitist, untrustworthy, and snobby.

Believe me, with family from both sides, I've heard it all.

And at that time, Ami was hearing a lot more of it, from giggling cousins to aunts and uncles teasing her about marrying a Punjabi man. The entire family had been in Lahore for decades by now, and she was often herself mistaken for Punjabi, thanks to her height and build, but once inside the gates of her family home, they poked fun at the "simpletons" they were surrounded by.

And then there was the food.

Here she was, hailing from Delhi, the land of Mughal culinary delights, with dishes developed in royal courts combining spices and seasonings and aromatics from across their vast empire. There were dozens of ways to prepare meat alone—roasted or fried into kababs, goat cooked in delicately aromatic broths, rich beef shanks stewed overnight, minced meat shaped into meatballs stuffed with boiled eggs, hunks of spiced chicken layered with fragrant basmati rice in biryanis. Not like

Punjabis, who subsisted on lentils and vegetables and waxed eloquent about their saag and daal as if they were princely dishes instead of village staples.

Farm animals eat like that, she thought.

The final blow to her pride, though, was this: Her groom-to-be, while referred to as Dr. Anwarul Haq Chaudry, was no real doctor at all. He was a veterinarian. Which meant he spent his days around large, fetid farm animals, knee deep in their manure, arm deep inside heaving, birthing beasts, his profession as undignified as his clientele. She could only imagine how he must smell when he returned home after work.

Ami wasn't completely wrong. After all, there wasn't much of a culture in Pakistan of raising household pets, cats and dogs were mostly street animals living on scraps, often scrawny and starving, despised scavengers not allowed into homes. No one kept pets. People had animals because they needed them. Chickens for meat and eggs, cows and buffalos for milk, but families like hers bought their dairy from shops, and didn't tie up some poor cow in their courtyard.

Raising animals was the provenance of the uneducated.

What she didn't know was that while, yes, Dr. Anwarul Haq Chaudry didn't attend to pampered kittens and poodles, he also wasn't stuck with farm animals all day. He was the head doctor at the national zoo, and his patients were elephants, bears, and tigers. She had no way of knowing this because she refused to meet him or his family, although a large contingent of his sisters often swung by, irritating her to no end.

Dressed head to toe in colorful burkas, all five of her future sisters-in-law would descend unannounced, causing a flurry of anxiety and activity as her parents, siblings, and cousins scattered to pull together a lavish chai service. That was the custom. One brother would be sent to fetch spicy, freshly fried samosas, while another was dispatched to grab ice-cold bottles of Coca-Cola. Her father would bellow to a servant to rush to the halwai, the sweet maker down the street, and bring back hot, crisp, cloying jalebis, which came in brown bags soaked with warm, sticky syrup.

Ami's sister, her only sister, a decade younger, would squeeze into the tiny kitchen with their mother, hurriedly putting eggs on to boil, shaping minced meat and lentil patties to fry into shaami kabab, and carefully measuring out spoonfuls of dark, dried loose-leaf tea into a cauldron of water. They had only two small gas burners at their disposal, and getting everything ready quickly meant first ensuring the gas tank wasn't empty, and then juggling pots and frying pans back and forth so everything came out hot and ready at the same time.

You couldn't have cold kababs and hot tea, or cold tea and hot eggs. That would be a disaster.

The best china cups and saucers and half-plates would be arranged on trays, and tiny old silver spoons, flecked with black, polished but unwaveringly dull, were fanned out on a small platter.

Ami sat in her room the entire time, listening to the hustle and bustle, knowing how much every visit cost her family in both time and money, how many dishes had to be washed afterward, how the younger siblings and cousins would sit and watch greedily as their guests bit into all the goodies they rarely got to enjoy. It wasn't that they were poor. They had never gone hungry a single day in their lives. But they weren't rich either, and there were six huge appetites in the home. Her bearlike father and her five brothers, who grew like weeds, becoming broader and taller by the week, each one easily reaching six feet by the time their adolescence peaked, had appetites that matched their physiques.

One of her youngest brothers, nicknamed Pummy, spent his days occupied with food. From the moment he could walk and figured out where the huge bin of whole wheat flour was kept in the house, he would peek into it several times a day, asking their mother if there was enough to make his rotis. As he grew older, their mother would have to shoo him out of the kitchen, where he hovered around, wanting to help in the cooking, dipping his fingers right into boiling pots of stew to poach bits of meat and vegetables. He was always just a bit chubby, and no number of growth spurts slimmed down his softly rounded belly or saved him from the chiding and teasing.

None of the others were fat, because the kinds of foods that could make a person fat, like the goodies they served the flock of my father's sisters, rarely made it into their mouths. Sweets and sodas only came into the home to be served immediately to guests. Otherwise, these luxuries were only had at weddings, or holidays.

Or, if there were leftovers. But with these relatives-to-be, there never were. Because the five sisters came with half a dozen or more of their children in tow, and by the time they left, no more than crumbs remained.

From her room upstairs, Ami could just imagine her own little siblings and cousins sitting there politely, hoping against hope something would be left for them, while these other grubby kids gobbled salty boiled eggs and licked syrup from their fingers.

If I'm to believe my mother, whatever was left over would be wrapped up in napkins and hidden into the folds of the sisters' burkas, leaving nothing behind.

If I'm to believe Ami, which, as I've said, is not always completely possible.

The only saving grace of this family, it seemed to her at this point in time, were the two distinguished elder men—her future father-in-law and her future brother-in-law. The brother-in-law, Dr. Abdul Haq, was impressive and intimidating, standing well over six feet tall (in direct contrast to her intended groom, who was disappointingly just an inch taller than she), with a grand booming voice, always dressed sharply in full three-piece suits and thick black glasses. He was shockingly fair-skinned and could have passed for a firangi, a white man, while her intended was as deeply brown as burnt rice. Most important, Dr. Abdul Haq was *a real doctor*. Not an animal doctor.

And then there was her prospective father-in-law, half the size of his eldest son, but handsome, proud, elegant. He had lost his wife nearly three decades earlier, when he was only in his forties, and was left with seven children to raise by himself, the youngest only eight years old. He never remarried, a fact that was nearly impossible to believe, given his circumstances. Most men with his means and with the monumental child-rearing task he faced would have quickly remarried, if for no other reason than to have help managing the household.

Ami respected the fact that he had not.

What annoyed her was the fact that he was the reason she was getting saddled with this relationship. Her father-in-law had noticed the attractive, no-nonsense woman pull up to the Girls College every morning like clockwork in the horse-drawn buggy and had asked around about her. When he learned she was single and in her late twenties, he decided she would be a perfect match for his youngest son, now thirty-three years old.

His son had been married years before, but not long after their wedding, the young woman had passed away from an illness shrouded in mystery. She had become weaker and weaker over months and finally had returned to her own family home to be cared for. She never returned, dying at her mother's home. She had been pregnant, and the baby died with her.

Dead four years now, there was nothing left to remember her by. Not even a photograph. It was well past time for his son to remarry. And Khalida was the bride he had been seeking for his son.

LIKE AMI'S FAMILY, Abu's family also survived the Partition without losing any loved ones. When India had begun rumbling with talk of being split along religious lines, refugees had begun fleeing riots and landing in camps along what was to become the border. At the time, Abu's older brother, Abdul, was finishing up medical school in Lahore and, like other young doctors, traveled to the camps to help take care of the hundreds of thousands of people who were cramming together, sick from hunger and disease, exhausted from travel and fear.

After over a year of service, months after the Partition had become official and Pakistan had been born, he was asked by the camp's United Nations administrators if there was anything they could do for him, to repay him for his endless labor. He said yes. He asked that they help get his family safely to the new nation.

Abu, who was seven at the time, and his five older sisters and mother were alone in Hoshiarpur, Punjab, without the protection of Abu's father, who was stationed as a regional postmaster up north, in Azad Kashmir. This part of Punjab was to remain in India and some of their relatives had already left to cross the border into Lahore, but Abu's family couldn't risk the journey by themselves.

Trains were still crossing the border both ways, but passengers didn't always arrive safely. At times, "ghost trains" would pull into the station, full of the dead, mutilated bodies of migrants. Violent mobs set out to terrorize, kill, and loot those who were now seen as enemies as they tried to flee to a new home. Trains full of the dead bodies of Hindus and Sikhs leaving Pakistan arrived in stations in India, and trains full of the bloodied bodies of Muslims fleeing India arrived in stations in Pakistan.

The UN officials who granted my uncle the favor that would change our destiny forever booked an entire train carriage for his family and sent along four armed guards to escort them to Lahore, all the way to the house Dr. Abdul Haq had secured. Not long after, safe passage was arranged for my grandfather as well, and they reunited in the new nation, in their newly adopted city of Lahore. They had left one side of the Punjab border for the other and were never considered muhajir. They were Punjabi and remained Punjabi.

Little did Ami or Abu know that they would grow up just miles from each other, both families having joined the millions that started life over with whatever they could carry with them, leaving behind living family and friends, buried ancestors, ancestral homes, and histories.

IN AUGUST 1973, after the wedding, Ami moved into Abu's home, not far from her own. The trek took her ten minutes, from Sham Nagar to Sant Nagar, both older, quiet neighborhoods in the suburbs of Lahore. It was a joint family home, which is as common now as it was back then. While daughters were expected to marry and move out, sons never did. Their wives joined their family and became a part of it. They raised their children in the presence of grandparents, took care of their husbands' parents as they aged, and then, when the elders passed, themselves became heads of the household. A very convenient circle of life. It was a rational system that gave support to both young families and aging parents, that built in a sense of responsibility and duty to care for one another, to rely on each other. It was mutually assured survival, even if it was not always comfortable.

Especially because no matter how many sons were in the family, they would all end up sharing a house that itself couldn't grow any larger than the land it sat on.

My mother was lucky she had only one brother-in-law, who had only one son with his wife of twenty years. The older Dr. Haq and his small family occupied the top floor of the home, which had a sitting room, kitchen, bathroom, and three bedrooms. My parents were given the lower floor of the house, which had a bathroom and two large bedrooms.

One of those bedrooms belonged to Dada Abu, my paternal grandfather, and he was a deeply fair-minded man. While traditionally the daughters-in-law who joined a family were expected to take on household duties, Khalida was a working woman and no one made demands that she stop working outside the home after marriage. Yet she did still have to be responsible for at least taking care of her husband, if not the rest of the household. So Dada Abu came up with a plan. He had a small kitchen made on the lower floor for his new daughter-in-law, and she was expected to cook for herself and her husband there, while upstairs the elder daughter-in-law only took care of her own family's needs. This way neither was a burden to the other. And between the two women, they would take turns making meals for their father-in-law.

Thus began a two-year unspoken culinary rivalry between my mother and her sister-in-law, a sweet, quiet woman who was decades older, decades she had spent mostly hunched over a stove.

I knew her as Taya Amma, "taya" being the title of a father's older brother, and "amma," meaning "mother." Her relationship to me, and my siblings, was as a mother elder, and from the remaining memories I have of her, she lived up to the title. Taya Amma was the daughter of a high-ranking military officer, a distant relative of my father's family, and was raised in relative comfort. Her life was to change drastically with her marriage to Dr. Haq, my Taya Abu, who lacked much ability for human warmth and connection. He was serious and straitlaced, and devastated Taya Amma shortly after their marriage by telling her that he was in love with another woman. He had met and promised to marry this woman well before his father had arranged his marriage without even asking him. And he was a man of his word.

Taya Abu married Taya Amma under pressure from his father, but religious law allowed him to take up to four wives, though it was a practice unheard of in his family. He would be the first, and last, in his family to be married to more than one woman at a time.

When Taya Abu fulfilled his promise to marry the woman he loved, both his father and my father stopped speaking to him—they abhorred the practice of polygamy—and refused to allow the other woman anywhere near the shared home.

Taya Abu thought marrying both women would absolve him of his guilt and make everyone happy. In reality his solution made everyone miserable. Taya Abu knew the price and condition of polygamy, and the reason most men avoided it was that every wife had to be treated equally and equitably, as literally as possible. One couldn't be favored over the other in any way, in time spent together, in financial support, or in affection. Taya Abu was exacting in this obligation, and spent one day at one wife's home, and the other day at the other wife's home, his time divided equally.

It wasn't like he was home much anyway, his days busy in his medical clinic and hospital, and at night he and Taya Amma slept in separate beds. That was partly because of the nature of their relationship, and partly because Taya Amma weighed over 300 pounds.

She had not always been this heavy, of course, but I imagine the weight came on over the many lonely years she spent confined mostly to the top level of that house, raising her son, Rehman. He was as handsome and strapping as his father, and just as serious and brooding. In the oppressive silence of the house, Rehman was her lifeline, and she was his. They shared a fearful respect of Dr. Haq, and mostly stayed out of his way.

Because of her weight, standing for long periods of time was impossible for Taya Amma. So a special stove was built on the floor of the kitchen, and there she sat, perched on a large woven footstool, for hours and hours a day. That was her throne, the headquarters from where she ordered around the house help, where she could look out of a small stone window into the garden and catch a glimpse of sky, and maybe a breeze. Everything she needed for her cooking—mixing bowls and spoons, a wooden mortar and pestle, a chimta (long steel tongs to flip rotis), even a sil wata (a large stone slab used to grind meat and masalas by hand)— were placed within her reach so she never had to stand up.

In the mornings she prepared the same breakfast daily for "Doctor Sahib," as she called her husband. Two fried eggs, two slices of buttered toast, and hot chai. He was not one for Pakistani-style breakfasts of spicy omelets and ghee-fried parathas, the tastier, layered flatbread sibling of the roti. Once Taya Abu left for work, the fruit and vegetable hawkers began making their rounds of the neighborhoods, and their offerings determined what would be cooked that day. Taya Amma would lean out of her second-story window and inspect the baskets perched precariously on bicycles or creaky wooden carts.

"What's good today? How much?" she asked, like all the neighborhood wives. Once a deal was struck, she would send down one of the help to fetch the okra or sweet peas or spinach or mustard greens or whatever was in season.

And then she would crouch again carefully on the stool, ready to prep. Doctor Sahib loved sweet peas, fried lightly with some salt and pepper, so at least a few times a week, on the days he was with her, she bought and shelled them fresh for his dinner. She first had to get lunch prepared, packed, and sent to the clinic by noon, so it arrived hot and fresh, along with a thermos of chai. Once that was taken care of, she turned her attention to dinner, sending the house help to pick up only what she needed for that night's meal. A few pounds of meat, some sprigs of cilantro, a small bag of garlic and ginger, and a handful of tiny, heat-packed green chilies, enough for exactly one dish, because there was no fridge.

The very idea of cold-storing fresh ingredients or leftover food was anathema. Who wanted to cook meat and vegetables that had been sitting around for days, weeks even? The flavor and quality of meat that had just been slaughtered, of vegetables and fruits just picked that morning, couldn't be compromised. And leftovers? Well, there was always someone needy passing by who would welcome a meal.

Preparing and serving these three meals to the three men in the house—her husband, son, and father-in-law—was Taya Amma's singular purpose every day, whether or not she wanted it to be. When my mother moved into the house, finally, after twenty years, Taya Amma had something new to occupy her time. New blood in that old stone house was exciting to everyone, and Taya Amma finally had someone to chat with in the evenings and weekends, someone to share family gossip with, and someone to share the duty of feeding her father-in-law with. She was eager to see if this working professional woman could even cook.

And Khalida was eager to prove that she absolutely could.

Ami made great show of differentiating her cooking from what her new family was used to. She brought the flavors of Delhi to this household of simple Punjabi eaters, and she reveled in their praise. Meat, she thought, was something that was simply beyond the ability of Punjabi women to handle. They chucked dozens of spices at it, stewed it in tons of oil and onions, the flavors heavy and greasy. There was no delicacy in their cooking, it was just solid and hearty. But my mother could take a pound of stringy, tough goat and create a light, aromatic shorba from it, coaxing all the flavors from the bone out into a broth that began with a base of browned onions and stewed tomatoes seasoned with cumin and black cardamom and clove and garlic and ginger. You could pick up a bowl of it and drink it down, or pour it over fluffy white rice, or soak chunks of roti in it.

The first time Ami made it and served it to Dada Abu, he paused after putting a shorba-soaked morsel of roti in his mouth, slowly licking his fingers. Then he called out in his huge voice to his elder daughter-in-law, who leaned over the second-floor rail, peering into the verandah below.

"Come here!" he bellowed. "Eat this! This, THIS is how you make a shorba!"

Ami smugly sent a bowl of it upstairs, happy to prove her domestic skills and stake her claim as one who was culinarily superior to these *simple* people.

This went on with dish after dish for the first year.

And then, I came along.

•••

WHILE MY FATHER'S five sisters had, between them, dozens of children, the Chaudry house in Sant Nagar had only seen one grandchild, Rehman, raised in it. There had been too many years since bottles and diapers and infant cries had filled up the space, and when Ami announced she was pregnant, the entire house buzzed with anticipation.

Dada Abu, full of excitement and pride, was going to ensure his daughter-in-law had the healthiest pregnancy possible by making certain she was as well nourished as possible.

Within days, a glossy black buffalo stood in a corner of the yard, tied to a stake, quietly munching on stacks of greens and hay. A servant was tasked to milk her as the sun rose, boil the milk, and deliver a tall brass glass, steamy and brimming, to my mother. She was to drink one glass each morning before work, and one glass every evening after dinner.

There was a reason Dada Abu bought a buffalo and not a cow. Cow milk couldn't hold a candle to buffalo milk, which left any vessel that contained it slick and greasy. Buffalo milk has twice the fat content of cow milk, twice as many calories, and a good deal more protein. A cup of pure, unadulterated buffalo milk forms a thick layer of cream after being boiled, and even after the cream is removed, there will remain globs of oil floating on top.

Not everyone can stomach the heaviness of it, or the fatty, rich, unmistakably buffalo-scented aroma. It made my mother nauseous, but she held her nose and chugged it down. How could she refuse when an entire living beast had been purchased just for her? Every drop of fatty goodness was captured from that milk. The cream was skimmed off, to be churned into butter or spread straight onto toast sprinkled with sugar. Buckets every week were turned into tangy, thick yogurt, which was then whipped into lassi, both salty and sweet.

My mother's tall, lanky framed filled out, and by the end of the pregnancy she was shaped, approximately, like her sizeable father. Unfortunately, he didn't live to see it. While he was able to witness his eldest get married, he never got to meet any of his grandchildren. He died a few months before I was born, but at least he learned I was coming. More important, it brought him a lot of relief knowing that my mother, who he half suspected would eventually refuse all the labors of marriage and return home, was now irrevocably tied to the relationship.

Not long after he passed away, my mother had an extraordinary vision about her father. Or rather, he visited her in a dream, as she tells it. In the dream, he gave her a gleaming silver bowl that shone like the moon, shone so bright you could barely look at it. That bowl, he said, was a symbol of the daughter she was going to have.

I've heard the story of the bowl hundreds of times, not in a "I knew you were going to be extraordinary and dazzling when you were born" way, but more like a "you're supposed to be extraordinary and dazzling, I'm waiting" kind of way. High expectations for a newborn, and I didn't immediately disappoint. My mother says (and, yes, I've decided to believe her on this one) that nurses told her I was one of the most beautiful babies they'd ever seen. I was rosy and plump but didn't look like the average newborn. My face wasn't all swollen, nose flattened, eyes squeezed shut from the pressure of delivery. I looked, she said, like my features had been hand carved. Nose pointed and delicate, large almond eyes like her own, and tiny bow-shaped mouth.

The disappointment took a few more days to arrive, when I was struck with jaundice. My creamy rosy skin began to yellow and the whites of my huge eyes turned a hideous, blood-streaked gold. I raged with fever, nothing the nurses did was helping, and my mother was certain I wouldn't make it.

When Taya Abu learned what was happening to his newborn niece, he was livid with the doctors and nurses at the hospital. He ordered that we be discharged and brought immediately home, where he had blocks of ice delivered. He put down towels on the ice and laid me there, completely naked, until the fever subsided.

My mother is convinced that if he hadn't done that, I wouldn't have survived. She's also convinced that the fever not only burned me up on the inside, but also burned up my wheatish skin and pink cheeks, leaving me looking as brown as if I had been left in the oven too long. There is an argument to be made that my carob-colored father's DNA has something to do with my skin tone, but my mother refuses to believe it. Besides, her brother-in-law told her not to worry, that by the time I turned sixteen my skin tone would return to its original fairness, a promise she banked on until I turned sixteen and nothing changed.

Well, at least I was still alive.

Alive, but now dark and scrawny.

The scrawny part, they weren't so worried about. But the dark part could haunt me for the rest of my life. The minute I was born, like other little girls from that generation and earlier ones, the score sheet of my future marriageability had gone live.

Now firmly in the dark-skinned camp, I had already lost a lot of ground.

It was the evil eye that got me, my mother was sure of it. That gaggle of sisters-in-law had all come to the hospital to quietly peer at me, size me up for one of their dozens of sons (cousin marriage is a thing on the subcontinent, for better or worse), and also pass judgment on my mother's womb.

The sighs were deep and heavy. A daughter. Their younger brother's first child was a girl. It wasn't the end of the world, but a first-born son was just so much more desirable. A son would grow up to take care of his parents, but a girl would be raised and basically just given away to another family. A son would bring home a wife, and the wife's dowry. A daughter meant you had to establish a dowry and give it away in order to marry her off.

Sons relieved you of burdens, and daughters brought them on. When you've been raised to believe that this is just how it is, it's natural to keep passing it on. My mother, however, broke the mold ever so slightly. True, she married and didn't take care of her parents financially, but she did work outside the home, unlike any of her husband's sisters. She wasn't a burden to anyone, financially or otherwise. And she wasn't about to raise a daughter who would be, either.

Still, she looked at my deep caramel skin and knew, twenty years down the line, it could be a problem for me, because that's just how it is. Fair skin was premium, something she knew from personal experience, because between her and her own much-younger sister, she was the darker one, and no one had ever failed to point it out.

Not to worry. Dada Abu had the fix. Dada Abu was not only the postmaster director of the region but was also an amateur hakim, having learned the practice of traditional, naturopathic medicine from his own father, who had been a well-known professional hakim.

Luckily, just like for scrawniness, there was nothing like doodh, dhai, and makhan—milk, yogurt, and butter, the trifecta of dairy products core to the Punjabi diet—to bring health, vitality, and glowing fair skin to babies and adults alike. Everyone knows you are what you eat. Lots of tomatoes mean rosy cheeks. Walnuts, which look like a brain, will make your mind sharper. Drink your tea bitter and dark? You'll end up the same color as it. And if you want bright, creamy skin, consume lots of light-colored dairy products, or as would-be-brides do to prepare for their wedding, just rub fatty cream directly onto your face.

And so, reenter the buffalo.

Dada Abu ordered my mother to give me bottles of fresh, full-cream buffalo milk day and night in lieu of the powdered baby formula the hospital had sent her home with. Ami had had every intention of breast-feeding during the pregnancy, but then had gotten caught up in the health campaign across the region to replace breastfeeding with formula. Breast milk, her doctors and nurses explained to her using fancy charts and showing her articles in English, could pass on illnesses from mother to child. But formula was specially created just for children, clean and pure, with all the vitamins and minerals needed to help children grow healthy, smart, and strong.

Besides, breastfeeding was for the poor and uneducated. Upper-class women, especially women in the US and Europe, only gave their babies formula now, which had the added advantage of keeping their breasts firm and perky and their schedules free. No more uncivilized bulging breasts, leaking milk through bras and shirts. After all, women were not cows meant to be milked, were they?

The propaganda worked, not just on my mother, but across the region. It was, we know now, a global scheme engineered by Nestlé to get mothers hooked on formula and to give up breastfeeding. Mothers were taught the risks of breastfeeding and discharged from hospitals armed with sample boxes of formula and baby bottles, ready to rear their children like their wealthy, wondrous, Western counterparts who had already bought into the marketing.

But when my grandfather examined the ingredient list on the back of the Nestlé tin can, he flung it across the room. "What is this nonsense?" Dada Abu raged. This was not milk from a living creature. Not from a goat or cow or buffalo or sheep. It was dead milk, made from dead, fake ingredients. And no way was his granddaughter going to be drinking this trash.

If Ami didn't want to breastfeed, fine. That was her decision alone. But I would get the next best thing to her milk—buffalo milk—and I would drink it day and night as long as Dada Abu had his way.

But he didn't have it for long, because shortly after I was born, my parents' entire world changed.

AMI KNEW THAT, like many of his friends and colleagues, Abu had applied for an American visa. In the 1970s America was opening its doors to professionals from around the world, having scrapped the previous national origin laws that favored immigrants from Europe. In 1965 the new Immigration and Nationality Act was passed, and immigration to America was no longer based on your race or national origin. Now it was based on your merit, on the skills you were able to bring to the most prosperous nation in the world to meet their labor and professional demands.

One of those demands was for veterinary doctors, and it wasn't that there weren't enough veterinarians to service millions of beloved American cats and dogs. Rather, the government needed the veterinarians to fill hundreds of roles in the US Department of Agriculture, and that's where dozens of my father's school buddies had ended up.

There were plenty of reasons Abu wanted to go to the US, but the slow exodus of his veterinarian friends was an influential one. Abu was always a social creature and cherished his pals, much to the chagrin of my mother. He had too many of them and spent too much time with them, as far as she was concerned. Friends were a waste of time, there were much more important things in life that needed attention, like religion and charity. This tug of war has lasted nearly fifty years now, but Ami has never been able to get Abu to shake his companions.

Dr. Emmanuel Gulab is one of those friends, and his relationship with my father stretched back to their school days and their time together in veterinary college. Uncle Emmanuel got his visa before my father and emigrated to the US with his wife, Sheila, not long after Ami and Abu had gotten married. And as soon as Uncle Emmanuel got his green card, he submitted an affidavit of support for my father's visa. In every sense, if it weren't for this couple, we probably would have never have made it America.

Uncle Emmanuel and Aunty Sheila first had a son. Then a daughter, when my future best friend, Shubnum, was born in the United States in January of 1974. Six months later I was born, on the other side of the world in Lahore, Pakistan. Almost immediately after I arrived, Abu's visa was approved.

You would think getting the visa was the hard part, but it wasn't even close. Leaving the father that raised him alone, the sisters and nieces and nephews, the streets and shops and neighbors he grew up with, the grave where his mother was buried—these were the emotionally painful costs of emigrating. His brother could take care of their elderly father, but leaving meant abdicating his own duty toward him.

And yet a place that seemed like a fantasy, the greatest land of opportunity that ever existed, beckoned. Everything he knew about America came from the movies, everything. Clean roads, high-rise buildings, perfectly planned suburbs, prosperity and abundance, adventures and excitement. That was what America stood for. If he stayed in Lahore, where he was already at the top of his field as a university lecturer and the head doctor at the national zoo, there was nowhere for his career to advance to.

But in America, people had pets. Everyone had dogs, it seemed. And they loved their pets, they treated them better than people in Pakistan treated family. They spent money on their cats and dogs, and veterinarians were respected and wealthy.

He couldn't say no, especially not now, with a wife and daughter, a family that he wanted to give a better life to. But unless his father gave permission, he wouldn't go. And he made that clear to my mother, so together they went to him and asked for his blessing. Dada Abu gave it, telling his son he was doing the right thing.

A few months later, my father sold his scooter, my mother sold a few pieces of their furniture, and they raised enough money for a single one-way ticket to America, with $500 to spare. That ticket would be for my father, who would get a job, get a place to live, and then send for us. My mother couldn't wait. After a lifetime surrounded by relatives at every turn, finally she would be able to have her own life, far from anyone who had any say over it.

By the time Abu could afford our two airfares ten months later, Ami had sold or given away everything she couldn't fit into two suitcases, handed over her work responsibilities to the new headmistress of the Girls College, gifted whatever amount she could to the help, and visited every relative at least once to say her goodbyes.

WE WERE A long way from home, but there was already a family of friends waiting for us in Northern Virginia, where my father had rented a small apartment in an immigrant neighborhood. They were surrounded by Pakistanis, Indians, West Africans, Arabs, Latinos, people from places they had only ever heard about. Uncle Emmanuel and Aunty Sheila were the only faces my mother knew, and they welcomed us in the new apartment with food, some housewares, and clothing their own daughter, Shubnum, had outgrown.

Shubnum was six months older than me, already walking, and bright, rosy, and chubby, in contrast to me: dried out from days of explosive diarrhea that plagued me the entire trip over, a big set of eyes looking out of a tiny little face as I crawled to keep up with her.

How, my mother asked Aunty Sheila, could she get me looking like Shubnum? Like the fat-cheeked NIDO baby on the infant formula cans back home?

Aunty Sheila, a nurse, looked me over and told me she knew just the thing. Here, in America, they sell a product called half-and-half, she told her. It was even richer than buffalo milk and would chub me up in no time.

Now, there is no way to know exactly where the wires crossed in this communication, but this exchange would end up haunting me for the rest of my life. Years later Aunty Sheila would swear she told my mother to add two teaspoons of half-and-half to my bottles, while my mother swore she'd told her to give me two full bottles of half-and-half a day.

Which is what she did. For the next few months, I grew larger by the week, as Ami plied me with one of the fattiest, creamiest dairy products one could drink through a bottle, a whopping 12 percent fat, almost three times that of whole milk. Beyond the half-and-half, I also chugged four, five, six bottles of whole milk throughout the day and night, some of which Ami would line up inside my crib at night, only to find them thrown across the room in the morning, sucked dry.

The teeth were also starting to come in, little razors pushing up through my baby gums, reducing me to tears and screams. Ami was away far from her own mother and aunts and cousins, the women who would normally help a new mother through the tough times. In Virginia she only had a couple of people she could ask advice from. They told Ami to give me something frozen to gnaw on to reduce the irritation and numb the pain. What, thought Ami, could she give me that was big enough to hold, wouldn't choke me, could be easily frozen, and wouldn't hurt my gums?

The answer came to her as she made breakfast one morning. Butter. Sticks of it. It was the perfect size for my grubby little hands, it would gradually melt in my mouth so there wasn't any fear of asphyxiation, and of course, if there was anything in the world healthier for babies than milk and ghee, it was butter!

You won't believe me when I tell you this, but as God is my witness, I can still taste the salty, cold butter in my mouth melting into heavenly pools. You have to wonder exactly how many sticks of butter I consumed to leave such an indelible mark on my memory. "Too many" is the only right answer.

The change couldn't have been gradual, I was consuming thousands of calories a day in dairy products alone. I very quickly out-chubbed

Shubnum, who was at our place every day because my mother had begun babysitting her—Ami's very first job in America. We spent hours together in the little one-bedroom apartment and napped in the same playpen. I was on the slower side, but Shubnum's little legs moved like lightening. More than once while Ami was catching a quick shower, Shubnum managed to climb out of the playpen, strip off her diaper, waddle over to the front door, and escape out of the apartment half naked.

Ami still remembers finding Shubnum outside of the playpen, trying to pull me out and over, so I could run off with her. From the start, Shubnum and I were each other's ride-and-dies, and the sisterhood that started in diapers turned into a lifelong best friendship. But it was only in the early months of our friendship that she was the plump one. Once the tables turned and I took the title, it stayed that way permanently.

That's because the land of milk and honey gave and gave, and I wasn't the only one expanding like our horizons. Never could my parents have conceived of a country where you could get an entire meal, greasy, hot, and ready, without ever even having to get out of the car. They were overwhelmed by the supermarkets, the fast food, the restaurants, the thousands of kinds of snacks and sodas and juices and desserts, all cheap and easily available. They'd never seen this many kinds of cookies and chips, cereals and breads. Prepackaged meat that you didn't have to go to pick up every day from the local butcher? Rows and rows of fruit and vegetables, from around the world, both in season and out of season, all in one place?

The sheer abundance was a promise fulfilled. By the time we flew back to see the family and loved ones my parents desperately missed, all three of us looked like "before" pictures in weight-loss stories, and no one in Pakistan would let them forget it.

TWO

Pakoray, Shakory

The story about what happened the first time we visited Pakistan a couple of years after having moved to the United States has been related so many times, it is now both legend and canon. I was two years old and clocked in, according to the lore, at fifty pounds. I refuse to believe this isn't an exaggeration but at this point it's too late. I'm stuck with that data point.

My mother emerged exhausted and disheveled from the belly of the Pakistan International Airlines plane, the airline of choice for all Pakistanis, thanks to their generous portions of greasy, masala-smeared chicken biryani. I clung to my pregnant mother, hapless white wool tights struggling to keep my thighs restrained, my arms twisted desperately around her neck as she negotiated a diaper bag, an oversized purse, massive international-size suitcases, and a large brown child through customs and immigration.

No one thought to bring a stroller, and while we had put humans on the moon by then, putting wheels on luggage hadn't yet occurred to anyone.

By the time Ami and I made it out, a good ninety sweaty minutes after landing, relatives from both sides of my family had grown weary. They had arrived bearing boxes of sweets and tinsel garlands, but as they waited in the sweltering heat, the tinsel went limp and the sweets softened into fudgy masses. Ami finally emerged and approached the melee, throwing down all the bags she had dragged from the baggage area. I still hung like a Christmas ornament around her poor neck.

Dada Abu, sprightly and fit even in his eighties, came toward us, gleaming in a bright white kurta and turban, cane swinging purposefully. But then his brow furrowed and his blue eyes narrowed with concern as he appraised his daughter-in-law and this unrecognizable child. The last time my grandfather saw me I was an acceptably chubby ten-month-old infant, but today he beheld his worst nightmare—an undeniably and alarmingly fat little girl.

My mother bent over, prying my sticky arms loose, and deposited me before him. Dada Abu handed her his cane and bent down to pick up the only child of his beloved youngest son. He brought me up slowly to his chest, bending backward to keep his balance, and then put me right back down murmuring "balle balle balle balle." At two years old, I was too damn heavy for him.

He then uttered the words my mother has since reminded me of a million times.

"What have you done to her?"

Dr. Abdul Haq appraised my girth carefully and turned his gaze to my well-fattened mother. They had seen pictures my father sent in the past couple of years, pictures in which his once-athletic frame had morphed into a classic desi dad bod—scrawny legs, and pants hitched under a paunchy gut. Clearly, this was a family affair. They had all looked perfectly fine when they left for America, what on earth had happened?

Ami tried to explain that there was just too much food in America, that it was easier and cheaper (and tastier) to grab burgers and fried chicken than slave over a stove, that finding desi spices and ingredients and goat meat and properly cut chicken was nearly impossible. And then there was this American family, a really kind family with four kids that lived on the same floor of their apartment building, and they had become obsessed with the chubby Pakistani toddler down the hall. Every chance the kids got after school, they would ferry me to their apartment, where we shared cake, cookies, chips, Cheetos, all the amazing American snack food my parents almost never brought into the house. In one faded photo I'm seated at their table wearing a tent-like dress, an entire towel tied around my neck, as I tuck into a hunk of cake.

These Americans, they were always eating. Snacking was, to my parents, a uniquely American phenomenon. In Pakistan, there were fairly set times to eat—breakfast, lunch, teatime, and dinner. But the kids in this white American family ate snacks all day, and now their snacks showed on me, too.

Taya Amma, who had helped raise me from the time I was born, murmured, "Goodness, she is shaped just like her father, isn't she," as she bathed me. A poorly disguised insult as far as my mother was concerned, especially coming from a woman of Taya Amma's size. But Ami knew the rule that married women could expand all they wanted to, having babies can do that to a woman, but unmarried girls had no business being fat. And an overweight girl toddler was one big red flag pointing to future unmarriageability.

Ami was happy to lay the blame on her husband, it wasn't her fault she had to sew veritable tents for their daughter because nothing would fit her. It was all Anwar's fault, he was a foodie before foodies were even a thing, he loved to try every restaurant, loved to spend hours feasting with friends, and lavished his little girl with fast food.

But if Abu's family sent out subtle signals of discomfort with the new shape of things, Ami's family was another story altogether. They didn't dare tease Ami, their intimidating elder sister they called Aapi. But this waddling two-year-old, her sheer chub both adorable and troubling, was totally fair game.

"How many Americans has she eaten??"

"She's a little bahns, our own baby buffalo!"

"Mota aalu pulpula, danda lay kar gir paray!" they sang to me, a song about a rotting fat potato who couldn't even stand with the help of a stick.

They recognized the abundance of America in every fold of my belly, in every dimple in my soft little mitts. Cleary, life in America was enviably easy. Or so they imagined.

Ami quickly disabused them of that notion. Life in America had its perks, but no one in Pakistan could imagine the amount of labor you had to do yourself, with your own two hands. First, and most tragically, there was no domestic help. If you needed groceries, there was no one to send to the store to fetch them for you. There was no one to make you a cup of tea, or sweep the floors, or clean the bathrooms.

My mother had never cleaned a bathroom in her life, she didn't even know how it was done when she first arrived on American soil. One of the other Pakistani transplants had to show her. Back home, cleaning bathrooms was a job relegated mostly to poor Pakistani Christians, who came every week to scrub and wash the squatty toilet and carry away human waste in baskets. And now here she was, cleaning toilets like an impoverished Eesai, an indignity Ami never thought she'd ever face.

Not that she had anything against Christians. After all, Emmanuel and Sheila were Christians, and they were good friends. But they were educated, upwardly mobile Christians. The right kind of Christians. Ami, like other Pakistani Muslims, liked to think they'd left behind the Hindu caste system with the Partition, indeed she felt superior to Hindus for it, but in reality they had just swapped out the players in the system.

Beyond the bathroom, doing laundry was nearly indescribable to her relatives. Every week you had to first hunt fistfuls of change, or go begging for it from neighbors, then haul your clothes to the dank apartment basement, wrestling bottles of detergent and bleach, where if you were lucky a public machine, shared with strangers, all kinds of strangers, strangers with who knows what hygienic practices, would be available. There you had the choice of either sitting for hours as the laundry was washing and drying, or leaving it and checking back periodically, risking your pillow covers and underthings and your husband's work clothes getting pilfered.

It was positively uncivilized, and Ami couldn't wait to leave our dirty clothes in a basket in my grandmother's home so it could be picked up, sorted, washed, pressed, folded, and returned by the only people who should be doing laundry—dhobis. In America, Ami was the dhobi. She was also the helper boy, the maid, the butcher, the cook, and the bathroom cleaner.

At least now, for a few months, she could relax back into what she was used to—and be cared for as she deserved to be, now in the final months of her second pregnancy. She turned me over to her siblings, who happily passed me around, taking turns bathing me, feeding me, and taking me for death-defying rides on the one rickety motorcycle in the household.

Back in Sham Nagar, Ami stayed up late into the night as cousins and aunts and uncles rotated through the house to visit with her, hear all about the land of milk and honey, and if lucky, pick up gifts she had brought from America. Electronics were most coveted, but not many returning immigrants could afford to bring those back. So instead, bottles of shampoo and lotion, sweaters, talcum powder, toothpaste, makeup, shoes, purses, bras, socks, candies, and a hundred other smaller items were dragged across the oceans to be distributed to dozens of relatives. And the very first thing that everyone did was to turn their gift upside-down, inside-out, looking for the Made in America label.

Rarely did they find it. Explaining to loved ones that most of America was made in China, or Bangladesh, or Vietnam was no easy sell, because more often than not they'd go away unconvinced, believing they'd been given a cheap version of the good stuff. The obsession with American-made products wasn't about the optics of the label, it was about the quality of the actual products themselves. No product available in Pakistan was the same quality as the same product in America and Europe. And so, they came for the almost-American gifts, and stayed for hours of endless cups of chai and the fried spicy things that go with chai—the ubiquitous nimko: a desi trail mix of sorts, comprised of fried, salty lentils mixed with nuts, golden raisins, chili-powdered corn flakes, crispy potato vermicelli noodles, and any one of a dozen other tiny fried varieties of snacks. There would be samosas if they were available fresh from the samosa-wala (no one wants a stale samosa, the fastest way to spend days of regret in the bathroom), or otherwise pakoras, because anyone and everyone could make those at home.

A quick batter of chickpea flour, seasonings, chopped onions, and chilies, dropped in dollops into hot oil, produced irresistible spicy hot dumplings, and new batches brought from the kitchen every five minutes to sop up green chutney were gone in less than half the time.

While Ami caught up with the latest gossip, I toddled around with whomever would play with me. In the mornings she would sleep in and my aunt and Nani Amma, my grandmother, would be up with me, washing my chubby hands and face for a breakfast of fried eggs and buttered toast, which is what they imagined an American child ate. They had their morning chai and paratha as I ate my continental meal on the open veranda that overlooked the courtyard, one of the most charming architectural features of Eastern homes, which is regrettably rarely found in the US. It's like a Western home turned inside out. Instead of outdoor living space—yards, patios, decks—surrounding a house, the courtyard is outdoor living space in the very center of the home, open to the sky, and surrounded on all sides by rooms that rise in stories, encircling it.

Some parts of a courtyard might be planted, but oftentimes they are paved with concrete or brick, making it easy to sweep and wash clean every day, and furnished with chairs and rugs and mangis, woven beds. They are places where family and friends can gather to share meals and tea, smoke hookah, read a newspaper or listen to the radio, and even sleep, on the nights when it's too stifling indoors.

It was in that courtyard that my mother often woke to find me being bathed, dripping wet in only my underwear, as one of her younger brothers lathered me up and washed me down with a hose like a farm animal. My thighs stuck together, love handles jiggled, my tummy hung in a soft brown mass over the straining elastic of my undies, and with my stick-straight black hair, from a distance I really did look like Anwar Chaudry shrunk down into a couple of feet.

According to Ami, the uncanny resemblance was only one of an entire list of reasons I should have been a boy, but no worries. There was a new baby on the way.

THAT SUMMER IN Lahore was milder than most Pakistani summers, if you can call temperatures in the high nineties "mild," and it was a good thing as my mother approached her due date, swelling steadily by the day. As she grew more uncomfortable, the days grew longer and warmer, and the streets began filling up with paper garlands of thousands of Pakistani flags, a stripe of white representing Pakistan's religious minorities, next to a block of green highlighting a moon and star, colors and symbols of the "Islamic" part of the Islamic Republic.

Pakistan Independence Day was August 14, a day before neighbor and rival India celebrated its independence from British colonialism. The weeks leading up to mid-August in these years were filled with the release of new patriotic songs, flags unfurled from windows and balconies, and on the only television network, the government-operated PTV, homages to the "Father of the Nation" Muhammad Ali Jinnah, blurry black-and-white images from the time of the Partition, and sentimental video collages celebrating the military.

The spirit that swept the young nation, which had seen its most recent war just years earlier, was heady and palpable. Ami had uncles and cousins in the military and had briefly joined a women's civilian regiment in 1971, receiving rifle training along with her little sister and other girls from the neighborhood. After all, Lahore was just miles from the enemy border, and they intended to be prepared to battle to the end if that border was breached. But one day all their fervor and bravado went out the window when an Indian fighter pilot buzzed them fast and low overhead. The women in training threw down their rifles and ran for shelter, scattering like pigeons as their instructor screamed bloody murder at them. Anyhow, the spirit was still there, and Ami had missed it while in America, so this year she was looking forward to seeing the fireworks and parades, dressing up in green and white, and eating sweets all day.

In the middle of all the excitement, though, on the day the homeland celebrated its twenty-ninth birthday, another patriot entered the scene to declare her independence. Independence from my mother's womb, that is. On August 14, 1976, my baby sister was born.

The second time, yet another girl, was worse than the first. This time, Ami was reduced to tears when one of her sisters-in-law mournfully looked at the baby and said, "Well, our brother is forever burdened." Another one tried to reassure her. So what if it was another girl? Sure, unlike Ami she had sons, but she also had half a dozen girls. Not to worry, one day God would give their brother a son, too.

It was enough for Ami to turn her head away from the baby and tell the nurse to take her away, refusing to hold her. Another nurse asked if she wanted to give up the baby for adoption, the nurse more than happy to take home the perfect little girl born with a cap of soft, dark curls. But of course, she couldn't and wouldn't do that. Her father-in-law had thundered, "So what if it's another girl, girls are blessings, the Prophet Muhammad had four girls and no sons!" admonishing his own brood of daughters. She felt better with his support.

They named my little sister Siddrah, after the sacred tree in Paradise, located all the way at the end of the seventh heaven, as far as any human soul is allowed to go, as far as the limit of human knowledge. Beyond this boundary lie all the unknown secrets of the universe, including the secrets of God Himself. Ami loved the name and hoped this time the name would stick. It hadn't with me.

The name she had chosen for me was Ayesha, after the beloved wife of the Prophet. Ayesha was known for her sharp wit, her compassion, her assertiveness, and her brilliance. Namesakes were important; they could shape a child's entire personality and even their destiny. Ayesha wasn't in the cards for me, though. Not long after I was born, a young girl in the neighborhood named Ayesha fell off the roof of her house and died. A bad omen, said Dada Abu.

He renamed me Rabia, after Rābi'a al-Basri, an eighth-century Iraqi slave-girl who would go on to become the Muslim world's first female Sufi saint. She was known for her love of God and for her ecstatic poetry, and a miracle: heavenly provisions were sent right to her chambers, where she would stay locked up for days and weeks in worship. Rābi'a al-Basri was revered not just for being a true mystic and intellectual, the teacher and master of both men and women of her time, but also for her fierce independence from men, preferring the single life. So fierce was she that famed Sufi theoretician 'Aṭṭār of Nishapur described her as being not "a single woman but a hundred men over."

Sadly I have no chance of ever living up to this namesake, especially not the part about staying locked up in a room awaiting meals from heaven, because for as long as anyone can remember, I've always been preoccupied with my next meal, even in childhood. Most kids would be busy playing, oblivious to a table set with tea and snacks, or a buffet laid out at an event, or all the other food offerings when you are either a guest or have guests. Not me. Instead, I was oblivious to the snickers and stares of kids and adults alike when I made a beeline to the food before anyone else could get there. I was the George Costanza of children, pushing myself through bodies to get to the head of the table, where I would stand, my eyes barely peering over the edge, waiting for the moment, the signal, that we could start eating.

Other mothers would have to tell their children to stop running around and come eat already, while my mother watched in silent resignation as I carefully carried a plate of food to a corner, tied on my own bib, and settled in to finish every last morsel all by myself. Ami marveled at how slowly and deliberately I ate, careful with each bite, like a meditation. I had the laserlike focus of a yogi, so the one saving grace of my unadulterated attention to the plate before me was that I never soiled my clothing. Not a single crumb, not a spoon of curry, not a kernel of rice, would escape the journey to my mouth.

Ami greatly appreciated that my clothes stayed pristine, given that finding clothes that fit me was getting harder and harder. Most of the waistlines in kid's clothing couldn't accommodate the tummy I'd grown, and they definitely didn't make cable-knit tights for thighs like mine.

It was a long-standing tradition for a new mother to spend the first forty days after giving birth with her own family, where she and the baby would be cared for by her own mother, sisters, aunts, and cousins. This period, the chillah, was also critical to helping a new mother heal. Her belly would be massaged daily to reduce swelling, her waist bound for six weeks to get her back to her prepartum figure, and she would be fed nutrient-rich foods all day to help build her strength back and ensure abundant lactation.

Ami rejected the first two of these practices, which she would come to regret later, because for the rest of her life, her belly stayed extended as if she were still pregnant. This, of course, had nothing to do with the fact that she embraced the third practice with vigor, and well beyond forty days.

Even before my mother returned from the hospital with the new baby girl, Nani Amma had begun preparing the panjiri, perhaps the most calorie-dense food anyone has ever dreamed up. The ingredients had been gathered—a sack of whole wheat flour, another of semolina, and pounds and pounds of almonds, raisins, dates, coconut, pistachios, acacia, kamarkas gum, the dried, fried seeds of the lotus plant known as makhanas or fox nuts, loads of ghee, and pounds of dense, caramelly jaggery to sweeten the dish.

Every single component of the panjiri was there for an Ayurvedic reason. Vitamins, protein, essential acids, minerals, and most important, calories. More calories than its weak Western cousin, granola, could ever hope to achieve. Calories meant to replace the calories burned by a breastfeeding mother, by a healing womb that had just created life, calories meant to heat up the insides, soothe aches and pains, and bring on the deepest slumber imaginable.

Each of the ingredients was slow roasted in ghee individually to cook out the rawness and deepen the flavors, and then put aside to wait for the rest of the party. Even the whole wheat flour and semolina were added to the pan with copious amounts of ghee over a low flame, until the starches turned a golden brown and filled the air with nuttiness. The roasted nuts and the gums and coconut were then laboriously ground together on a stone slab until they turned into a coarse crumble, and finally mixed with all the other components, jaggery added by the handfuls as sweet as one wanted, resulting in mounds of a delicious, nutty, sweet, rich, chewy superfood that would last for months in an airtight container.

Every day, all day, my mother would scoop up handfuls between naps and meals, first thing in the morning and last thing at night, and as she passed the huge jar that sat on the table on the veranda, inviting others to steal mouthfuls, too.

Thousands and thousands of panjiri calories were consumed by Ami in the first month after Siddrah was born, and this was, if anything, a fitting segue into the time of year when Muslims gain the most collective weight. Ramadan. The month of fasting between sunup and sundown, which that year began just weeks after Siddrah was born.

Every year when it rolls around, the non-Muslim world sends us both condolences and expressions of admiration with some variation of this message, "I could never do it, amazing you can go all day without eating or drinking anything—FOR THIRTY DAYS!" Little do these poor, empathetic souls know that Ramadan is less the month of fasting, and more perfectly described as the month of feasting. At no other time in the entire year will you find two billion people worldwide more focused on food than during Ramadan.

Once upon a time, back when the tradition began, the whole point of the month was to experience the deprivation as a spiritual cleansing and as a way to understand the daily sufferings of those without. Now, Ramadan is about how much food we can stuff into our bodies during nonfasting hours, starting from breaking the fast with the evening iftar meal, all the way to the predawn suhoor meal, and plenty of night-time snacking in between. Every Muslim culture has developed its own Ramadan food rituals, creating special dishes made just that month, holding lavish iftar parties, and even gathering together before the sun comes up for Instagrammable suhoor spreads.

Well before the advent of social media, however, Lahoris had already turned Ramadan into a month-long culinary festival. The restaurants, bakeries, and street vendors flipped their schedules around, closing all day as the sun shone, and preparing for their customers a couple of hours before dusk.

By the time the call for the evening prayer sounds, the streets and bazaars are packed with blazing cauldrons of oil deep-frying iftar treats, young men slapping dough stretched over a cloth pad to smack fast and furiously into underground tandoors. Minutes later they pull out steaming hot naan and roti with long-handled hooks and fling them toward waiting customers. At street-side open-air markets, huge aluminum deghs of pulao and biryani cook over wood fires, both brimming with savory combinations of meat and rice, and sweet shops churn out hundreds of pounds of milky, fudgy, syrup-filled desserts.

The actual tradition, dating back nearly 1500 years, is to break your fast with a few healthy, nutritious dates and some water, go pray, then have a light dinner. But dates and water are just an afterthought in Pakistani iftars. They're always there, on the table, so everyone can grab at least one date to fulfill the tradition, but on the subcontinent any iftar worth its name is a spread to behold, the dates and water usually lost among the samosas, pakoras (without which, to this day, my father won't break his fast), the patties, the cutlets, the chutneys, and the chaats.

The humble chaat deserves some pause and explanation, because even those most experienced in South Asian foods may not have ever eaten a chaat. I don't blame them. As foods from this part of the world go, these may be the most intimidating. A reductive way to describe a chaat is that it's kind of a salad eaten as a snack. But in no way like any salad that you may imagine. A chaat is an explosion of flavors and textures, layers of spicy and savory ingredients doused with a variety of sweet and fiery chutneys and whipped yogurt, tiny diced onion and tomato and cilantro, finished off with yet more crunchy goodies.

A chaat could consist of boiled, cubed potatoes and chickpeas, a smashed-up samosa topped with chickpeas in a tangy sauce, or fried lentil dumplings, with layers of papri, fried crackerlike wafers, piled up high with chutneys and sev—thin, crunchy gram-flour noodles broken into bits to garnish. But a chaat could also be made of fruit, and fair warning to anyone who bites into a fruit chaat expecting a refreshing, cool fruit salad. Instead, you'll find a perplexingly delicious combination of diced fruit, often mixed with chickpeas, in a saucy dressing of mango pulp and its very own special masala blend.

There are dozens of variations, but every chaat has that masala blend in common—chaat masala, not to be confused with the heady, deep combination of spices known as garam masala. Chaat masala is its rebellious, tangy, pungent cousin, a mixture of at least a dozen dried, powdered ingredients like red chili, dried mango, and asafetida, but the only one that really matters is the star ingredient: Indian black salt.

The only resemblance on the tongue that black salt has to regular table salt is that it's salty. But to really savor the saltiness, you have to first get past its sulphuric, gassy smell, which is also what you first taste when it hits your mouth. There's a reason kids call chaat masala "fart masala," and that reason is black salt. You could say it's an acquired taste, but mixed up in the pungent, rotten egginess of black salt is also an unmistakable umami that heightens the flavors of fruit and vegetables, and when chaat masala infused with black salt is sprinkled generously on a mound of chaat, it leaves you licking the bowl clean.

That's why chaat masala, spicy, heady, sour, stinky all at once, is non-negotiable in all chaats, and is also a favorite seasoning sprinkled on anything deep-fried and savory, or just on fresh sliced fruits and vegetables. Trust me when I tell you that french fries sprinkled with chaat masala might be the very best way to eat fried potatoes.

Ami wasn't fasting that Ramadan, exempt from the religious obligation because she was still in her forty-day chillah period, as are also those who are breast-feeding, ill, traveling, or elderly. But that didn't mean she didn't join in the early morning meals of fried eggs, rich beef trotter stew, and thick, hearty kulcha naan studded with sesame and nigella seeds. Hasty cups of chai were downed as the call to the dawn prayer rang out from the neighborhood mosque through an ancient, crackling speaker system, signaling the time to stop eating and drinking.

With a collective burp, everyone would say their prayers as quickly as possible and roll back into bed, snoring well into the day to kill as many daylight hours as possible. I've known people who sleep all day during Ramadan, and stay up all night, thereby completely mitigating any risk of getting thirsty or hungry as they "fasted." Not everyone has that luxury, of course, but in many parts of the Muslim world, office hours even get adjusted during Ramadan, allowing folks to start the workday later and wrap it up sooner.

The streets were therefore quiet on Ramadan days, and the nights lit up with shopping and cooking and eating. And in the homes, most of the day was spent planning and preparing food, trading trays and baskets and bowls of treats with neighbors and family, handing out food to the poor that came by and knocked at your gates, or doling out plates of rice at local shrines, where the homeless and impoverished congregated.

And at the end of the month, so many who had fasted for thirty days ended up with higher cholesterol, spiking blood sugar, and a few more pounds than they carried weeks earlier.

That Ramadan in Lahore, I imagine, groomed my young palate toward desi cuisine in a way that it had missed out on in America the previous two years. But I'd be returning to America for a newly invigorated culinary education, with my father at the helm. And my mother would be returning with dozens of packages of spices and seasonings wrapped carefully in plastic, tins of sweets, sacks of loose-leaf chai, jars of achaar—her mother's homemade pickles that had soaked up the Lahori sun all that summer—cumin- and cardamom-studded biscuits and nimko, and all the tea snacks she could carry back.

The one thing she wouldn't be returning with was her newborn baby, Siddrah.

THREE

Attay Ki Bori: A Sack of Flour

"You know how hard it is to leave a two-month-old infant behind?"
Ami asked yet again, a question she's raised with no expectation of an answer for over forty years now. "My milk, it was still leaking when I left her in Lahore and brought you back with me. I would remember her and my milk would run, I would cry and my milk would flood. It took months before the milk finally dried up." It's never been clear to me whether or not Ami regretted leaving Siddrah behind, but the pain she had at doing so is less ambiguous.

It was the hardest calculation of her life. She saw how her widowed mother reveled in the new baby, how Siddrah brought hope and joy into a home that had fallen into a quiet sadness since her father died. And she also knew that it was time for her to find work in America, and when she did, she couldn't afford childcare for two children. Plus, if she left Siddrah in Pakistan, Ami would have a pretense to send a little bit of money to her mother. They needed it, her father's pension barely covered their expenses, and otherwise they would be too proud to accept it.

Abu, who was still in America and had not even seen the new baby, agreed to the plan, understanding the practical benefits to everyone. To everyone but perhaps Siddrah herself. She may have been surrounded by loving uncles and an aunt and grandmother who doted on her, but you cannot replace the love of parents, or a child's natural need for them. But these are the choices immigrants often face—whom to leave behind, when, and for how long.

Ami and I returned to America in the fall of 1976, without my little sister, and I once again enjoyed the pleasures of being an only child, the only one my parents had to raise, and the only one they loved to feed, and fed to love.

I could read by the time I was four years old, and for that I have America's fast food restaurants to thank. It was rather ingenious of my father to come up with a virtually Pavlovian system. "A is for Arby's, B is for Burger King, C is for Coca-Cola, D is for Dairy Queen . . ." and so on and so forth. Let's just say it was an alphabet befitting me. I could recite it by the time I turned three, around the same time we finally moved away from the comfortable cocoon of our northern Virginia immigrant community and encountered new kinds of people and an unfamiliar cuisine—Italian.

Up until that point Abu had been taking whatever jobs he could come by—in research labs, as a security guard, in banks—but desperately wanted to return to his profession. He had passed the exams required in order to practice veterinary medicine in the US, but still needed an internship. That finally happened when he came across a classified ad for an animal clinic seeking a veterinary assistant. He responded and was called in for an interview.

The clinic was housed in an old brick rancher and clearly had been around for decades. There Abu met an elderly man who introduced himself as Dr. Keller. He was in his eighties and, while not quite ready to retire and close the place down, couldn't run it full-time anymore by himself. He asked my father where he was from, and when Abu told him Pakistan, Dr. Keller said, "Oh, you've probably never met a Jewish person then."

Indeed, Abu hadn't. There was no Jewish community in Pakistan to speak of, and all he knew about Jews was this: Hitler killed millions of Jewish people, and of those who survived, some fled to America and others uprooted the Palestinians to create their own state, Israel. There was little distinction for him between Jews and Israelis, and Palestinians and Muslims. The plight of the Palestinians was, by extension, an attack on the global Muslim body. And it was all Israel's fault.

At least that's what Abu had learned growing up, but he was never very political himself and he certainly didn't harbor any enmity toward anyone because of their religion. And so, there he was, hoping this elderly Jewish man would give him a job and wondering whether Dr. Keller would hold Abu's own religion against him.

He didn't. Dr. Keller offered Abu an internship, seeing patients and running the clinic from 5 to 8 p.m. and on weekends, which allowed my father to work elsewhere during the day. Abu had been hoping for full-time work, but it was a start, a foot back into the veterinary field. It would require a lot of running around, though, from our apartment in Seven Corners, Virginia, to the day job he had across state lines, to the clinic in Potomac, each location over an hour away from the other. Dr. Keller asked him why he didn't just move closer, and Abu explained that he wasn't alone, that he had a wife and daughter, and that he couldn't afford another place that could house us all.

Dr. Keller had a solution. Right next to the clinic was another old home. It belonged to him and it was empty. It needed repairs, and the basement was prone to flooding, but if Abu agreed, we could stay there in lieu of compensation for work. Abu agreed, and my parents soon packed up and moved out of the apartment community where most of their friends lived and into the rural little house where you couldn't smell frying onions or roasted cumin anywhere.

But every time they stepped outside, they could smell something else, something they couldn't quite place, and it was coming from another rickety old house next door. The aroma was garlicky and savory, but nothing like their own spices. It wasn't long after they moved in that Ami answered a knock on the door to discover an elderly lady in a flowered apron and thick horn-rimmed glasses, her white hair curled into a cloud around her head, holding a tinfoil-wrapped pan that she handed over.

That's how we met "Mama," the only name any of us ever knew her by, because that's what she told us to call her. Mama was the matriarch of her once-large Italian family, but time had taken her husband, opportunities elsewhere had lured away her children, and now Mama lived alone. Her house was rarely empty though. There was a steady stream of friends and relatives in and out of her door, and she stayed busy tending a garden bursting with tomatoes and basil and turning the bounty into sauces for her loved ones.

"It takes hours," she told my mother.

Hours? To make a sauce? That made absolutely no sense to Ami. In hours she could cook six dishes plus a dessert. The only thing that should take hours to make was paya, beef or goat trotters that need the time to break down into sticky, gelatinous glory.

That first warm pan that Mama brought over, a cheesy, heavy lasagne, was our introduction to authentic Italian food, which Ami and I loved. My father remained ambivalent. Pizza? Well, he had enjoyed that particular Italian food without realizing it was Italian, even though the cheese took some getting used to, because none of us had ever had it before coming to the States. While many Indian dishes contain paneer, a homemade cottage cheese, I can't think of a single time I have ever eaten cheese in a Pakistani home or restaurant. Cheese on pizza and burgers, however, made perfect sense. That salty, melty, gooey goodness gave these foods the flavor that they otherwise lacked.

What confused Abu about Mama's dishes was that they all seemed like variations of the same thing to him—tomato sauce, pasta, and cheese. He couldn't tell the difference between spaghetti and linguini and ziti and lasagne other than the shape of the noodles. They all tasted the same, and pasta itself didn't seem right to him. It looked like uncooked dough, pale and flabby. Who boils dough? Dough should be baked or fried. Pasta was a neglected doughy stepchild that didn't quite complete the journey to being *actually* cooked.

To be fair, Abu's exposure to pasta before this was almost nil. Pakistani Punjabi food is almost completely lacking in pasta and noodles of any sort, notwithstanding a few sweet dishes. Seviyan, made from extremely thin vermicelli noodles, was prepared a couple of ways, but in each dish the noodles were first roasted in ghee until brown, and then either cooked in milk, sugar, and cardamom to make a pudding-like dessert, or cooked with a bit of water, sugar, and cardamom so you ended up with a sweet, caramelized dish of noodles that looked like slightly sticky golden-brown pasta garnished with nuts. Yes, these were noodles Abu was willing to eat, but at least they were fried first!

He didn't have the heart to say anything to Mama, though, and turning down food from a friend was no less than a sin, so Ami and I did our neighborly duty and cleaned up all the variations of pasta and sauce that Mama made for us. Hands down, though, lasagne was our favorite, and I ate it regularly, like Garfield, because once Ami found a job, Mama began babysitting me. Not for the money—my parents could barely pay her a few dollars an hour—but for the company of a child that couldn't get enough of her food.

The pasta packed the pounds on my frame, and Ami would ask Mama to hold back with it, but she couldn't help herself. Mama loved to feed me and I did not object. Pictures from that time show me standing in a snowy driveway, straining the fabric of my coat, my hair in two long ponytails tied high on opposite sides of my head. The size of my face is approximately the same size as my father's, and decidedly bigger than my mother's, but that likely has as much to do with the fact that I inherited Abu's remarkably large, blocky head, and a face full of cheeks that fit nicely across it.

I've only ever seen my hair two ways in childhood photographs—in those two ponytails or cut into the shortest bob possible. It wasn't until I got older that I understood why I never appeared in a single ponytail or braid. That blocky head, completely flat from behind, made those styles nearly impossible. Imagine gathering a ponytail on the back of a cardboard box, where exactly do you position it? My flat head was no accident, and Ami wasn't about to let Abu's genetics take all the credit. She had purposefully and lovingly shaped my head that way, in the time-honored desi tradition of head-shaping infants. God forbid I ended up with an oval, pointy head like white people—a beautiful head was broad, and she painstakingly made sure that for the first six months of my life I slept on my back with my head resting on a board.

Other desi mothers would ask her how she had managed to get such utter flatness on the back of my head, and she would smile slightly, stroking my hair, pleased with the maternal discipline it took to achieve this permanent result. Unfortunately Ami had neglected to direct her mother to make sure Siddrah's head was shaped likewise, which she would later regret, as she stared at my little sister's perfectly oval noggin. It was shaped much like her own head, because Nani Amma had never had the time or inclination to shape the heads of her seven babies while taking care of a house of in-laws.

So two ponytails it was, until Ami started working, at which point it was just easier and faster to manage my thick, pin-straight hair by whacking it all off. She needed all the help, and extra time, she could get since she didn't have a village to raise a child like she would have had in Pakistan.

Lucky for her, America was nothing if not the land of edible convenience.

AMI'S FIRST REAL job in the United States had nothing to do with her experience or training in education. A friend had convinced her that the future was in a new technology, the emerging field of computing. Like most people in 1977, she knew nothing about computers or computing, but there were jobs in the field that she could still get if she knew how to type.

Of course she knew how to type, how else did civilized people write papers and letters and run schools? She thanked her lucky stars and applied to a data-entry position and was called in for an interview almost immediately. Leaving me with Mama, she took one bus to another to another, until she arrived at an impressive high-rise. She was dressed in the best approximation of Western garb she was willing to accommodate: a long kurta, the collarless shirt reaching her knees; baggy pants; and a three-yard dupatta (shawl) tied like a scarf around her neck. She couldn't bring herself to wear a short shirt that showed off her rear end like she saw American women dressed in, or to leave the house without a headscarf, both options being scandalously immodest for her. There were some Pakistani and Indian women who apparently forgot where they came from, threw away the scarves and tucked in their shirts, but Ami vowed to never cheapen herself that way.

The interview lasted longer than expected when the middle-aged white man in charge of hiring for the department realized Ami was from Pakistan—he loved Pakistan, he declared! He had visited once and had fallen in love with the people, the culture, and the food. Could Ami cook Pakistani food, he asked? Of course she could, and after promising to one day make him the dish he craved the most—chicken biryani—she left with a job offer in hand.

Unfortunately for him, and ironically, Ami's new job made it harder for her to make home-cooked Pakistani food, and my parents began relying more and more on American convenience foods from the supermarket. Into our home came, for the first time, processed cheese slices, cookies and chips and crackers, frozen cans of juice, ready-made pizzas, jams and jellies, donuts and snack cakes.

Mama's cooking had primed me to become a cheese lover and it had been fattening for sure, but at least it was freshly cooked from whole ingredients. The daily addition of processed foods to my diet may have been the nail in the coffin of any possibility of me not being overweight for the rest of my life.

Not long before I started kindergarten, we finally returned to Pakistan to bring back Siddrah, and in the years that had passed since we had left her, things only looked worse for me. Ami was downright apprehensive about going, knowing full well that everyone would blame her for my weight problem, a problem her husband didn't yet think was a problem.

"She'll grow out of it, she's just a chubby child, everyone loves chubby children" summed up Abu's philosophy, but Abu hadn't been there the last time, when Dada Abu had raised the question Ami could never forget: "What have you done to her?" This time, though, Abu returned with us, and Ami made sure everyone knew *he* was the foodie; the tubby kid was all his fault and so was his own girth spurt.

The abundance of America strained at our skin and clothing, and our relatives were torn between embarrassment at us returning like sheep fattened for slaughter, and mild jealousy at how good the living must be in the States. We looked like attay ki bori, the monstrous sacks of flour they stacked monthly at home.

It became apparent why when we opened our suitcases to pass out gifts to the dozens and dozens of relatives on both sides. We had carried (along with all the beauty and toiletry products hauled there the last time) some of the processed American delights Ami and Abu were sure everyone would marvel at and enjoy. Fudge-striped shortbread cookies, candy bars, boxes of macaroni and cheese, pudding and cake mixes, Little Debbie snacks and peanut-butter-stuffed crackers—foods they'd never even heard of, foods we loved.

These were also the treats we wanted to shower Siddrah with. We hadn't seen her in over two years, other than the occasional picture my grandmother sent with her letters, and phone calls only happened once monthly, with international rates being so high. Both Siddrah and I knew we had a sister, somewhere far away, and one day we would finally get to be with each other. I was always, according to Ami, insisting that I wanted my little sister home, and on the other side of the world, according to our grandmother, Siddrah would look at my picture and ask why they took the fat kid and left her behind.

By the time Siddrah was one, she had been dubbed "Lilly" by our grandmother, a nickname that has stuck ever since, and was already a complete chatterbox. Nani Amma would sit her by the phone so she could hear our voices and we could hear hers through the staticky line. The calls weren't ideal, but at least they had a phone at home, one of the very few residential phones in the entire neighborhood. It was installed through sheer willpower and repeated bribes to cut through the bureaucracy of the government agency that owned and operated the network. Having a phone added some prestige to the family, when most people had to make and take calls from local merchants who charged by the minute. The downside, though, was that Nani Amma's number had become the default number all the neighbors passed on to others as their contact. All day, every day, people dropped by requesting to make phone calls, and calls constantly came in for the aunty down the street or the uncle around the block and someone would have to be sent to relay the message or fetch the party to take the call.

It was a headache but worth it for Lilly. They needed to be able to have contact with us at any time in case there was an emergency, and vice versa, and so we could have some semblance of a relationship with her. It must have worked because the minute we walked through the airport doors, Lilly forgot about our grandmother, who she had called Ami until then, and attached herself firmly to our parents, insisting we all go back to America together, immediately.

She wasn't so enamored of me, apparently, and the story goes that she slapped me around a bit after we first met, though I was twice her size.

But I had half her personality and gumption. She was raised among five rabble-rousing uncles who tossed her onto the backs of their motorbikes for rides at all hours of the day and night, taught her all the dirty Punjabi words, and took turns having her sleep on their chests at night. I, on the other hand, had been raised in relative isolation, with no relatives around and few friends, quietly entertaining myself with lasagne and potato chips.

I was just slightly terrified of this spitfire of a little sister.

Before we returned to America with her, Taya Abu, ever stately and severe, had a talk with Abu. He looked down through thick, black, square-framed glasses upon his portly little brother, who had once been the captain of the Punjab cricket team, lithe and athletic.

Now look at him. How, asked Taya Abu, could Anwar live in the most highly educated, most advanced country in the world but show utter disregard for his health, and the health of his child. "Anwar," he said, "you should be ashamed of yourself."

And with that final admonition, we left Pakistan, not knowing we wouldn't return for many years.

A COUPLE OF years later, Ami had to take a hiatus from work, a much longer hiatus than expected, thanks to the arrival of our little brother, Saad, in 1980. Finally, the boy, the son, the inheritor of bloodlines and the family name, the one everyone had been waiting for, was here. Boxes and boxes of sweets were ordered and distributed to hundreds of relatives back home in Pakistan and to friends in America to celebrate.

Like Lilly, he had a head of curly hair and was fair. He was long and lanky, with chubby cheeks and little upturned eyes that looked nothing like our almond-shaped ones. He was a quiet, easy baby; everything about him was easy, including his delivery. On the day he was born, Ami was at work. When she realized she was in labor, she clocked out and drove herself to the hospital. Easy peasy.

Every family picture from that time shows all of us huddled around Saad, buzzing like bees encircling a flower, proud and protective, thrilled with this new, sweet toy. Years earlier Ami had filed an immigration petition for her mother, who had shown little interest in coming to America then. But now with a new grandson as added incentive, she was willing to get on a plane and cross the oceans for the first time in her life. Saad had been born in September, and Nani Amma arrived a few weeks later to a cold, wet, gray, and dreary American East Coast.

She stayed a mere few months. She missed the Lahore winter, chilly but full of sunshine, her Pakistani government-run television station, the sound of neighbors and street vendors, the smells of the gutter and cement and fried fish and stalls of spices mixed together, and the endless loop of relatives that streamed in and out of her gates. It was so quiet in America, too quiet. The streets were clean, yes, but empty. Not a soul to be seen outside, as if she weren't among the living at all. If the price of neighborhoods bustling full of life was littered alleyways and smoggy rickshaws, so be it. It was better than this, and she wondered if her eldest daughter could truly be happy in this colorless, sanitized country.

She was unimpressed with the food, too, and though Ami and Abu excitedly tried to introduce her to pizza, their first culinary love in America, she dismissed it out of hand. She picked up a slice and examined it, asking, "Why is this roti only cooked on one side, why does this tomato sauce have no cumin or ginger or turmeric or chili, what is this soggy, stretchy white mass across the top?"

She felt sorry for us all, knowing that her daughter, who almost never cooked before marriage, certainly couldn't be expected to, afterward, with three kids. That's what she was here for, though—to cook and clean and help Ami get through the first few months with a new baby.

Nani Amma may have done some home cooking for us while she was here, but the truth was that, by the time Saad was born, it was too late to backtrack from our collective addiction to American convenience

foods. Little did we know that we were swapping out healthy, wholesome eats for products that some societies wouldn't even call food. My
parents, like many immigrants, had a naivete about America, believing
that everything here was the best, cleanest, safest, healthiest. America
had regulations and standards, laws and rules the food industry had to
abide by, the most cutting-edge science and technology in the world. The
doctors and scientists of this country knew better than anyone in the
world what was good for the human body, and no way would America
feed its citizens anything but the best.

We thought that eating like Americans meant eating healthier, so
began the years of stuff-that-makes-a-cheap-and-fast-school-lunch products, and the very foundation of those school lunches was cheap white
bread.

God, did I love it. I was obsessed with Wonder Bread commercials,
which joyously promised that its bread was enriched with calcium and
vitamins, a veritable health food, slices of Americana wrapped in the
happiest polka-dotted plastic. Other kids in school had neatly cut sandwiches made with Wonder Bread—peanut butter and jelly, ham and
cheese, tuna salad, pressed between the soft, pliable, premium white
bread—but Ami only ever bought the generic version. Wonder Bread
was, like so many brand-name versions of grocery store items, never, ever
in our budget.

I imagined it to be heftier than the store brand, and in my mind at
least two slices of the cheap white bread were the equivalent to one slice
of Wonder Bread, which meant I could eat more of them. And I did.
I discovered there was nothing that didn't taste better stuffed into, or
slathered onto, white bread. Softened butter and jam, neon yellow cheese
and pickles, plain sugar, and even other carbs like pasta or rice. Toasted
and smeared with butter, then sprinkled with salt and pepper. Flattened
and rolled up with mayonnaise or leftover omelette.

I learned the joy of bologna, cheese, mustard, and lettuce on toasty bread from my best friend, Shubnum. Shubnum's family had moved years earlier from Virginia to Delaware, while we had a brief stint in Kansas after Abu left the veterinary clinic, applied for a government job, and we moved there from Maryland. Both of our fathers, now employed as supervisory veterinary doctors by the US Department of Agriculture, were doomed to go where the slaughterhouses beckoned.

But after living in utter isolation in a double-wide in Kansas for a year—a year in which we lived in a town without any other people of color, hundreds of miles from the closest desi grocer, or Muslim family—Ami had had enough. We had to get back to civilization. And so Abu applied for, and received, a transfer to Delaware, where low white structures stretched for miles, housing tens of thousands of chickens, raised en masse on family farms that supplied Perdue and the like. It might also have been rural but at least Shubnum and her extended family lived there, and we were only a couple of hours away from DC.

I had written to Shubnum, my only friend ever, all the way from Kansas and it felt like I would never see her again. Moving to her town, then, was a dream come true. We weren't there long, just a matter of a few months, months in which Shubnum and I actually went to the same school and rode the same bus to and from school. Sometimes I would get off at her stop and hang out at her house until Abu picked me up in the evening, and those were some of the best school days of my life.

Both of Shubnum's parents would be at work, though her older brother, Asher, would often be holed up in his bedroom, which was off limits to us losers. Shubnum's house was next to a large pond, large enough to canoe across, and surrounded by woods, so we would spend hours by the water or playing among the trees, watching television, giggling over magazines, two best friends on their own. It was a fleeting few months, and one of my clearest memories is of bologna sandwiches.

I had never had bologna before, and I thought Shubnum and her parents were so cool to have something *so American* in their fridge, along with other *very American* foods like hot dogs and frozen dinners, convenience food frontiers my parents had yet to cross. I was instantly hooked on that salty, rubbery Gwaltney chicken bologna, and the best part about it was slowly tearing off the red plastic coating around each slice.

Yes, I know you may be shuddering right now, and for all the right reasons. Still, those processed, pink chicken slices were magical, and I was so greedy that they sometimes didn't even make it to the bread, I just rolled them up and ate them whole, hoping Shubnum didn't catch me doing it. I was starting to learn to hide my voraciousness, which was clearly not shared by Lilly or Saad or even my best friend. But I was just hungrier than them all.

Somehow Ami was eventually convinced to start buying Gwaltney bologna, too, and I began experimenting with it at home—open-faced on top of a cream-cheese-smeared piece of toast, stuffed in a grilled cheese, fried and slathered with mayonnaise.

Finally, I had some respectable sandwich options for school, though my most common lunch was still a sandwich of leftover saag or okra or chickpea stew, curried and spicy, oozing between the bread I loved. This practice didn't help my popularity at school, but then it couldn't really hurt what didn't actually exist. I remained undeterred. If those kids could taste the spicy, creamy saag squished between the fluffy white slices, they wouldn't be so fast to turn their noses up at the green, admittedly unattractive mess. I loved the way the stewed curries seeped into the spongelike bread, making it even soggier, upping the gummy factor exponentially in my mouth. I relished the way the bread balled up into a dense lump of starch, sticking to my palate. I didn't know then, and wouldn't for decades, that it was worse than pure sugar, but it probably wouldn't have mattered anyway—I was already addicted and there was nothing this bread couldn't do.

Cheap, easy, tasty, it was a working mother's dream and a brown mom's salvation from making homemade desi flatbreads—naan, rotis, and parathas. This was in the "before times"—before Pakistani and Indian grocers stocked with a hundred varieties of frozen and fresh desi flatbreads dotted the US like they do today. The halal grocer carried only a single kind of mass-produced naan, sold in tubular packs of twenty-five. They had little flavor, always seemed just slightly stale, and they were made with white flour instead of whole wheat. Hardly healthy contenders to replace the kinds of daily fresh roti we should be sopping up our curries with.

Healthy or not, they were convenient, and I learned fast that giving them a quick toast and spreading them with salted butter was game changing. After school, I downed glasses of cold milk with one, two, three of these toasty naan, or nearly half a loaf of white bread that I surreptitiously ferried out of its plastic bag a few slices at a time, hoping to cover my gluttonous tracks.

These were the years I learned to eat in secret, to hide my insatiable hunger, to wrap food in napkins and press it between the pages of my books, to inhale entire mouthfuls without chewing when someone suddenly entered the room. And these were also the years I realized I may have been a bit chubby because it seemed everyone had begun commenting about my weight and noticing what I ate and how much I ate. I understood that if I was going to eat the things I loved in the amounts that satiated me, I had damn better hide it.

I envied Lilly, who didn't seem to care much for cookies and crackers and bread. She would munch on apples or oranges after school, which I couldn't even understand. Who ate those things voluntarily? The only time I touched fruit was when Ami cut plates of it for us to eat, mandatorily, a few times a week after dinner. Lilly picked fruit over bread, icy sherbet over creamy ice cream, hard candies over chocolate. She liked to suck on lemons and limes and I liked to suck the center out of an Oreo. Her palate was on the opposite end of the spectrum as mine, but at least it meant more junk for me.

I imagine now the American diet must have been a shock to her system, after nearly three years of being raised on home-cooked meals, made fresh daily from ingredients picked up every morning from the butcher and fruit and vegetable stalls right outside Nani Amma's gates. And I also imagine those early years shaped her food choices and physique her entire life, as did, unfortunately, mine.

She must have especially missed fresh roti, but frankly, for Ami, it was just too much damn work. Kneading the dough wasn't too bad—the whole wheat flour in America was highly processed, unlike that back home. You could bring it together into a pliable dough with some water, salt, and oil, by hand, in about five minutes. The flour in Pakistan, authentic atta, was coarser and took nearly thirty minutes of working before it developed enough gluten to roll out into anything that could be edible. If it wasn't worked enough, you'd end up with stiff, heavy boardlike rotis instead of airy, soft, foldable ones that soaked up sauces and gravies.

The process of rolling out on a floured surface, by hand, every roti, was menial work as far as Ami was concerned. Truth be told, she had never made roti in her life before getting married and moving to America. And neither had her mother. Her family, while barely middle class, had a hired woman who came by the house every day just to make their daily roti. They were one of many families on the roti-making-woman's circuit, and roti-making had become the work of domestic servants instead of the average Pakistani housewife.

Roti is best served hot, as people are seated around the table, the roti brought to them right off the tawa, the heavy, flat iron pan that puffed up the bread into airy perfection when superheated and left lovely dark brown freckles across its surface. The timing of the process has to be exact.

It was a one-person factory-conveyer-belt operation that left flour across the kitchen counters and floors and in nasal passages and hair, and Ami hated it. While she had become a pro at making roti, at some point in time, she eventually simply stopped making it altogether, and there was only one time in the year we would smell the aroma of fresh whole wheat dough and see her slapping thin disks of rolled-out dough between her palms, *flap flap flap*, as it grew miraculously bigger and rounder in her generous hands.

That time was in the wee early morning hours of Ramadan, when we had to pry ourselves from deep slumber to eat and drink something before the sun's first rays made an appearance. Technically speaking, kids aren't required to start fasting until puberty, but in many families younger kids like to join in with the grown-ups, and start off by "fasting" from the predawn meal to lunch, then from lunch to iftar time when the sun goes down, all the while drinking water throughout the day.

Look, it's the thought that counts here. By the time I was six, I had started observing these pseudofasts, feeling very proud of myself for only eating three meals a day with no snacks, but I kept my first real full-day fast around the age of nine. I don't deny that the greatest motivator to fasting wasn't the feeling of accomplishment and superiority over the other kids, it was so I could eat parathas in the morning, since it was the only time of the year my mother made them.

Paratha and roti, for the uninitiated, are both made from the same basic dough. The difference is this: while roti is made with no oil or ghee, just rolled out and cooked dry on a tawa, the paratha is layered, pastrylike, with some kind of fat or oil, and then rolled out and cooked with a bit of grease on the pan itself. Roti is often eaten at night, because it's lighter and healthier, and parathay are a mainstay of breakfasts and brunches.

On the Ramadan mornings that Ami blessed us with parathay, the dough would be made the night before, and a good hour before dawn, as we slept, she would be in the kitchen deftly rolling out half a dozen smooth balls in a row while the tawa heated up. One at a time, she'd lightly press a ball of dough into a small disk with her substantial fingers, slap both sides of it in a bowl of whole wheat flour to give it a light dusting, and then press it out some more directly on the countertop until it was slightly bigger than her hand.

Then she would spread one side of the flattened dough with vegetable oil or ghee and roll the disk up, turn it into a chunky length of dough, and then twist the length into a spiral.

Here is where my mother showed old-school, real-G moves. She never used a rolling pin to actually roll out a paratha, at any point in the process. She would take that spiral and roll it back into a ball between her palms, press it into the flour and then out onto the countertop a second time, this time with the dough softer from the layers and oil, then pick it up in her hands and begin, with speed and vigor, to slap it back and forth between her palms.

I have never not been enthralled by watching her do this. The dough passed from left to right and right to left, faster, faster, growing in diameter from the sheer centrifugal force of the action, until it was the size she wanted, nearly the size of the pan. As one side cooked, she dribbled oil around the edges and a bit on top, waiting a few minutes to flip the paratha, and drizzling a little more oil on the other side. By this time she was almost ready with the next paratha, holding it on her left palm as she wielded a spatula in her right hand, working the one on the stove. Once the paratha was golden brown on both sides, with the edges nice and crispy, into the folds of a kitchen towel it went, to keep warm until it was joined by another, then another.

We were usually awake by the second or third paratha, aroused by her calls from the stairs, but mostly persuaded by the warm smell of dough sizzling on a tawa. And all thirty days of Ramadan, we ate those parathas with plain yogurt and goat shorba. Yogurt to help digest a meal eaten hastily around 4 a.m., and shorba because the savory bone broth was rich in nutrients, but light enough not to make us feel sick. We sometimes tore pieces of paratha into a bowl of shorba and let it soak up the goodness, like chunks of bread in a soup, and other times folded pieces of paratha into little funnels that were perfect to scoop up a little broth and a bit of meat with and quickly pop it into our mouths.

It was enough to fuel us all through the school day.

After school we ran around the neighborhood until dark, climbing trees, collecting rocks, going door to door knocking to see who else could come out to play. Georgetown, Delaware, wasn't exactly a teeming metropolis, but it was definitely not the country. Most of our neighbors in Georgetown were Black and we felt at home in a way we certainly didn't in Kansas. We ran up and down the block after school, playing with the many kids that lived in our neighborhood, while avoiding the one house directly across the street that had four very energetic pit bulls we were terrified of.

The houses in Georgetown were old, tall, and narrow, with chain-link fences around each property and sheds in most of the backyards. We made good use of the shed by housing a dozen or so chickens and a single duck there. Ami and Abu hadn't planned on raising chickens but it all began when Abu came home from work with a box holding the largest white chicken we had ever seen in it. He had been driving down a two-lane road on his way back from a poultry farm, trailing a couple hundred feet behind a flatbed truck hauling broiler chickens in hundreds of wire cages. Suddenly, he saw a chicken fly out of the truck—how and why he had no idea—and land on the side of the road.

Abu pulled over to take a look. It was a huge bird, common in industrial farming, more meat per bird for the slaughter. The chicken sat in a big white lump, in shock, so Abu leaned down and stroked it, carefully examining it for injuries. It seemed fine, no bleeding, no tenderness as he felt around it. Abu picked up the bird to help it stand, and it plopped back down. He picked it up again, and again, it plopped back onto the gravel.

That's when Abu realized that because it had been raised in such cramped quarters and grown to such a size, its legs couldn't support its weight. The poor bird had probably lived its entire existence in a massive windowless shed along with thousands of other birds, squeezed together, never getting a chance to run, walk, or stretch. And it had grown fatter and fatter at an alarming rate thanks to genetic modifications and feed packed with hormones. He put the chicken in a cardboard box and brought it home to us, and we promptly cleaned out a space in the shed and named the huge white bird Bonnie.

A couple of weeks after Bonnie joined the family, Abu came home with a box containing three tiny ducklings given to him by one of the farmers on his inspection rounds. We lined the box with towels and kept the little ashy-brown fluff balls in the kitchen by the screen door, where they could get sun most of the day. One day Saad, who was three years old at the time, saw that the ducklings were huddling together and gave the box a few strong, swift kicks. Later that day we found two of the ducklings dead, and while it may have had nothing to do with Saad, my nine-year-old self was convinced he murdered them.

We named the surviving duckling Bill and moved him into the shed once he was big enough to be safe there. Bonnie took Bill under her wing and they became inseparable. During the day the two would hang out together in the yard, Bill waddling behind Bonnie, who stayed as plump as the day we found her but had begun moving fairly well on her own. She still couldn't stand, her legs were permanently bent underneath her, but she had somehow learned to scoot her body around.

Other birds soon joined Bonnie and Bill, but they weren't meant to be pets. Getting halal meat was still no easy task, so my parents thought it would be a great idea to slaughter our own chickens, an idea they gave up after seeing what a mess it created. Turns out that killing a chicken, draining the blood, cleaning out its insides, disposing of the head and feet, plucking the feathers, skinning and carving it into pieces, was way more work than it was worth.

They'd stick to the trays of cleaned-up, packaged chicken from the local supermarket, and Allah would certainly understand. Whatever chickens escaped my father's knife, we kept, but they didn't feel like family the way Bonnie and Bill did. The entire neighborhood, and friends that visited, marveled over their friendship, and we spent the entire summer of 1984 watching them eat together, play together, and snuggle together to sleep. And then, a few months after we'd moved to Delaware, Abu got news that he was being transferred two hundred miles away, to Chambersburg, Pennsylvania, which was devastating to me. Once again, I'd be far away from my best friend, Shubnum, and once again, we'd move in the middle of a school year, away from all the kids I'd made friends with at school and in the neighborhood.

The upside though, according to my parents, was that about forty minutes from Chambersburg in Hagerstown, Maryland, there was a small Pakistani community, so we would certainly find friends there. Abu lined up a few places for Ami to check out, and one Saturday morning we locked up the house and drove to Chambersburg to look at potential homes to rent. We stayed the night and returned the next day to discover utter carnage in our backyard.

It was a scene out of a horror movie. Blood and feathers and guts everywhere. None of our birds to be found anywhere. We stood dazed, staring at what was apparently a massacre, when the next-door neighbor came running over to the fence to tell us what happened. The previous afternoon, an hour or so before the sun set, the dogs from the house across the street somehow not only escaped their house but also got into our backyard. The neighbor didn't know how, she only heard a squawking, quacking commotion and looked out to see the dogs running wildly after the birds. Most of the chickens could fly enough to make it over the fence, and escaped, and Bill was able to fly out of reach to the top of the shed.

But chunky, land-bound Bonnie couldn't. According to our neighbor, when Bill saw the dogs tearing up his adopted mother, his best friend, to bits, he flew down to try and save her. He flapped in the air, biting and pecking and screeching at the dogs, until one of them grabbed Bill in his teeth.

It was all over in a matter of minutes, and Bonnie and Bill were left in pieces across the yard.

I always had a soft spot for animals, and these two were the closest thing to pets we ever had. I sobbed and sobbed, heartbroken at their demise, but also at Bill's bravery and loyalty. Decades later I still tear up thinking about it. It was my first lesson in friendship and fidelity. To my parents, though, it was a lesson in the facts of life, and part of growing up was understanding that nature was often brutal. Ami handed me a garbage bag and told me to go pick up the bloody hunks of feathered flesh that littered the yard.

Through my tears, I did.

A FEW MONTHS later we were pretty well settled into Chambersburg, a scenic, quiet borough in the Cumberland Valley, population 15,000. Every Friday, we drove an hour to visit with the other Pakistani families for weekly potlucks. We got to know the Amish farmers down the street, and made friends with the neighbors in our community of townhouses. Once again, we found ourselves the rare brown family in a village of mostly white people.

Upon moving in, my mother was immediately scandalized by our new neighbor lady, who insisted on frequently sunbathing in a bikini, in her front yard. Every time the sun was out, there she was, barely dressed, for the entire world, and Abu specifically, to see.

I was amazed by her sheer audacity, her confidence in her body, her refusal to care what man or God thought. Ami, on the other hand, often muttered, "Thank God we're Muslims and have to keep covered up, instead of showing the world all our blubber and flaws."

A field stretched far and wide behind our row of townhouses, edged by trees perfect for climbing. I spent hours in those trees reading books, because my appetite for food was matched only by my appetite for reading. I perpetually had a stack of books next to my pillow, trading out half a dozen at a time every week at the local library, and reading became the thing I thought made me special. Every so often, I splurged on the library's old book cart and spent a quarter to purchase one of the books, because returning books to the library was nearly heartbreaking, like leaving behind friends you'd never see again.

One of those books that I got to bring home and keep home was a ratty, mustard-colored hardcover called *Ginnie and the Cooking Contest*. Written in the fifties, it was the story of a bored eleven-year-old named Ginnie who discovers a cooking contest in the newspaper. So begins Ginnie's quest to collect recipes and learn how to cook all kinds of dishes that perfectly captured the era—gelatin salads, soufflés, and chicken loaf. After spending months trying her hand at these fancy foods and a last-minute screwup on a soufflé, Ginnie decides her entry for the cooking contest will be decidedly simpler—bread.

I read that book maybe two dozen times, obsessed with the idea of someone that young cooking. I had never been allowed to cook anything. Ami didn't want any of us in her kitchen unless we were there to wash the dishes. Letting three kids loose cooking would just create a mess and it was a headache she didn't want.

But here I had this book, and it was telling me a girl my age could cook, that she would not necessarily blow anything up or destroy a stove or cut a finger off. I asked Ami if I could bake a loaf of bread, using the very recipe in the book. I promised I wouldn't need the stove, so no open flames would be involved, and the bread didn't have spices or onions or anything else that could stink up the place or leave turmeric stains anywhere. Plus, it would give us a chance to use the oven, which my mother had never used until that point, and for that matter, has still never used to this day.

The oven was and always has been a place for Ami to store pots and skillets and the woklike karhai vessel that was permanently filled with four endless inches of oil to fry pakoray or fish or whatever needed to be fried. Every so often Ami would filter the oil, add some more, and return the karhai to its holding area. Nothing in her repertoire demanded an oven. She hadn't grown up with one, no Pakistani food she ever made needed one.

She knew some of aunties we potlucked with liked to show off with their American baked goodies, like cake and brownies and roast chicken. Well, Ami didn't need an oven to roast chicken. She could do it right on the stove in a heavy iron pot, low and slow. And she didn't bake desserts, all her desi desserts were made on the stovetop, too. Abu had recently bought a fancy new microwave the size of a television and we had a small toaster oven to heat up stuff and those worked fine for Ami.

All I needed to buy to make the bread was white flour. The previous tenants of the townhouse had inexplicably left behind three things—a humongous tin can of unsweetened cacao powder, a five-pound bag of confectioner's sugar, and a box full of yeast packets, abandoned on the top step of the stairs leading to the basement. No one knew how old anything was, but we weren't about to throw them out. My ingredient needs being minimal, Ami finally gave in.

I spent an entire Saturday making that loaf of bread. Kneading it and proofing it and pounding it back down and proofing it again. All day the house smelled malty and sweet. It was better than lighting candles, or in our case, incense sticks. To me, it made the house smell homey, even it if did take hours. Finally, though, it was ready to bake.

I turned on the oven to preheat and it felt near miraculous that I had entered a food frontier even my own mother had never ventured into. I shaped the dough into a loaflike approximation in the bottom of a steel cooking pot, given we didn't have a bread tin or a baking sheet or a cake pan. I slid the pot into the oven and then gleefully discovered the oven had a light. As I furiously scrubbed all evidence of bread baking from Ami's kitchen, Lilly and Saad crowded around the glowing oven door for the next forty minutes to watch the loaf rise and turn golden right before our eyes.

If the kitchen had smelled freshly yeasty before, now it was full of an indescribable toasty warmth, like the air had become a soft, cozy blanket. We had never smelled anything like it, but if sunlight had an aroma, it would smell like that bread. We watched the clock and finally, finally it was time take the bread out. It was magnificent, high and round and golden and crusty and perfect, the very first thing I had ever cooked.

I knew from the book that the best way to eat warm bread was smeared with butter, so I had already taken a stick out to soften. The loaf was too hot to handle but I threw a kitchen towel over it and quickly cut some slices. The butter melted as soon as it hit the bread, and the bread itself disappeared between the five of us within what seemed like minutes. No wonder Ginnie won the cooking contest with bread of all things. The whole family licked salty butter off our fingers and marveled at how tasty something so simple was, at the difference between the cheap white store bread and this homemade loaf. Lilly and Saad wanted more, my parents wanted more, and I wished I had made two loaves instead of one.

Now that I had breached the oven, though, I wasn't just limited to bread. The possibilities seemed endless. I could make cookies or cakes, pastries and pies. Meatloaf! Casseroles! An entire world of American foods were now mine for the cooking. I was, however, limited by the fact that Ami had already made clear that she wasn't going to be financially supporting this new hobby and buying ingredients we otherwise never used or needed. So I contemplated what was left of the ten-pound sack of all-purpose flour, the yeast, confectioner's sugar, and the cocoa powder tin.

I baked the same bread a couple more times, and then found and clipped a recipe for a dessert called tip-tops, a sandwich cookie with two cakelike fluffy chocolate cookies held together with whipped cream. Basically a whoopie pie, but bite sized. That was the first dessert I had ever made, and like the bread, a huge hit. I made tip-tops as many times as I could before everything ran out.

This happened, unfortunately, right before fifth grade began, a lost opportunity to raise my popularity through baked goods. I had been banking my popularity on trying to be the smartest kid at the tiny Portico Elementary School—perhaps not the best strategy, but I thought I could succeed by learning every word in the English vocabulary. I would read the backs of shampoo bottles in the shower and cereal boxes at the breakfast table. I would look up the words I didn't know and write and rewrite them. I would read and read and read, at lunch and dinner, and under the covers with a flashlight. I even embarked on memorizing the dictionary and got through half of the *B*s before giving up.

It drove Ami crazy. She was convinced I'd go blind reading so much and hated watching me sit in one place for hours with my face buried behind a book. I was like an old, retired man instead of a kid who should be running around playing. But I was ravenous for pages and pages of words and was also certain that reading made me superior to my siblings and classmates, unsophisticated mongrels with no curiosity about the world. Reading would elevate me above them all. It was the only thing I was good at, so it had to.

I did weird things like memorize the entire Gettysburg Address and tell everyone who would listen that I'd memorized it because I loved the majesty of it. I was sure this, *this*, would make me popular and beloved at school. Surprisingly, it didn't work. I was still a chubby brown wallflower with greasy black hair in a hairband, the same hairband, every day, and had recently achieved the distinction of needing glasses. Fifth grade was when I really started noticing the little white girls in my class, their blue eyes and blond hair, in waves or curls or in a straight shiny wall down their backs. How their cheeks turned pink when they ran around the playground, while I went from brown to blue as the blood rushed to my face. I noticed how delicate they were, and I felt the heft of my Punjabi genes. My looks, certainly, were going to win me no popularity contests.

A chance to shine came with the school's annual holiday fundraising sale, the first time I had ever seen such a thing. We were all given impressive color brochures and a very official-looking envelope to collect orders. The class that raised the most money would win a pizza party, and the student who won would get to have breakfast with the principal.

I knew, as soon as I took a look at the prices for the assorted boxes of chocolate, gourmet popcorn candied apples, nut-coated caramel pretzels, and sets of cheese, crackers, and sausage, that I wasn't going to make a single sale in-house. No way were my parents going to shell out $13.99 for candy they could get for a few bucks at the grocery store. And it wasn't like we were going to be giving any Christmas gifts, so the festive snowflake-and-Santa-covered packaging would do nothing to sell Ami and Abu.

I would have to pound the hard streets of our subdivision to win that prize. Ami and Abu were mortified at the very prospect of sending children out to sell things door to door to strangers. What kind of warped tradition was that, and why didn't the school have enough money when the government took so much in taxes? I finally convinced them to let me do it, on the condition that I took Lilly and Saad along.

So I dragged my siblings with me from townhouse to townhouse, quickly realizing that I was up against other kids with the same idea. At the end of days of meekly trying to make some sales, I had three. Two sausage and cheese baskets and one order for chocolate nonpareils. I had never heard of these candies but from the picture they looked like tiny chocolate buttons covered in sprinkles.

When the goods finally came in a few weeks later, we picked them up at school to deliver to our customers, who had already prepaid. I dropped off the sausage and cheese baskets that afternoon, but when I went to deliver the candies, no one was home. I took the one-pound cellophane bag bursting with the festive little chocolates back home and put it under the bottom bunk of the bed I shared with Lilly. When it was time for bed, I lay in the dark, thinking about the chocolate under my bed that no one knew about. I wondered what they tasted like. The bag wasn't sealed, it was just tied with a twisty bow thing on top.

I could try just one, and close it back up, and no one would ever know.

I couldn't see if Lilly was asleep unless I climbed the ladder to the top bunk, but it sounded like she was. She hated sleeping on top, she was scared, but we didn't have a choice. Once or twice when I had slept on top, my mattress had fallen right down on top of Lilly. Ami and Abu decided the slats weren't strong enough to hold my weight and Lilly had to sleep up top or risk getting crushed by me in her sleep. I thought it was kind of an overreaction, but better safe than sorry.

I slowly took the bag out from under the bed and untwisted the tie. The smell of chocolate hit me like a shot of adrenaline. I popped one tiny nonpareil in my mouth and let it melt on my tongue. I wanted to crunch up the candies in my teeth but was afraid to wake Lilly. Just one more, I thought. And one more. Maybe one more. Okay, one last one.

Before I knew it, the bag was empty. I had eaten every last nonpareil, and now I was a thief. A thief who had committed her crime in the dark of the night, like a born-in-the-blood criminal. I should know, I had read enough Nancy Drew books. What was I going to do now? I would be turned in, not sure to whom, but I would definitely be turned in to someone, somewhere. And if I escaped the long arm of the law, Hell still awaited me.

I had never stolen anything before. Okay there was that one time I swiped some candy from a Brach's display in a grocery store, but I was six and it kind of looked like the candy was free. What if the sweet old lady who had ordered these showed up at our house demanding the candies? What if I had to pay her back, where would I get thirteen dollars? What would Abu do if he learned his daughter was a criminal?

I spent the next few days in despair, scheming. Maybe I could fill the bag with Hershey kisses, or something else, and just drop it at the woman's door and run? She didn't know where I lived. Could she call the school? The days went by, then the weeks. Then came Christmas, and nothing happened. I was wracked with guilt, but relieved that it was all over. Maybe she had forgotten. Maybe. The problem was, I wouldn't ever forget that I was a thief. To this day, the sight of nonpareils, which I haven't eaten since that dark time, fills me with shame-ridden dread.

Of course some classmate whose parents and grandparents and aunts and uncles bought dozens of items won the fundraising contest, an unfair and discriminatory advantage for kids who actually did celebrate Christmas. After all, if it had been a saag-and-paratha-selling contest, I definitely would have won.

My holiday glory had been stolen, but spring brought with it a new possibility. The school potluck approached, a once-a-year spring affair in which every family came and brought something to share. Ami wouldn't buy me more dessert ingredients, but I could still make other recipes (as long as they were confined to the oven; I still wasn't allowed to use the stove) from what we had at home. My big chance to break into savory foods coincided with one more chance to become spectacularly popular at school. Plus, the very thought of Ami showing up with a pot of fiery chickpeas or goat shorba gave me anxiety. I had to step up. I found the most amazing recipe and I imagined everyone would be awed by my dish. They would whisper "I can't believe Rabia made this, she's only ten!" nod and murmur about how special and smart and talented I was, they would finally *see me*.

I had surreptitiously torn out the recipe from a magazine at the doctor's office, convinced if the receptionist saw me, she'd call the police. But the recipe was worth the risk. It was a meatloaf, but not just any meatloaf. It was a spiral meatloaf, with a layer of rice rolled up inside a sheet of ground beef, topped with tomato sauce and baked to savory perfection. The color photo showed a glistening loaf sliced open, revealing glorious whorls of browned meat and fluffy rice flecked with parsley.

I imagined unveiling the tray holding the meatloaf at the potluck, the undeniable impressiveness of those spiraled slices. Oh, how they would gasp. The kids would talk about me for weeks.

We always had pounds and pounds of ground beef stacked in the freezer, after all; we had to buy nearly a quarter of a cow at a time from the halal butcher, and we never had anything smaller than a twenty-pound sack of basmati rice at home. It wasn't the regular, stodgier American white rice, which was probably best used in the recipe, but at that time I had no idea there was even a difference between them.

We didn't have parsley, we never used parsley, but we had a veritable harvest of cilantro Ami planted everywhere we moved. It seemed close enough. Worcestershire sauce? I had never heard of it. But we had soy sauce, and they looked similar, so that would do. Breadcrumbs weren't ever a staple in our house, but I knew Ami added besan, chickpea flour, to her meatballs to keep them soft, so besan it was.

If you know the show *Nailed It!*, in which contestants try to recreate exquisite dishes, often with disastrous results, well, my meatloaf "nailed it" decades before the show was a twinkle in the eye of a network executive.

I seasoned the beef with spices as close to the recipe as possible and flattened it out on a piece of foil. I layered on steamed basmati rice and began rolling it up, like a meaty, garlicky yule log. Finally I topped it with plain ketchup because we didn't have brown sugar to make the tomato sauce, which seemed like a weird thing to add to a meat dish anyway.

Because we still didn't own a loaf baking tin, I cooked it on the foil, and it went from the fairly decent looking log that I had patted into shape to a flattened, uneven mass about two inches high and eight inches wide. All kinds of juices spurted out from under the beef. Was it supposed to have juice? What was I supposed to do with the juice? Ami had no idea, but I figured if I cooked it long enough, the liquid would evaporate. So I just kept it in the oven until all the moisture, both in and out of the meatloaf, disappeared.

It looked hideously unappetizing, but the potluck was in an hour and there was no option left but to take it. The aroma was more like a Pakistani meatloaf, given the besan and cilantro, than what I thought an American meatloaf was supposed to smell like, but I was sure it had to taste better than it looked. When we arrived, I quickly deposited the graying brown loaf in the middle of a long, crowded table and stepped away, refusing to claim my ugly creation. I watched from a distance in horror as people in line poked and prodded it, shrugged and cut off a piece to try. Then I watched, breath held, as they ate. I was waiting for the grimace, the gagging, the spitting out, the throwing it all into the trash.

But no one did. No one seemed to throw it away, but no one went back for seconds either. I finally worked up the courage to try it, pretending not to know who made it, just casually taking a hunk to bury among the other food on my plate. It wasn't nearly as bad as it looked, though it wasn't exactly good. It was just confusing. That may have been the first and last time in history that besan and soy sauce met in a dish.

By the end of the night about a quarter of said loaf remained on the table. As others picked up their empty bowls and platters and pans, I refused to retrieve our dish. I didn't want anyone seeing me pick it up and peg me as the person behind the least identifiable food on the table. I told Ami I would get the dish from school the next day and beelined out of there. My dreams of becoming an overnight celebrity at Portico Elementary were dashed, but I was yet to hit bottom.

For the first entire year at Portico, I spent every recess reading as I pretended not to watch the other kids play together. I didn't have the dexterity or muscle to play like Lilly, who bounced from the swings to the balance beam to the monkey bars with ease and grace. I would watch her from across the playground as she pulled herself up and over a bar, twirling like a bead around a string, or reached her long, strong arms out from bar to bar, moving with ease. I couldn't do those things—my arms just weren't strong enough for my weight.

I had never weighed myself because, as far as I remember, we didn't own a scale at home. There must have been doctors' physicals over the years, but I have no recollection of ever being made aware of what I weighed. My very first memory of seeing my weight on a scale was in those final weeks of fifth grade, thanks to the goddamned Presidential Fitness Award program.

If you've never heard of this program, you were spared the utter humiliation that the majority of kids of my generation went through as we struggled in front of dozens of other students to complete a series of sit-ups, crunches, and pull-ups and a timed one-mile run. Because Portico was so tiny, all five classes did the challenge on the same day, so it wasn't just one class witnessing your failure, it was the entire school.

My day of shame began with an achievement that I certainly didn't want. The very first thing we did that morning was take off our shoes and line up to step on a scale in front of everyone to get our height measured and to get weighed. The gym teacher stood to the side with a chart while one of the teachers weighed us one by one and called out the number to be written down, and so of course everyone else could hear it, too.

"Fifty-three."

"Forty-nine."

"Sixty-one."

And then it was my turn.

I knew I wasn't the smallest girl, but I definitely wasn't as rotund as I was in my toddler years. I had a prepubescent chubbiness, but that didn't equal *fat* to me. I wasn't athletic like Lilly, but I could still climb trees and jump rope when I really felt compelled to. The point being, until that moment, I didn't think my body was a problem.

Then I stepped on that scale.

The teacher bent over as I kept my eyes straight ahead, stood back up, bent back again to double-check, and then yelled out, "One hundred. She weighs ONE HUNDRED POUNDS."

Then he turned to me and said, "Well, looks like so far you have everyone beat, you weigh more than any of the other kids in the school!" He grinned as if congratulating me on a hard-earned victory.

Everyone heard it and my face and ears burned with heat, glasses fogged up, hair band askew, as I walked past the other kids, past the gym teacher with raised eyebrows, past Jonathan Widney, the most popular boy in school, the boy whom I had the most furious crush on.

A hundred pounds? How could I weigh so much more than my classmates? I didn't think I looked like I weighed that much more . . . but maybe I didn't really know what I looked like.

The day didn't get any better when I couldn't manage a single pull-up, did barely a dozen crunches and push-ups in a minute, and slow-jogged an eleven-minute mile, all the while certain I was going to puke and pass out. That was when I really, truly understood that I was as physically fit as a pile of mashed potatoes, and that I was fat.

I didn't get the award, but Lilly did. She brought home the certificate with the presidential seal, signed by President Ronald Reagan himself, and my parents were thrilled. The *actual president of the United States* had signed their daughter's certificate, proving she had the fitness expected of an American. It was truly an honor for our immigrant family.

But despite my athletic ineptitude and failure to get the award, I suddenly started to get asked to play kickball at recess every day, the only activity I actually felt comfortable doing in front of everyone. My new and unexpected popularity was due to the explicit invitation of Jonathan Widney, the blue-eyed, blond, buck-toothed, bow-legged heartthrob of Portico. Every girl in fifth grade had a crush on him, but he was cool as a cucumber about it. He never responded to the notes the girls left him, to the eyes they made at him, to their giggles as he passed by.

I shared everyone's crush, but also lived in utter terror of him, of his popularity and his laid-back confidence. I mostly avoided him until I couldn't: when in the last quarter of the school year, the teacher lined up my desk right next to his. Now, Jonathan Widney would know what my lunches smelled like, see my thighs strain through one of two pairs of jeans I owned, and discover how unequivocally uncool I was. I felt sorry for him, getting stuck next to me.

But every day Jonathan tried to have conversations with me, sharpened my pencil when he sharpened his, and traced the pictures I had drawn onto my jean leg in marker with his finger.

And every day Jonathan Widney, who was naturally a team captain in every game he wanted to play, picked me first to be on his kickball team, a move that confused and confounded me and every other little girl who harbored puppy love for him.

It was the first time in my life, but not the last, that I discovered that boys can like big girls, too.

FOUR

Jal Bin Machli: A Fish Out of Water

The year was 1985. I was eleven, firmly in love with Michael Jackson, deeply confused by Madonna, and hating life in my new middle school. No more adoring Jonathan Widney, who had tried but failed, thanks to my glaring parents, to hang out with me during the summer break. No more Lilly across the playground, who at least brought some comfort—she was still back in Portico.

I found myself lost once again, this time the only brown fleck in a sea of hundreds of white children rather than one of dozens of them at small Portico. Thankfully the nightmare was short-lived, because two months into sixth grade, I left with Ami, Lilly, and Saad for Pakistan to attend my aunt's wedding, and we didn't return for five months.

The aunt getting married was Ami's only sister, born after a string of four boys, though there was one last son born after her. Still, she was one of the babies of the family and this wedding was going to be a *very big deal*.

I hadn't known until then that her real name was Fauzia, because we all called her Zuby. It's a thing, nicknames in Punjab, and even though Ami's family wasn't Punjabi, some of the customs stuck. My own sister, of course, had gone from Siddrah to Lilly, and somewhere in my toddler years I had become Bobbi. Except it wasn't really pronounced the way

Americans said "Bobby." It was more like "Bo-*bee*," with the eeeeees stretched long when I was being called.

"Bo-*beeeeeeeeeeeeeeeee*, where are you?!"

Zuby Aunty's wedding was a big deal, not just because she was one of the youngest in the family or because at the ripe old age of twenty-seven she hadn't yet been married off, but because for the first time in a decade the seven siblings had assembled, like a dysfunctional team of Avengers, from across the world.

Ami and her younger brothers, Iffi and Khalid Mamu ("Mamu" being the proper way to address a maternal uncle) were flying in from the US. Babar Mamu came with his family from Dubai. Pummy Mamu lived in Karachi, some 700 miles south of Lahore, and Khan Gul Mamu lived a few hundred miles north of Lahore, in Pindi. Zuby Aunty and Nani Amma, my grandmother, were the only ones still living at the old house in Sham Nagar, and the sons who lived in the country took turns stopping by.

I had never before been with them all together. We saw Iffi and Khalid Mamu in the US every so often, and Pummy Mamu, who worked for Pakistan International Airlines and got free international tickets every year, would also pop by, but I'd no recollection of the others—Zuby, Khan Gul, and Babar—whom I hadn't seen since I was four.

The five brothers were all tall and swarthy, with the exception of Khan Gul, who had light skin and green eyes. I couldn't believe I was related to someone who looked like that, until my mother showed us pictures of cousins with blond hair and blue eyes. "The seed of Sikander e Azam still lingers," she said, blaming Alexander the Great for leaving behind his DNA all over the region.

Zuby Aunty was the only one who was petite like her mother, and I was most fascinated with her because she was the bride, and there's nothing like a bride—the closest thing there was to a princess—to light up the imagination of a little girl. It was also the first proper Pakistani wedding I'd ever attended. It promised a mehndi (henna) party and a house decorated with lights and days of music and wedding rituals and trays of sweets and platters of kababs and curries and rices, and a reception with a dramatic, grand, weepy giving away of the bride, just like in the Bollywood movies I loved.

We had been to the American wedding of one of Abu's colleagues once, and it was a quiet, colorless affair. We sat in somber rows in the church in utter silence, the bride dressed in white as if she were at a funeral and not a wedding, the couple all alone at the altar as if they were the only ones that mattered, families be damned—no wonder, said Ami, the divorce rate in America was 50 percent.

It only got worse at the reception, where we had finger sandwiches and bland pasta salad and dainty hors d'oeuvres. "Even the food is colorless. And they're sending their guests back home starving!" Ami hissed, and Abu nodded. Completely unacceptable.

The chaotic joy of a desi wedding, the bride and groom's families with them every step of the way, the noise and colors, the jewels dripping off the bride and pretty much every woman in attendance, now *that* was a celebration.

Ami's eldest brother, Babar, had gotten married a few years earlier in Pakistan, but we hadn't been invited to that wedding. In fact, we didn't even hear about the wedding until afterward. That was because my mother was adamantly against Babar marrying this woman, a cousin she loathed. Marrying your first or second, or any, cousin was a fairly common practice in Pakistan until recently, when people learned that the children of such unions had higher risks of genetic disorders. It was a way to keep families close, a sure pool of marriageable candidates whom you were intimately familiar with, and at times it was just a matter of keeping inheritance and property in the family. There was always a tense expectation around whose kids would marry whose kids. Aunts and uncles kept their eyes on nieces and nephews as they grew up, weighing good future matches and sometimes arranging engagements years before the kids were even of marriageable age. There was every reason to expect that Lilly and I would eventually get proposals from cousins, too, when the time came.

Ami knew the cousin whom Babar wanted to marry, she had known her all her life, and she couldn't stand her. She didn't think she was good enough for Babar, and Ami was positive this woman had cunningly seduced her naïve brother after being rejected by other suitors. Ami wrote letters of protest from America when she learned that there was talk of an engagement, but Babar Mamu was in love, and that was that. When she found out that they had gotten married anyway, Ami wrote pages and pages in anger to everyone who'd let it happen.

A few days after we arrived in Lahore, Babar Mamu flew in from the Gulf with his wife and their baby daughter. The house was already full, every room held three or four people, except for one room, Zuby Aunty's. No one was to bunk with the bride-to-be, she needed her space and rest.

One of the bedrooms held two beds, a massive bed that four adults could sleep on and a smaller one perpendicular to it. Ami and a couple of her brothers were reclining on the big bed watching television. I was on the small bed, facing the windows, and saw a large man walk past outside with a woman and a baby, and a minute later they entered the bedroom.

The room went completely silent and it was clear something was about to go down. Babar Mamu and his wife took a seat on the chairs and Ami sat up in bed, glaring at them. Babar Mamu finally said "Salaam," but before his wife could get a word out, Ami leaped up and slapped her across the face. She raised her hand again, but Babar Mamu caught it, roaring, before the other brothers grabbed my mother and dragged her away.

That was when I knew that this was going to be a wedding, and a trip, that I'd never forget.

•••

THERE IS A stereotype about Punjabis, that they're loud and unruly and quick to fight and quick to make up, and while there may be a kernel of truth to all of that, I didn't see a bit of it in Abu's side of the family, the Punjabi side of the family. All the drama, fights, tempers were reserved for Ami's family, the non-Punjabi side.

Going from Nani Amma's home in Sham Nagar to Dada Abu's home just a few miles away in the Sant Nagar neighborhood felt like leaving a war zone and entering a safe haven. Not just because of what was going on inside at Sham Nagar, but also because it sat on an incredibly busy, crowded street, which might have been nearly empty when they moved there during the Partition but by the eighties had gotten so narrow from storefronts and vendors and house additions that two cars could barely pass by each other without touching. The cacophony of cars, bikes, dogs, donkeys, scooters, rickshaws, and streams of people was unrelenting during the day, and even after midnight there was plenty of life on the street. It was a great place to people-watch, but a terrible place to nap.

Dada Abu's house, on the other hand, was on a wide, clean street so quiet that when the occasional bicycle vendor came through hawking fruit or vegetables, his voice would echo. You could look out of a window for hours and see just a handful of people walk by. It was just as quiet inside the house. You'd hardly know anyone was home.

We were always told that I was the darling of Abu's family, and Lilly the darling of Ami's family, so I felt a special affinity for Dada Abu. I vaguely remembered Taya Amma, the one who watched me, bathed me, fed me, and loved me while my mother worked, before we moved to America. But she had passed away a few years earlier, her heart unable to survive the strain of her size. She hadn't even gotten to see her only child, Rehman, get married.

There were new faces in Dada's house now. Rehman (whom everyone called Poppa) had married the previous year, and he and his wife were living with their newborn twin boys in a new bedroom built upstairs.

Taya Abu, in his seventies, still worked in his clinic, and had been joined by Rehman, who was also a doctor, and neither of them were home all day. Dada Abu, in his late nineties and completely blind, stayed alone in his room on the ground floor, as he had most of his life, and upstairs Rehman's wife had recently been restricted to months of bed rest as the twins grew bigger and bigger in her tummy.

An old blind man and a heavily pregnant woman couldn't be left alone all day at the mercy of servants. They needed a family member at home to keep an eye on them, to keep the servants doing their jobs, to make sure everyone got home-cooked meals and got the shopping done and sent the laundry out, to communicate with the rest of the family, and to run the entire ship itself. And so, Taya Abu's second wife, the woman he would not abandon even though his father had arranged his marriage elsewhere, the woman my grandfather forbid to set foot in his house decades earlier, had moved in.

Dada Abu refused to talk to her, still bitter that she was the reason his son had disobeyed him, she was the reason his daughter-in-law had lived heartbroken until she died. Rehman likewise lost no love on her, and it pained him to see her take the place of his mother in the house, in his mother's kitchen, in his mother's bedroom. It was a restrained resentment, though, without the kicking and screaming of Sham Nagar. Everyone dutifully played the hands they were dealt, prioritizing dignity and peace in the house over their pride and anger.

Dada Abu might have lost his vision, his teeth, and some of his hearing, but was still mentally sharp, fit, and physically active. He had everything he needed placed around his bed so he could feel for whatever he wanted—fruit, nuts, medicine, water, socks, towels. Every morning he gathered fresh clothes from his dresser himself, threw his towel over his shoulder, and made his way down the path outside to the bathroom to bathe with cold water.

There was no hot water in the plumbing system, so bathing in warm water required that a bucket of water be heated to boiling upstairs in the kitchen, then carried down and mixed with cold water in a plastic bucket in the bathroom. There was no tub or shower stall in his bathroom, or in the bathroom at Nani's house either. The room had a sink, a toilet, a faucet a few feet off the ground, and a hole in the floor where the water from bathing would drain. You sat on a stool, filled up the large bucket from the faucet, and then washed by pouring jugfuls of water over you.

For me, taking a bath in Pakistan was actually more fun than in America, but going to the toilet wasn't. In both Dada and Nani's homes, like in most of the country at that time, the toilet was a squatting potty, flush with the ground. There were ceramic footholds on both sides of the bowl where you positioned your feet and squatted to do your business.

Ami's brothers knew that we wouldn't be able to manage a squatting potty, so they thankfully had had an aboveground toilet installed before we arrived, but at Dada Abu's house it was just that hole in the ground. I had no idea what to with it. Did I have to completely take off my pants to go? How did I make sure my tunic didn't fall into the hole? How did I wash and wipe afterward if I was using my hands to balance myself as I teetered on my toes? What if I fell in?!

Falling into the hole was my biggest nightmare, because my legs just weren't able to squat with both feet firmly on the ground. Clearly, this was a learned skill that my soft American body couldn't manage. Dada Abu heard about my distress and came up with a novel solution. He had a hole cut in the seat of a plastic chair and then positioned the chair over the ominous hole. It was ingenious, but more important, it was so deeply loving of him to care about the toilet fears of an eleven-year-old.

I was the first born of his last born, and he had a very tender spot for me. Even at ninety-seven, shrunk to about five foot five, he was a commanding man. His huge voice had an authoritative tone, but the minute he addressed me he lowered it, softened it, called me puttar—"my child." I had never felt so much love as I did in that one word.

He was the oldest person I'd ever been around, and I took advantage of his blindness by staring without shame at the lines of his face, his wrinkled hands, his thin calves sticking out from under the dhoti wrapped around his waist. I wanted to memorize him, and I did.

I was fascinated with his blindness and was already obsessed by the story of Helen Keller. A year earlier, when I'd started wearing glasses, I became convinced I'd eventually go blind, too. I watched Dada Abu intently to learn how he navigated his life, how he walked from one place to another, one hand never leaving the wall as he shuffled along.

He insisted on feeding himself, dipping a finger in every dish on the trays delivered to his room to check what everything was, and where everything was. Once he had the configuration of the tray figured out, he would fish for his dentures, which usually rested in a glass of water by his bed, pop them in and adjust them, and eat with ease, slowly and deliberately. When he was done, he'd reach for a tin can, which he pried open to retrieve a chunk of carmel-colored jaggery. He would break off a piece and offer it to me, and then savor a bit himself to end his meal.

"Chew each bite twenty-five times," he advised me. This seemed like overkill, but he explained that by chewing twenty-five times, you saved your digestive system a lot of trouble, and it moderated your intake so you would eat less but enjoy it more. I tried it, but I just couldn't stretch a bite for twenty-five chews—by the time I counted to ten, there was nothing left to chew.

One morning I decided to make an omelette for his breakfast as a surprise. I perched on the wooden stool in front of the double-burner gas stove on the floor of the kitchen, whisked some eggs, added salt and chili powder and turmeric and cumin seeds, and poured it into a pan of sizzling ghee. I made it the way Abu liked his omelettes, cooked until golden on the outside, no pale, fluffy American-style omelettes for him.

The paratha was already ready, and so was a bowl of sliced fruit. I carefully carried the tray down to his room and plunked it down proudly. Dada Abu reached toward the plate and picked it up, feeling around to determine if he was getting a fried egg, or a boiled egg, or an omelette that morning. He picked up a piece of paratha and a chunk of omelette and popped them in his mouth. He chewed once, twice, and then suddenly slammed down the plate and spit out his entire mouthful into a handkerchief.

"WHAT IS THIS?!" he bellowed.

But he wasn't bellowing at me. He was yelling at the woman he thought had made his breakfast, his son's second wife whom he otherwise refused to talk to.

"Are you trying to poison me? It's ALL SALT! Don't you know how to make an egg?!"

His face was red and puffed up, his hands trembling in anger. I panicked, ready to book it out of the room and let her take the fall.

Instead I confessed. I made the poisonous omelette, I reluctantly admitted.

Dada Abu's body immediately went soft and he hung his head. Then, he reached for the plate again and began eating the salty disaster.

"Puttar," he said gently, "you should always taste the food you make before serving it."

And with that, he finished it, the entire thing, without so much as wincing, just because I had made it. It was an early lesson in cooking, learned.

Some days I would sit with Dada Abu as he soaked up the sun in the courtyard, reclining on his mangi pulling smoke through a gurgling hookah. I loved the smell of the hookah, though once I learned that there was goober, dry bovine dung patties, burning along with the tobacco, I was a little grossed out. It didn't smell like dung, and I knew pretty well by then what that smelled like. Nearly every day in the early afternoon, an entire herd of sleek ebony buffaloes was guided down the quiet lane in front of the house. I would run to an upstairs window when I heard the jangling of the huge bells that hung around their necks and watch as they lumbered by, gently urged on by an impossibly scrawny man with a switch in his hand.

They always left behind mounds of dung steaming in the sun. It didn't occur to me until later that the dung would disappear at some point in the day, until I was told that it was collected to be mixed with hay, slapped into patties to dry, and ended up as fuel in hookahs and stoves across the city.

Dada could sit in silence in the sun for hours, and sometimes I wondered if he knew whether I was there or not. Once I was sure that he wouldn't know if I snuck away, I felt less guilty running off to play or explore. It was hard not to get restless because when I sat with him outside, I would see little dusty heads pop up over the wall that bordered the yard. A family of nine daughters and one son lived right next door, in a tiny sublet section of a larger house.

They were the most beautiful Pakistani family I had ever seen. The parents were so young they looked like kids themselves, and all ten children had light brown wavy hair and hazel eyes. Their eldest, a girl a couple of years older than me, wore her hair in a long, single braid that hung to her waist, and this made me embarrassed of my short, greasy black bob.

The parents had daughter after daughter, a new baby every year, determined to keep having more until they had a son. They needed a son. Who would take care of them in their old age? Who would help earn enough to get all the girls married? And so, the older daughters always seemed to be carrying a little sister on a hip, their mother perpetually pregnant, praying all nine months for a boy every time until one finally arrived.

"So ignorant," Ami said. "Having children in litters like animals.

How are they going to raise that many children, how will they marry off that many girls?? That poor son will be crushed under the burden of nine sisters."

They were fascinated with me, this numpty from America who wore her hair like a boy and wore glasses like an old man. My Urdu was weak. I could understand it but barely speak it, and couldn't read it to save my life. They in turn didn't know a bit of English, but we got past the communication barrier and played tag and hide-and-seek, and I would smuggle them candies and cookies from the stash in Ami's suitcase. Twice I went inside their home, where I saw that all twelve of them lived in two rooms, with a stove set up in the courtyard. The rooms were neatly stacked with schoolbooks and folded clothes, with a tired-looking mangi in each room leaned up against the wall during the day.

The poverty was unmistakable, but so was their dignity. Everything in their tiny home was orderly and clean, just like the kids themselves, and there was a contented peacefulness in their home that I envied. I also envied the eldest daughter, delicate and sweet, big light eyes and a generous smile. She didn't seem to have a self-conscious bone in her body. I had become even more acutely aware of my boyish bulk since landing in Pakistan, and of the fact that everyone expected our relative prosperity to mean we would be more elegant, more polished, more *American*.

Instead Lilly and I showed up with terrible homemade haircuts and clothing, relying on Ami's skills for both, because we certainly didn't have the money for salon cuts and boutique Pakistani clothing. Why didn't we look like the Americans they saw in the movies, they wondered? It was because Ami and Abu were raising us the way they had been raised, thrift being the guiding principle. At the same time, they wanted desperately to keep us as Pakistani as possible, having convinced themselves that one day soon we would all return to Pakistan forever. The minute we got home from school we had to change into shalwar kameez, the traditional desi dress, and my father's dream of both his daughters wearing their hair in long, oiled, tightly wound braids was thwarted only by Ami's insistance on hacking it off every few months so she wouldn't have to deal with it.

There wasn't a thing posh about us, but ironically, the one thing that reflected our American abundance was my heft. Kids did not get that rotund unless there was excess in the home.

The last time Dada Abu had seen me with his own eyes was when we had come to pick up Lilly eight years earlier. Ami had repeated the "what have you done to her?" story many dozens of times over the years, and I'd been worried that he would be newly mortified by my size, so it was a small blessing that he was blind.

Unfortunately no one else was.

Meeting his five daughters, my phuphos, as paternal aunts are called, was like being inspected for market. The older aunts had kids in their thirties, already settled down, but the younger ones had sons that could very well be matches for Lilly and me.

One by one we made the rounds to their houses to pay our respects, deliver gifts, and catch up. The four eldest all lived in the area, never having moved too far from their father's home, so that all day their kids, my cousins, could stop by to check on him and provide some company. Visiting them was like meeting 80 percent of your family tree at once. In every home, Lilly, Saad, and I were introduced to the many cousins we didn't know, eight or ten in each family, and to their spouses and their kids. We had to try and remember Cookie, Mona, Babloo, Twinky, Pinky, and a hundred other nicknames, their actual names, and how exactly they were related to us.

We'd sit quietly in the living room as the entire family streamed in to say hello, eventually surrounding us, appraising us with welcoming grins, as we squirmed awkwardly and tried to avoid their stares. If staring was a competitive sport, Pakistanis would win. Everywhere you go, people will look directly at you frankly and openly for uncomfortably sustained periods of time without even trying to hide it. Culturally, it's not considered rude to stare. Everyone does it, but it's almost too much to bear. How long can you stare back and smile and nod? Eventually you have to look away, look down, look anywhere hoping they'll finally stop. But they don't.

And surrounded by dozens of new people, all staring at us as they sized us up, we were expected to eat while they didn't. The minute we arrived, boys would be sent to fetch cold bottles of Coca-Cola, samosas, and sweets, and in the kitchen a kettle of chai would promptly be started. It was wintertime so we kept being served the same "hot foods"—not food that was hot to the touch, but foods that heat up the body. An ancient approach to food in the East is that every food and spice is assigned to either the hot, cold, or neutral categories and it's best to eat according to the season. Hot foods in the winter, to warm you up, and cold foods in the summer to cool your body down in the unforgiving heat. Everywhere we went, we were presented with two traditional hot foods: bowls of steaming gajar ka halwa—a sweet dish of carrots cooked down in ghee into a caramelly mash with nuts and globs of khoya, sweet, thickened cooked milk—and platters of boiled, halved eggs.

No amount of scrutiny from elderly aunts and staring cousins stopped me from eating my fill at every stop. I was in the middle of eating yet a third boiled egg at one stop when the second-to-oldest phupho, whose house we sat in surrounded by her daughters and granddaughters, asked Ami, "How old is Rabia again?"

Ami looked at me sitting there in my glasses, hairband holding back a short bob of greasy, stick-straight black hair, and responded that I was eleven.

"Eleven? What do you feed her? She looks eighteen. She has a full jism."

I continued to eat my egg, listening but not overly concerned because the salty, buttery warm yolk, so much more golden than the eggs in

America, had my attention. When I looked up, Ami, the phupho, and a half a dozen assorted female cousins were assessing me. "Jism?" I thought. I had no idea what a jism was.

Ami seemed flustered and muttered, "Well you know in America girls grow up so much faster, they develop younger, I didn't become grown until I was almost sixteen, but Bobbi, she became grown just a couple of months ago."

"*Hawwwwwww*," phupho exclaimed, as the others raised eyebrows and let out small gasps.

I suddenly understood what they were talking about. A few months earlier, on my birthday, and right before the start of sixth grade, I had gotten my period.

Thanks to fifth grade health class, I wasn't completely blindsided, and had a basic understanding of puberty and the birds and the bees. After much prodding from me, Ami had finally signed the consent form for sex education, but it came with a threat. "Whatever you learn, don't you ever ever ever talk about it with your brother or sister. Or Shubnum. Or anyone at school. With no one, ever."

The threat worked and I never mentioned anything I'd ever learned to anyone until years later, when I finally worked up the courage to ask Shubnum *how* the sperm got to the egg—something the nurse declined to explain—and then absolutely refused to believe the answer.

The morning I got my period, I came bouncing down the stairs gleefully and whispered the news in my mother's ear as she sat hemming something. Her face turned red and she put down the fabric and stuck the needle back into a spool of thread. "Follow me," she said.

I bounded up the stairs behind her, and she locked us in the bathroom where she showed me where the pads were and explained what to do with them, all the while avoiding my grinning face. Then she looked me in the eyes and said, "Don't you ever ever ever tell anyone that you are now grown. No one. Ever."

And I didn't. But now, here we were, in a room full of women, telling them all that I had gotten my period, as Ami explained that the American diet was so rich and full of protein that girls there became "grown" years earlier than girls in Pakistan.

Everyone looked glum. This was truly terrible news. The longer a girl stayed not-grown, the better. Once she got her period she had to fulfill all the religious obligations, and technically, she was of marriageable age. But the rule that a girl could get married once she hit puberty was definitely not created at a time that girls got their periods at nine, ten, eleven years old.

"Well, that explains her jism," the phupho said, staring at my budding chest. I pulled my shoulders down and hunched a bit when I realized what all the fuss was about, a plate of egg halves still in hand. Phupho sighed, troubled for her niece. Everyone knew that once a girl had her period, she would stop growing any taller, and start to fill out, gain a few pounds in certain places. That didn't bode well for me, and my marriageability, at barely five feet, and already thickly proportioned. Phupho had hoped that I would one day make a good match for one of her sons, but it was clear that what I was carrying wasn't baby fat. This was grown-up fat, and no sudden spurt in height would fix things.

She delivered her verdict. "American food made her grown. And it made her fat. Think of her prospects. Who will marry her?"

"OYE MOTI! NO one will marry you!" my middle uncle, Pummy Mamu, crooned at me back at my Nani's house, half teasing, half concerned.

Moti, fat female, was one of many nicknames I collected during that trip. I was also "gol guppa," shaped like a spherical street snack stuffed with chickpeas and potatoes.

"Fatty fatty boom boom," my Taya's son, Rehman, said affectionately to me, as we were having breakfast one morning.

I halted mid-bite, but he softened. "No, no, eat. See, I'm a fatty fatty boom boom, too."

And he was: Rehman was huge, nearly six foot four and likely 250 pounds. But very quickly, I learned it didn't matter for men.

I pointed out to Pummy Mamu, who had gone through multiple engagements but was still not married, that he was no Mr. Universe either, with his paunchy gut. He leaned close and said, "Moti, don't you understand, men can look like anything, as long as they have good jobs and homes. But girls cannot look like middle-aged women before they're even married. Girls should have a kamar, not a kamra."

Kamar: a waist. Not a *kamra*: an entire room. It was a clever play on words, I had to hand that to him.

We were by then only a few weeks out from Zuby Aunty's wedding, and with each passing day the house got more frenetic. Zuby Aunty was supposed to stay strictly at home for at least the month before the wedding, the proper thing for a bride to do, but she just couldn't deal with all six of her siblings and their kids pressing in on her at once. That, and she was used to being out and about all day, going to university, visiting friends, wandering bazaars, and exploring local food and jewelry vendors, her two favorite things in the world.

I was enamored of her. Unlike the other siblings, she was quiet and reserved, and also absolutely beautiful. I wondered what it was like to be so pretty, to have an entire household whirl around you in excitement, to be the center, the star, of a monumental event. She would often snuggle with us, her nieces and nephews, secretly sharing candies and biscuits in bed, but she told me she most loved snuggling with me because I was soft and fleshy. She may have been the only person, during the entire trip, that didn't say a negative thing about my weight.

One day, as I watched her get dressed to surreptitiously head out before anyone caught her, she saw my mournful eyes and asked, "Do you want to come with me?"

I jumped up, ran to put on my sandals, and told Ami I was going out with Zuby Aunty.

"Stop going out in the sun! You'll get all brown before the wedding, and what will the neighbors say, the bride-to-be traipsing all over town without a hint of shame!" Ami yelled at her as we headed out of the iron gate.

Zuby Aunty grabbed my hand and said, "Okay, first stop, I'm getting you a burger." I didn't even know you could get a burger in Pakistan, and by that point I was desperately missing American fast food. We began walking, and walking, and walking.

She walked everywhere, she explained. She didn't want to spend money on a rickshaw and she hated dealing with the throngs of men on buses, so it was just easier to walk. And that way, she could also keep her eyes peeled for new shops that popped up in tiny enclaves and slivers of buildings, new food stalls set up in slender alleys off the main roads.

We walked hand in hand, navigating the tight space between road traffic, street vendors, motorcycles and cars parked in any and every possible opening, and the steady line of open gutters that ran alongside homes to drain into the sewers. It was the first time I was really exploring the streets of Lahore. Up until then I had been stuck behind the gates in Sham Nagar and Sant Nagar. It was exhilarating and overwhelming, and I felt an indescribable sense of belonging. We reached a roundabout with no discernible lanes, with traffic whizzing by, vehicles crisscrossing, entering and exiting through what seemed like ten different lanes that fed into it. Every driver, it appeared, was leaning on their horn in one long, unbreaking honk.

In the center of the roundabout in a grassy circle stood a stunning monument that looked like a small Mughal castle, four majestic pillars on each corner of a blocklike structure with massive arched, open doorways. It was so oddly out of place, this ornate, decaying structure, something out of Aladdin, in the middle of traffic and shops and piles of garbage and garish, colorful billboards.

Zuby Aunty saw me staring and said, "That is Chauburji. It means 'four towers.' It's four hundred years old and it was built for the Mughal princess Zeb-Un-Nissa as a gateway to a royal garden, a place where she and her ladies-in-waiting could relax. Back then, a stream flowed through the huge center doorway . . . but now it's not even worth looking at."

It was worth looking at for me because I had never seen anything like it. It was built for a real princess! And the place had once been surrounded by gardens and streams!

I thought we were going to walk up to Chuaburji and through to the other side but my aunt said absolutely not. "See those men lying in the grass all around it?"

I did, and I figured they were taking naps.

"They're charsis, drug addicts and petty criminals. They're homeless so they camp around Chauburji, sell and buy their drugs there. It's not safe, we'll just walk around."

We walked around the circle and down alleyway after alleyway, and finally stopped at a wooden cart. A stack of elongated buns and a tub of boiled eggs sat on one side, and a dozen containers of chopped onions, tomatoes, chilies, lettuce, spices, and sauces on the other. In the center, on a small raised burner, there was a large circular tawa, over two feet in diameter. This was the burger joint.

My excitement grew. Not only had I not walked around the city before, no one had let us eat from a street cart until now. Everyone on my father's side of the family strictly forbid it. They wouldn't even eat street food themselves. It was completely unhygienic, open food that attracted flies, from vendors who wiped their noses or scratched their crotches and then got back to the business of serving customers with their bare hands. And, they warned, for Americans with tummies not used to the local organisms in the water, it would be a recipe for disaster.

Ami's family was much more adventurous in their consumption, and every day my five uncles would bring food home from some restaurant or food stall or another, but they never took us there to eat. This right here, this open burger cart, was a full-on adventure. Zuby Aunty signaled for the tall, lanky man in a turban to make us two burgers and he reached under his cart and pulled out four patties. But they didn't look like beef patties. "What are *those*?" I asked her.

"They're shaami kabab, made from daal and beef ground up together. Watch how he makes a burger of them."

I realized then that this was not going to be the kind of burger I expected, and clearly my aunt had never had a real burger. The vendor pressed the patties on the tawa and poured a ladle of ghee on them, and as they began sizzling he threw a few boiled eggs on the pan, too, and began roughly chopping them up with his spatula. He tossed the patties over and covered them with two buns, pried open, as the chopped egg bits popped and hissed, the egg whites slightly browning.

Finally he took the patties, and instead of placing them in a now warmed bun, he smashed them into the bread, spreading the patty like a hunk of butter, before topping them with a pile of egg crumbs, all of the fresh fixings, a sprinkle of chaat masala, and spoonfuls of ketchup and spicy green and sweet red chutneys. The burger had every texture possible. Soft patty, chewy egg, crunchy onion, juicy tomato. It wasn't a burger in any way I could have imagined, but that vendor was light years ahead of the recent egg-topped burger trend in the US. We stood by the side of the road and scarfed our burgers down, chutney dripping down our fingers, and then washed our hands with the jug of water at the cart.

By then we'd been walking an hour and my sedentary American lifestyle was catching up to me, so Zuby Aunty agreed we would take a bus to our next destination—her old college canteen. She led me to a street corner, where there were absolutely no signs for a bus stop but where apparently buses still knew to stop and people knew to wait for them. Every minute or so another bus or small van would pull up, stuffed to the gills with people, and a handful would burst out as a conductor yelled out the stop. Another handful of people would scramble to make it inside before the driver took off, and inevitably a bunch of people were crowded out and had to wait for the next one.

It was absolutely terrifying chaos. We were surrounded by a throng of mostly men, and my aunt squeezed my hand tight. "Our bus is almost here, whatever you do, don't let go of my hand, I'll get us onto it."

Our bus arrived, and like many of the others, it had two entries—at the front and back—but no actual doors, so passengers who couldn't quite get inside just stood on the bottom steps half hanging out into the street. My aunt surged ahead, elbowing people left and right until she made it to the door. In a matter of seconds she was up the steps and inside the bus, but I had let go of her hand and was still standing outside. Zuby Aunty began screaming, "That's my daughter, that's my daughter, help her on, get out of the way, help her on!" and someone grabbed me up and onto the first step of the bus as it took off.

I could see my aunt from a distance yelling, "Bo*beeee*, Bo*beeee*!" straining to figure out if I had made it, until someone yelled, *"Fikar na kaar bibi, tere bhans ka bacha char gaya!"* ("Don't worry lady, your baby buffalo made it.")

A bunch of men guffawed and my face flushed red. I was hanging on to a bar for dear life, trying not to fall right off that bottom step as the bus drove wildly, but part of me now wanted to hurl myself into traffic. At the next stop, once some passengers got off, someone pulled me further into the bus and I finally got to my aunt, who gave me a tight hug. "There is no way that's your daughter," someone said. "You look like *her* daughter."

Zuby Aunty barked, "Bakwas band karo" (Shut your nonsense up), and it worked. When we finally got off the bus, I was in tears. "This city is full of assholes," she said, and took my hand and marched us through the gates of her old college.

The rest of the day made up for the horror of the bus. We had pakoray and pistachio kulfi on sticks, better than any ice cream I'd ever had, at the canteen, and then late in the afternoon walked to the famed two-hundred-year-old bazaar, Anarkali. There was no discernable rhyme or reason to the bazaar, it just looked like lane upon ancient lane filled with open shop fronts, some as small as ten feet across, bursting with reams of cloth, shoes, toys, clothing, and rows and rows of glass bangles. But my aunt knew the bazaar like the back of her hand and led me deeper and deeper in, until we reached a shop where a man sat perched atop a high platform surrounded by pomegranates and pineapples, oranges and bananas.

A curtain hung on one side and my aunt swept it aside, revealing a series of simple benches where a dozen tired-looking women, shopping bags piled around their feet, hidden from the rest of the bazaar, sat drinking huge mugs of fresh fruit juice and eating bowls of fruit chaat.

"This," said my aunt, "is the most famous fruit chaat in all of Lahore."

We took a seat and Zuby Aunty ordered one regular chaat, one ambrosia-like cream chaat, and a pineapple shake.

Just outside the curtain, I spied a young boy surrounded by piles of dirty mugs and dishes, who was quickly dunking them into a bucket of water a few times then passing them on to another boy, who gave them a quick wipe with a grayish rag. Oh, I was definitely asking for trouble now. I thought about all the diseases and bacteria my cousin Rehman had rattled off to me—hepatitis, typhoid, worms, and a dozen other ways to ensure diarrhea and vomiting.

But once the small silver plates brimming with chaat and a frosty mug were placed before us, I forgot everything. We topped our chaat with even more chaat masala, and doused it with plum and date chutney, tangy and sweet and infused with red chili powder. It was magical, but not necessarily any better than chaat we made at home. What made it magical was the experience—sitting in the middle of an ancient bazaar, hidden in a quiet spot where no one could see us, sharing a tight space with a bunch of weary aunties as my aunt told me about the seventeenth-century legend of Anarkali.

Anarkali, which means "pomegranate blossom," was the name of a beautiful courtesan who fell in love with a Mughal crown prince. Prince Saleem had first laid eyes on Anarkali in Lahore and was immediately smitten. The problem was that this courtesan belonged to the harem of his father, Emperor Akbar, and she was one of his father's favorites. When news of the love affair reached Akbar, he was so livid, he ordered Anarkali entombed alive behind a wall in his palace. Some say she died buried in that wall, and others that she escaped. Either way, Prince Saleem was heartbroken, and when he ascended to the throne as the Emperor Jehangir, he built a gorgeous tomb for her in the heart of the old city.

Inscribed in the tomb were the ninety-nine names of Allah and a poem the emperor wrote for her that read "Ah! Could I behold the face of my beloved once more, I would give thanks unto my God until the day of resurrection."

The story filled up all the romantic pathways that Bollywood had already carved into my impressionable psyche. I wanted to see the tomb, I said, as I spooned up the last bits of juice released by the macerated fruit.

"Well, unfortunately while Jehangir was really romantic, today's men aren't," my aunt told me. "The tomb still stands, but it's been turned into a government building now, full of records and archives. It's like Anarkali was killed all over again."

THE FINAL WEDDING countdown was on, a week to go, and so much left to do.

Dowry gifts our family bought to give the groom and his family began piling up in one room, including dozens of household items Zuby

Aunty would haul to her new house. Technically, Muslims aren't supposed to send their daughters off with dowries, as if purchasing a groom. Instead Muslim grooms are obligated to provide a dowry to the bride, in accord with what the bride's family asks for, and it can be gifted up front or given to her later in the marriage. And yet, the Hindu customs from the old country, India, remained. Pakistani brides got a dowry from their grooms, but also were expected to enter the marriage laden with gifts.

The greater the gifts, the greater the prestige. Gold rings and bangles and fancy clothes and shawls for the groom's mother and sisters, watches and cologne for him and his father, a dozen suits and sweaters and coats and pairs of shoes for him, tea sets and fine china, blankets and comforters, appliances, stainless steel cooking pots and pans, furniture for the new couple's room, and even, for the most well-off bride or greedy groom, a brand-new car. These were the kinds of dowry gifts families of daughters would begin collecting, along with wedding jewelry for her, when their girls were very little, knowing that they likely wouldn't be able to bear the expense all at once.

Zuby Aunty's dowry was internationally sourced. Those of us who had come from overseas for the wedding brought coveted gifts from America, Europe, and Dubai. Ami had bought her brother-in-law-to-be suits and leather shoes and cologne, and purses and sweaters for the women in his family. The elder siblings had divvied up more expensive stuff, a washer and dryer from one brother, a watch for the groom from another, gold rings for the women of his house from another.

The household goods would be delivered to the groom's home after the wedding, but all the personal gifts couldn't just be shoved into bags and handed over. They had to be beautifully displayed on huge trays and baskets, decorated with tinsel and flowers and wrapped in clear cellophane to be presented like royal offerings. It was a lot of work, and it took many hands to fold the garments just so, pin them so they didn't shift, arrange them artfully on trays or baskets with accessories, and then wrap the whole thing tightly so nothing moved from its place until dispatched to the groom's family on the day of the wedding in a grand show.

The only gifts exchanged before the wedding were the actual wedding outfits. The groom's family would provide the gown and jewelry the bride was to wear for the wedding, and the bride's family would provide the groom's outfit. It may seem nerve-wracking not to know what you'll be wearing until just days before your wedding, sometimes not even until the night before, but until recently that was how it was. The families would trade measurements, and then hope for the best.

I had never seen Zuby Aunty's intended but had heard about him. He was a captain in the Pakistani army and came from Gujranwala, a city a couple of hours away. Over the weeks when I got to be alone with her, I had asked if she loved him, or liked him, or if he was handsome, or if she was excited, and every time she would look away without responding.

"Stop it," Ami hissed, "a bride isn't supposed to be excited and happy to be getting married. She's leaving her family forever, she's sad!"

It was very confusing because I remembered the American wedding we had gone to, and how happy the bride was, which seemed like the right way to be.

One morning, a few days from the wedding, mild pandemonium broke out in the house. The plan had been for two of my uncles to travel to Gujranwala to drop off the groom's wedding ensemble, but when they called ahead, they were told not to bother. The groom and his family had errands to take care of in Lahore and would stop by themselves in a couple of hours. No one was remotely in any condition for guests. My aunt had a head full of coconut oil, half the men were sitting around unshaven in their undershirts, and Ami and Nani were out shopping.

Zuby Aunty rushed to change out of the clothes she had been wearing for two days, smoothed and tied her hair in a braid, then headed to the kitchen to frantically scrounge up something to serve her future in-laws and husband. Others ran around cleaning up the courtyard, clearing riffraff off the dining table, and straightening up the sitting room, where a half dozen of us slept every night, couches moved to the walls, bedspreads and pillows all over the floor. This was the least pleasant of surprises for everyone but me. The unexpected guests had put a wrench in their afternoon plans, and there was so much still to be done before the mehndi party, now two days away. I, however, was bursting with excitement to meet the groom.

Eventually we heard a banging on the gate and the sound of greetings and chattering as my aunt's betrothed arrived with his mother and sisters. Ami and Nani Amma had just returned home moments earlier and were scrambling to get the groom's outfit properly packed, leaving my aunt to get everything ready in the kitchen. I stood by the small two-burner stove frying pakoray with Zuby Aunty, whose face was beet red. One of my uncles came and asked us if the trays were ready, and they were, so he grabbed one, and I grabbed one, and followed him to the sitting room.

By this time I'd become fairly adept in the sport of staring, now that I knew I could get away with it. From the second I entered the room I focused all my attention on the slender, balding, mustachioed man in the center of the sofa. I put down the tray of nuts and eggs and pakoray and kababs without taking my eyes off him, and then stood behind Ami, who occupied the most prominent chair in the room.

The groom's family was meeting the elder sister for the first time and Ami was determined to impress them with how American she was. Ami launched questions in English, throwing me off. She never spoke English at home, not even in America, unless she absolutely had to. This was definitely an attempt to cement her superiority.

To my surprise, the groom, sitting very sophisticatedly with his legs

crossed, responded in perfectly proper English. He was, after all, an officer in the military. Once Ami had tested the waters and realized she
wasn't going to gain any points with English, she reverted to Urdu pleas-
antries. I continued to stare at the groom and every so often he would
glance at me and smile.

Finally he asked, "What's your name?"

"Uh. Rabia."

"You can call me Uncle Israr."

I liked this guy. Most of the time kids were completely overlooked,
not spoken to and not expected to be heard from, but he had specially
paid a few moments of attention to me. I skipped across the courtyard
and back to the kitchen and my aunt whispered, "Did you see him?
What do you think?"

I bellowed, "He's really nice and HE HAS NO HAIR AND A FACE
AS ROUND AS AN EGG!"

I didn't know until weeks later, after the wedding, that he and everyone in the sitting room had heard my declaration.

They left late in the evening, and by then only Thursday remained
between the events of the weekend: the henna party on Friday; the rukh-
sati, or giving away of the bride, on Saturday; and the groom's reception
on Sunday.

I had discovered a dusty old cassette player in one of the cupboards
and gotten one of my uncles to buy a bunch of wedding music tapes,
songs from Bollywood, old folk songs, fast-paced henna party songs, and
slow, sad away-goes-the-bride songs. I blasted them, as loud as the old
machine would go, day and night to build up the wedding spirit.

It wasn't working though. My aunt grew more sullen and withdrawn,
and the rest of her siblings got more and more anxious and aggressive
with every passing day. On the day before the henna party, a handful of
workers showed up with buckets of paint to do some quick whitewashing

and hang reams of string lights to deck out the house, from the front facade facing the street, to the roof, to the inner courtyard. A house with a wedding had to look like it.

I loved it. I had only ever seen string lights in America at Christmas, where I admired their twinkly wonder from afar, since we didn't celebrate the holiday. By dusk, the house was lit up in the most festive way, just like in Indian movies, but unlike in Indian movies, the family of the bride was in a terrible mood. Ami snapped at her mother, who snapped at her sons, who snapped at each other, while Zuby Aunty locked herself in her room.

Sensing the tension, I went up to the roof, one of my favorite places, where I could see across the neighborhood and onto other roofs. Every house had an open, flat roof edged with a rail made of iron or bricks, furnished with some chairs and mangis. There were kids playing, young men flying kites, women hanging the wash, trays of chilies and jars of pickles soaking up the sun, old men drinking chai; I loved peeping into these other lives. It was the best place in the house to get some direct sunlight in the cold Lahore winter, and sometimes we would sit up there during the day, eating sliced cucumber sprinkled with salt and chili powder and drinking freshly squeezed carrot juice spiked with black salt.

I wanted desperately to sleep on the roof, which was something I knew my father had grown up doing on hot summer nights. I had begged my uncles to let me sleep up there but they said absolutely not. First of all, girls didn't sleep on roofs, that was just inviting unwanted attention, only boys did. But second, and more important, I could get murdered. "The Hathora Group will get you!" I was told.

The Hathora ("hammer") Group was the name given by newspaper reporters to whoever was responsible for a series of grisly murders in the country. The victim was always killed as they slept outdoors—on a roof, or in the street if homeless—by a blow to the head with a hammer. Sometimes the victim's head would be smashed to pieces, I was warned.

That's why, my uncles said, I wouldn't see people sleeping on the roof anymore. The city was terrified.

They had me sufficiently scared not to linger too long when I did climb the rickety ladder to the top, but sometimes I did it not to spy on other people but to be able to see down into our own courtyard without anyone seeing me. Especially when I wanted to overhear what the grown-ups were talking about.

That night, from two stories above, I peered down into the courtyard, where a few of the uncles were sitting around, breaking open pine nuts and walnuts, and resting from the day's work of preparing the house for the henna party. Suddenly, their conversation got loud. And louder, and louder.

This wasn't an unusual thing though. I'd seen at least a dozen fights between the siblings since we'd arrived and each one was like the clash of the titans. They were big men with huge voices and they thundered cuss words I'd never heard before, cuss words involving doing things to mothers and sisters and body parts I wasn't even allowed to mention. Most of them I wouldn't understand until years later.

Having never heard my father even raise his voice, I wasn't used to being around loud, angry men. It was somewhat scary, but also kind of amazing, like watching a car wreck take place right before your eyes.

I watched as two of them jumped up and began shoving each other.

Uh oh. This was an escalation.

"Fuck YOU, what have you ever done for her?!?"

"You sister-pounder, I did more than your ass ever did, getting fat overseas!"

They were fighting over who had neglected their poor, widowed mother more over the years. The competition was stiff and the allegations grew by the second.

I happened to have the tape recorder with me and hastily checked to see what cassette was in it. It was *Wedding Songs* by Musarrat Nazir, a big hit in that era, but I'd have to sacrifice the tape so I could record the fight over it. I had this plan: if I were able to record one of their epic, raunchy fights and then play it back to them when things had calmed down, they would be ashamed enough not to do it again. That, or I could use it for blackmail, though I had no idea what I would blackmail anyone for.

Now was my chance. I hit record as the fight raged on.

One of them was in a headlock now, roaring profanities as Nani Amma stood on the veranda pleading with them to stop humiliating her. The whole neighborhood could hear their fights. I heard pounding on the gate and ran to the front of the roof so I could see down into the street. A few men stood outside, neighbors, and they were yelling at my uncles to have some shame, it was ten o'clock at night, people were trying to sleep, and their daughters and sisters and mothers could hear the horrific obscenities that no decent person should ever be subjected to.

No one answered the gate of course.

I ran back to see how the fight was progressing just in time to witness one uncle raise a chair and bring it slamming down on his brother from behind, screaming, "Oh yeah, WELL I FUCKED YOUR WIFE!"

At the time I had no idea what he said, because he said it in Urdu and I didn't know what the word meant in that or any language. But it definitely felt like a turning point in the fight. They both grabbed pieces of the broken chair and began swinging at each other. Nani Amma had retreated to a bedroom in tears, but two of the other brothers came racing out and finally ended the death match by wrestling the challengers apart and into separate rooms.

Finally, it was quiet. I waited ten minutes, straining to hear if things were going to erupt again, and then tiptoed back down the two flights.

Ami was in the bigger bedroom, watching television in bed as if nothing had happened, and Nani Amma lay next to her with the covers pulled over her head. One uncle, Iffi Mamu, the one who never ever got involved in fights, sat on the smaller bed reading a newspaper. I quietly walked past and into the adjoining room, my aunt's room. She lay in the dark, the lights turned off, but I could see her in the faint glow from the strings of wedding lights hung outside every window. She was on her stomach with a pillow over her head.

I retreated out to the veranda and sat down, surveying the bits of broken chair. I knew the uncles were split up in different rooms, combatants cooling off apart from each other. A little while later Pummy Mamu walked out into the veranda and said, "Chal moti [Come on, fatty], let's go get something to eat."

I climbed behind him on his motorcycle and we took off in the dark. There was still plenty of traffic on the roads; Lahore comes to life at night, and restaurants often stayed open into the wee hours. I sat sidesaddle, because he said that was the proper way for a lady to ride. I was certain I would slide right off with every turn, so I clutched him for dear life and buried my head in his back, not wanting to see all the near misses.

We finally arrived at an open-front restaurant with lines of motorcycles and bikes jammed into every inch of space on the street before it. An open front meant exactly that, there was no wall to the restaurant facing the street, and all the cooking was done out on the footpath, right there for everyone to see. You could sit at the tables inside behind the cooks, or snag a bench or random overturned bucket out front.

My uncle pointed to the sign posted above the restaurant. "Read that."

I couldn't.

"Haji Sardar Ki Machli," he read. Haji Sardar's Fish.

Two vats of oil bubbled ferociously as one man weighed out slabs of batter-coated fish on a scale and passed it on to be deep-fried, fresh for the customer. The men frying the fish squatted on platforms above the vats and looked like they could fall in any minute. But they were nimble and practiced, able to keep an eye on everything in the oil, knowing exactly when to pull out or drop in the fish or the sliced potatoes and eggplants that were coated in the same batter and fried to be served alongside.

The fish was sold by the kilos, and the pieces were huge. All the fish I'd ever seen had been in slender fillets at the local grocery store back home, but these were behemoth, cylindrical cuts the size of small logs, and I could only imagine how big the fish they came from had been.

I waited on the motorcycle as my uncle made his way through the crowd, finally returning fifteen minutes later with three steaming plastic bags full of food. We sped back to Sham Nagar, and Pummy Mamu emptied the bags onto the dining table in the verandah. Half a dozen smaller plastic bags tumbled out, filled with chutney and grated radish, along with a pile of newspaper-rolled packs of fish and naan and potato pakoray.

"Yaar, aajao sab, garam garam machli hai!" he yelled into every room, telling everyone to come because the fish was hot and fresh.

One by one, the family emerged, some begrudgingly, from three different rooms, and pulled up chairs to the table. All but my aunt, who had been on a virtual hunger strike all week at home, surviving on glasses of milk but otherwise barely eating.

The feuding uncles sat across the table from one another and no one said a word about what had happened just an hour ago. Pummy Mamu filled my plate up with fish and potatoes, grinning as he pinched my cheek. "Eat up moti, we like you this way."

Your wish is my command, I thought. I took the plate and sat on the verandah steps under the cool night sky, the fish steaming through its crispy, spicy besan batter. Ami cautioned, "Be careful, there are kantay. The bones can get stuck in your throat."

I broke off pieces of the fish and massaged them to remove any tiny needlelike bones, drizzled the thin, tangy brown tamarind chutney over what remained, and scooped up radish-topped bites with the chewy, warm naan. Crunchy, soft, chewy, tart, sweet, spicy, it was all there, in every bite. The fish was meaty but flaky, the pieces the size of a decent steak. Ami explained it was called rohu, a river fish found only in South Asia, and they could grow to over a few feet in length, which explained the huge slabs of it.

It was an exceedingly simple meal, but one of the best I'd ever had. Plus, it signaled the end of the worst fight I'd ever seen. It was nearly midnight and everyone ate in silence, warming up their insides, and then turned in early. Early, given that they usually stayed up until 4 a.m. laughing and eating and fighting and gossiping.

But tonight too much had already been said, and we had a big weekend ahead of us.

FIVE

Daal May Kuch Kala:
Something Black in the Daal

Every morning I watched Pummy Mamu wash up in the basin installed outside the bathroom, dry his face, and then head back into the master bedroom, where he pulled out a pink tube of cream hidden in a tiny drawer. Clearly this secret cream was just his, not meant to be shared with anyone else. He would squeeze out a dime-size amount of the white paste, slip the tube back in the dresser, and massage the cream into his face, carefully inspecting his full, brown cheeks, tilting his head up to check underneath his chin.

I had no idea what he was looking for when he examined his face, but one day when I got a chance to be alone in the room, I carefully pulled the tube out of the drawer and read it: Fair & Lovely.

I knew exactly what that was, I had seen a thousand Fair & Lovely commercials on Pakistani television, seen billboards for it everywhere, and seen the pink cartons stacked up in the market. The television ads invariably showed a young woman held back from her aspirations, love or career, or denied basic human respect by family and peers, because of her brown skin. Enter Fair & Lovely, which lightened her skin, and brought her joy and success. Now, she was worthy of affection and ready to land the job of her dreams.

No wonder Pummy Mamu was so furtive about his morning routine. If anyone found out, he'd be ridiculed for using a women's product to lighten his skin.

I twisted open the cap and took a sniff. Nice and floral. I quickly squeezed a teeny tiny bit into my palm, enough that it wouldn›t be missed, and rubbed it all over my face, hiding the tube just as it was before. I repeated this ritual every day leading up to the wedding, praying that it actually worked because I'd already heard much concern about how very *brown* I was from my relatives.

Not long after we arrived in Pakistan, Ami left Lilly and me with our middle phupho while she went shopping. This aunt didn't even look related to my father, though she was his elder sister. Her eyes were a soft blue and her skin was the color of cream. She looked at me intently with those soft blue eyes and asked if I used a jhanwan when I bathed. I had no idea what she was talking about. She led me to the bathroom and showed me what looked like a brick whittled down into a slender bar with a handle.

"They don't have these in America? Your mother never used this on you?"

I couldn't even figure out how it was supposed to be used.

When it was clear I was completely lost, she finally understood the magnitude of this lapse in my mother's child-rearing. She had to take matters into her own hand. She ordered a bucket of water heated up and had Lilly and me strip down to our underwear.

We took turns sitting on the stool in the bathroom as she lathered us up and then scrubbed the living daylights out of us with the jhanwan. She moved it in circles over our arms and legs, murmuring, "No wonder they're so hairy," and up and down our backs and behind our necks.

My skin felt like it had been set on fire, but afterward my body was aglow. I had never felt so clean in my life.

Phupho showed me her own arms and legs. "See any hair?" she asked. None at all.

"Body hair makes you look darker than you are, and you two are plenty dark enough. Look at the other women in the family. Look at your own mother and aunt. Are they covered in hair like men?" she pressed.

Nope, the only hairy girls in our family, it seemed, were me and Lilly.

Girls were supposed to use a jhanwan from the time the first peach fuzz sprouted anywhere on their body, moving it in circles to rip the fuzz and any errant hair up from its roots. You'd never have body hair for the rest of your life if it was taken care of early on. Plus, it removed layers and layers of dead skin and grime. No wonder I was coffee-colored, I was carrying around a decade of soot in my very skin, she declared.

How could Ami have completely neglected this vital aspect of our upbringing? How, when we marveled at her incredibly smooth skin without a single hair on it, or held our cocoa-colored arms next to her latte-colored skin, could she fail to reveal this secret? How had Nani Amma and Zuby Aunty never mentioned it?? We were being raised like beasts, doomed to be hairy and brown!

We left armed with new jhanwans and showed them to Ami. She nodded and said, "Good, I guess you should start using those. It's not too late, you're still young, and your Taya said your original, fair color could return by the time you're sixteen. The jaundice just burned you up completely," she sighed.

I believed that jaundice story for a long time, until I learned about DNA in school and took a good hard look at my father and realized my skin color had nothing to do with jaundice.

Whatever caused it, I now had a jhanwan and, more important, Fair & Lovely to lighten me to an acceptable shade, and I religiously stole a bit every day from Pummy Mamu for weeks. The Fair & Lovely didn't make a lick of difference before the wedding, though it did say that it had to be used for months to see the results. Still, I was disappointed that I'd have no breathtaking transformation, turning heads at every event as people wondered, "Who is *she*?"

The day of the henna party, we all began getting dressed as dusk settled around the house, where the festivities would be held. Strings of lights illuminated every wall inside the house and outside its gates; strings of flowers, real and paper, hung in doorways, and in the court-yard three deghs had been bubbling since early afternoon, the pots big enough to cook an entire person in them. The henna party's menu was simple and traditional: chicken curry, chickpea curry, salad, and a sem-olina halwa roasted in ghee and studded with nuts and coconut and raisins. Steaming bags full of fresh sesame-seed-topped naan were lined up on a side table. No rice tonight, and no red meat. Those were reserved for the next two days.

Nani Amma had been ironing three-piece shalwar-kameez suits, a long tunic over flappy pants and matching three-yard-long scarves, for hours. For herself, Ami, Lilly, me, and of course, the bride-to-be. Over a dozen of us juggled between the bathroom and the bedrooms and the few mirrors in the house to get ready, and finally Zuby Aunty emerged from her own room, wearing a simple cotton suit the color of an egg yolk and a sheer scarf with a gold border pulled down low over her face, and sat on the bed in the master bedroom in silence, hunched over, waiting for when we would lead her into the sitting room for the party.

I stayed with my aunt, concerned. Why wouldn't she look up, why wasn't she talking to anyone? "Zuby Aunty. Zuby Aunty. Zuby Aunty?!" I kept prodding her but got nothing.

Pummy Mamu finally intervened. "Don't you know a bride is sup-posed to be shy, and not supposed to make a sound or talk to anyone or look around. It's not easy to do, but you just have to do it for the wedding, otherwise everyone will think you're a shameless girl who's *actually happy* to be getting married."

I made a face. I still didn't get why a bride couldn›t be happy at her own wedding. I wouldn't know for years that a bride was expected to exhibit shy sadness both because she was losing her family and because she was saying farewell to her virginal innocence. Only an absolute hussy would be excited for that loss.

"Moti, I can already tell you are dying to get married, aren't you? How will you ever put on the shy act?" he laughed.

I thought about that for a second and said, "I can do it, I can sit quietly like her, too."

Pummy Mamu leaned down. "Okay, let's see. If you can sit there with Zuby, just like her, until the party starts, I'll give you a reward."

I quickly pulled my scarf over my head and hunched over, eyes on the floor. I could totally do this.

Twenty minutes later when it was time to escort Zuby Aunty into the room full of guests, I was still sitting with my head bowed, my neck starting to strain from all the shyness.

Pummy Mamu laughed and pulled others into the room to look at me.

"Kya baat hai! Amazing, you've proven yourself, moti! You are definitely ready to get married, but the real question is, *who will marry you?*"

I jerked up to glare at him.

"Whoever marries you will have to bring a crane to drag you home and, by God, I will salute him!"

Pummy Mamu struck a pose saluting my unknown future groom and Zuby Aunty giggled. Then she stood up. We raised a silky red shawl covered in embroidered golden flowers and beads above her head, and led her to into the party room, where nearly a hundred women sat crushed together. Back in the good old days, the mehndi party was only ever for women, though times have changed and today it's a full-court event.

Back then, though, while the guys were banned so the ladies could cut loose, there was still a solid tradition of young men spending hours trying to catch peeks of gyrating hips and swaying waists every time the doors opened or a curtain moved.

Zuby Aunty took the seat of honor in the center of Nani Amma's old couch, while we sat crossed-legged on the floor in front of her, crowded around that one friend who knew how to work a dholki, a two-headed drum played by hand that was a mandatory part of any henna party. I clapped along with the others as they sang familiar wedding songs, from Bollywood anthems to Punjabi folk tunes, and around the perimeter of the room some of the girls were applying henna decorations to themselves and others.

Two women tackled my aunt's hands and feet, and they would move up to her arms and legs through the course of the night. The rest of the bridal party would get fairly simple designs, which took less than half an hour to create, but a bride's henna required hours, it was that intricate. Somewhere hidden among the swirls and flowers and paisleys running up and down her hands, the henna artists would disguise the name of her groom, for him to find on their wedding night.

After rubbing the dried designs with oil and holding your hennaed limbs over burning cloves, you had to keep the henna paste on overnight, all to ensure a deep maroon result once it was scraped and washed off the next day. Getting that color right was imperative. The darker the color, the more your husband would adore you, they said. If it turned out light and orangey, that wasn't a great omen. Plus it would look like you had rubbed Cheetos on your skin.

I was going to wait until the end of the night to have my henna done. I didn't want to have to sit in a corner waiting for it to dry and miss out on the dancing portion of the party. For that, I had been preparing my entire short life. It wasn't easy, in the seventies and eighties, to get ahold of Bollywood movies in the US. Abu had shelled out nearly four hundred dollars for a VCR player after we had moved to Pennsylvania, and then it was just a matter of renting VHS tapes of Indian movies, Pakistani dramas, compilations of music, and once in a while some religious lectures, though they were definitely an afterthought.

The Pakistani halal shop that we visited about once a month, because it was all the way in Rockville, Maryland, had begun stocking all the latest juicy titles, and on every trip we picked up a couple of tapes and returned a couple. Sometimes, though, a movie or drama was so good you didn't want to return it.

Luckily, someone in our network of desi families had figured out how to copy a VHS tape using two VCR players, and before you knew it, everyone had their own private collections. The centerpiece of our private collection was two Indian films that were played nearly every week for years in our home, films that reigned supreme at the top of the Bollywood hierarchy. No other films could, or would, ever touch them.

Umrao Jaan and *Silsila*. The heroine in both of these blockbuster movies, still hailed as some of the best films to ever come out of Bollywood, was the inimitable starlet Rekha.

She went by one name, just like Madonna.

Rekha was sublime in both her beauty and talent. She had dusky skin, huge almond eyes, full petal-like lips, a slender, delicate nose, and the darkest, deepest, waviest hair, which reached down to her waist. Imagine a carving of a dancing girl from an ancient Hindu temple come to life. That was Rekha.

She danced like a dream, entrancing her audiences with a swing of a voluptuous hip and the twist of a bangled wrist. Her expressions were iconic—a single raised eyebrow, a slight smile staring straight into the camera as if she shared a deep, sweet secret with you—her ability to convey the meaning of every word of a song with just her face was legendary.

In a word, she was exquisite and her acting talent unmatched. Abu threw out the religious rules when it came to Rekha. It didn't matter if she wasn't Muslim, he said, she would still make it to heaven because she made so many people happy.

In *Umrao Jaan*, titled for the lead character, a young girl is kidnapped and forced into the life of a courtesan, dancing for rich, entitled men. In *Silsila*, the love of Rekha's life is forced to marry his brother's widow, and she then marries a man she doesn't love either. The tragedy of the stories resonated with me. So did the fact that Umrao was overlooked when she was young, kidnapped, then sold to a brothel for a low price because her skin was darker than the other girls. She had a distinctive beauty mark in the center of her chin, a mark that, later in life, helped her mother recognize her.

When I looked in the mirror I saw a dark girl with a beauty mark on her chin. It wasn't until that film that I thought the black dot on my chin was attractive. And if Umrao blossomed, so could I. Night after night, alone in my room, I copied Rekha's dance steps from both movies, having recorded the songs by holding up a tape recorder to the television. I draped a scarf this way and that way, imagining myself as the innocent courtesan from *Umrao*, or the seductive siren from *Silsila*, and I secretly thought I was a pretty good dancer for a chubby kid with no training.

So on the night of my aunt's henna party as a song from *Silsila*, one of the most famous wedding dance sequences in all of Indian film history, began playing, I knew it was my time. I knew every step of the dance, every inflection of the song. I took the floor, alone, tied my scarf around my waist, and began.

I tried to avoid looking at the faces around me, instead focusing on the words of the song, but pretty quickly the giggles and half-mocking encouragement were unmistakable. I realized I didn't look anything like Rekha as I pretended to dance along with a handsome hero, but I couldn't abandon ship, I just had to get through it. I kept dancing, my face hot and swollen from embarrassment, my glasses completely fogged up, to the damn song that seemed to never end. A few minutes in, folks were losing interest, some got up and left the room. I wanted to die but kept bouncing, pumping one hip up and down, until it was finally over.

I got some half-hearted applause, which was probably because they were at last liberated from the awful experience. But Zuby Aunty beamed at me, until someone yelled out, "Next time, do an *Anjuman* dance, that would suit you better!" and everyone snickered. Anjuman, I would later learn, was a Pakistani Punjabi heroine built like a brick house. She often towered over her leading men, and likely outweighed them by dozens of pounds. She hadn't started out that way, but as she got older, and bigger, she refused to give up her trademark moves, leaping and gyrating ferociously so her bosom and stomach and hips filled the entire screen. She was equal parts beloved and scorned.

I thought I would never live down that night, surely it would be the thing that everyone remembered from the wedding. I had nothing to worry about, though, because the wedding was all downhill from there.

THIS IS HOW it was supposed to go: The wedding would be taking place at a military officer's clubhouse, an exclusive venue, not open to the public, but we had enough military officers in our family to make it happen. The bridal party would arrive by 3 p.m., stash the bride into a private room, and prepare to shower the groom's procession with trays of rose garlands and flower petals.

Once the groom had been properly received in the princely manner he deserved, he would be led to a stage at the head of the venue, where either a couch or thronelike chairs were set up against a background of lights, flowers, tinsel, drapes, and whatever else was considered decorative at the time. The groom's party would be given a respectable time to settle in and then the nikkah, the ceremony that rendered them husband and wife, would commence. The parties would each separately declare, thrice, their acceptance of the marriage—the groom in front of the guests, and the bride in her private room with witnesses—then sign some papers, and be a married couple before they saw each other. Then the bride would be led in by the women of her family and seated next to the groom so that thousands of photographs could be taken with them and every combination of family and friends possible. Finally, the moment everyone waited for would arrive: everyone would eat. There might be some music and dancing, and at the end of the night the bride would be tearfully given away, get in the groom's car, and drive off to her new life.

Again, that's how it was supposed to go. Here is how it went:

Pummy Mamu took Zuby Aunty to the makeup and hair parlor around 11 a.m., plenty of time to create the teased-up bouffant and stark white makeup that turned everyone into a geisha—*the* signature bridal look of the eighties. And then of course you needed time to arrange all the bridal jewelry, the layers of gold necklaces that cascaded down her neck and chest, forearms full of bangles, shoulder-length earrings that needed to be triple secured, a glittering headpiece with jeweled medallions, and a large but delicately thin ring of gold in her nose. Finally, on top of all this, the heavily embroidered bridal veil, weighing pounds and pounds, had to be draped and pinned so it wouldn't slip off her head for at least the next ten hours. Not until the groom himself took it off.

Four hours should have been enough to get ready, and Pummy and Zuby should have been at the wedding hall by 3 p.m.

Three p.m. came and went, and at 4 p.m. on the dot the groom's procession arrived, hundreds of relatives spilling out of a dozen cars and vans. The official police band had been booked for the occasion, seeing as it was the wedding of the daughter of the former Deputy Superintendent of Police, rest his soul.

The groom and his entourage, amid falling rose petals and bedecked by reams and reams of garlands around their necks, marched slowly behind the band as they played the classic wedding songs. So far, so good.

Once the groom was seated on the outdoor stage and the tents filled up with guests, my family started getting nervous. The bride hadn't arrived yet and the groom and his family *could not know this*. No one knew what salon they had gone to, so they couldn't make any calls. This was well before the advent of cellphones, and all Ami and her brothers could do was smile nervously at the groom's family and friends and wait.

Five p.m. . . . Six p.m. . . .

Zuby Aunty still hadn't arrived. By this time there were murmurs that the bride had run away. Different members of the groom's family kept approaching Ami and the brothers trying to ask where the bride was, as delicately as possible. Nani Amma hid herself inside the clubhouse in the private room meant for the bride, alternately weeping and praying.

Something terrible must have happened, there was no other explanation for not having heard from Pummy all afternoon. What if the groom's party got up and left?? The thought of the dishonor that would bring to them all was almost too much to bear.

Ami heard that some of our guests and the groom's guests were about to leave, so at 7 p.m. she hurriedly had dinner announced, which was enough to get people to linger a bit longer. Behind the tents a dozen cooks had been laboring all afternoon over sputtering deghs and skewered meat that sat on a row of open fires. Gleaming silver buffet servers and huge, round tawas meant to keep grilled meats sizzling were already laid out on numerous long tables in two different areas of the tent, dividing the male and female guests. Servers began carrying in trays of grilled meat to empty onto the tawas, and before they could even retreat, guests began lining up.

Except they didn't line up in any kind of line I had ever seen before. They crowded up and down the tables, rows of people behind them, everyone trying to work their way to the front without looking greedy but ultimately looking exceptionally greedy. Plates were passed up and down the line, and I waited behind a horde of perfumed, brightly dressed women for my turn at the buffet. From a distance I could see hunks of goat glistening in dark brown korma gravy; platters of biryani; plump red tandoori chicken legs; rich, thick stewed chickpeas; spinach and potatoes swimming in ghee together; and stacks of sesame-coated naan.

I waited, and waited, but my turn was apparently not coming. Instead of carrying their plates back to their seats, guests were standing with feet firmly planted in front of the serving dishes, refusing to leave the buffet, as if they intended to eat right above it until it was all gone. If I was going to get food, I would have to elbow my way in as I saw others do it. And once I got there, I, too, refused to move until I'd had my fill.

I might have been the only member of the bridal party who actually ate that night. My siblings were running around with cousins, never as concerned about food as I was, and the elders were still biting their nails over Zuby Aunty. I had dinner, then dessert, then headed into the club-house and back to the private room, where at last, the bride had shown up.

Zuby Aunty sat with tears streaming down her face, mascara drawing rows in her pancake makeup, lipstick smudged, bouffant askew, as her siblings raged. Everyone was piling on—Pummy Mamu and Zuby Aunty had humiliated them in front of the groom, his family, and all their guests—and Pummy Mamu kept screaming back. The car he had borrowed from a friend for the day had broken down in the middle of a traffic circle with a fully made-up bride in the back seat. He couldn't find a taxi, he couldn't very well stick her in a three-wheeled rickshaw or a horse-drawn tanga, he couldn't leave her alone in the circle to go find a mechanic, and he couldn't make her get out and walk through streams of traffic and dust and mud.

Traffic kept rushing around them and no one would stop, but eventually he was able to flag down some men to block the way and help push the car to the side of the road. Zuby Aunty still sat inside, silently weeping. They didn't have the number for the clubhouse and everyone he knew was already at the wedding, so there was nothing for him to do but try and get the car moving again as quickly as possible. A shop owner who saw it all unfold called a mechanic, who tinkered for two hours before they could get back on the road.

They were both starving, and thirsty, and miserable, and now everyone was yelling at them. "You just *had* to go get ready in a fancy salon across town, eh?" "The neighborhood parlor wasn't good enough for you?" "You couldn't do your own makeup, look at you now, you would've looked better than *this*!"

Hearing all the commotion, a cousin had popped in and realized no one was even trying to clean up the bride. She quickly began dipping a cloth into a glass of water and wiping down my aunt's face until all traces of her tears, and most of the makeup, were gone. Then Zuby Aunty was hastily escorted out and seated next to Uncle Israr, who smiled for the first time in hours. His bride, thankfully, had not run away.

Most of the guests had left by then, but family remained. After an hour or so, we decided that the groom's party had been made to wait long enough, and since their drive back to his town would take a couple of hours, it was time to give the bride away.

Iffi Mamu brought out a Quran, carefully wrapped in ornately embroidered velvet. As he held it over Zuby Aunty's head, she struggled to stand up and follow her siblings to a car decorated with whole roses, stems and all, taped all over the hood, the back, and the roof. The bride was to leave her old family under the shadow of God's word, and in His protection.

But, just to be safe, a female relative was sent along with her. This was immutable tradition. After all, she was marrying into strangers, strangers to her, and pretty much strangers to her family, too. So Ami, the designated "plus-one," tagged along to make sure everything was legit, that the bride's possessions arrived safely, and to give her some moral support.

Ami squeezed into the back of the wedding car next to the groom's mother as Zuby Aunty said her final goodbyes. This time everyone—brothers, cousins, aunts and uncles, friends and neighbors—cried along-side her. Nani Amma threw herself onto her new son-in-law's chest, wailing, "Take care of her, promise you'll take care of her!" and he assured her that he would. As the car drove off, my uncles breathed a collective sigh of relief. Their baby sister was married off, a duty fulfilled. Nani Amma was still being consoled by her own sisters, who gave her a sedative to calm her down. Zuby was her baby, the one she slept with close to her heart after being widowed so young. Her sons were scattered all over the country and the world, and now she would be alone in the house she had lived in for nearly half a century.

We went back to Sham Nagar and slept like the dead behind the yellow gates, utterly spent from the day. We had to be up and ready fairly early for the final event, the walima, the groom's reception, the next afternoon.

Ami had left our outfits behind with Nani Amma, not having told me or my siblings that she'd be leaving with Zuby Aunty, so we got washed and dressed the best we could. There was already a traditional spread of halwa puri—fluffy, chewy fried flatbread eaten with a chick-pea and potato curry—and bright orange, sweetened semolina halwa, out on Nani Amma's verandah. The sweet, spicy, salty, greasy flavors come together perfectly, but it's not the kind of brunch you eat every day. It was for lazy weekends or special occasions, and that morning my youngest uncle, Khan Gul Mamu, had ordered enough halwa puri for fifty people and then driven all the way to Gujranwala on his motorcycle to drop off the breakfast with Zuby Aunty's new family, leaving behind a few portions for us.

Sending the couple and the groom's entire family breakfast the morn-ing after the wedding was a ritual Nani Amma wasn't about to abandon just because they lived so far away.

Two of Nani Amma's sisters arrived at the house around 11 a.m., ready to accompany us to the groom's reception. It was customary for a small bridal party to attend the groom's reception; you didn't want to burden them with hundreds of your own guests, so only about a dozen of us were going.

That was when everyone realized something important had been completely neglected. In all the work and hustle of the previous two days, no one had remembered to book a van for Sunday morning to get us to the reception.

The only motorcycle in the house was now already in Gujranwala, and there was no car at home because no one who lived in Sham Nagar drove a car, and while the uncles didn't mind riding rickety, doorless, three-wheeled rickshaws for two hours, they couldn't possibly load their mother and aunts and us three kids onto them. And, most important, if we arrived in a procession of a dozen rickshaws, Ami and Zuby Aunty would kill us.

Pummy and Khalid Mamu headed out to try and find a van or minibus or taxi, or any decent ride, and returned after an hour with a van and a tiny little car. The car they borrowed from a friend, and they could squeeze themselves into it with a couple of kids, but the van was for Nani Amma and her sisters.

We stared at the van, not sure how this would work, because it wasn't a van with any windows, or even seats. It was a cargo van. The cab up front could seat one woman along with the driver, and the other two had to sit in the back. How? Khalid Mamu had a solution.

He swung open the doors to the dark interior and signaled Pummy Mamu into the living room. Together, they carried out Nani Amma's couch and loaded it into the back of the van. "There," he said, "now you can ride in comfort."

Khalid Mamu helped Nani Amma and her youngest sister up into the van, and I hopped in with them, as excited as an eleven-year-old could be to ride on an unsecured sofa in the back of a van. "We will stop every thirty minutes so you can get some fresh air," he said, "and I'll drive slow, but if you need anything, just bang on the wall and I'll hear you up front!" Then he closed the door, leaving us pressed together on the couch in the dark.

As soon as the van made a right out of the gates, we knew this was a terrible idea. The couch slid left and right, forward and backward toward the doors, as my grandmother and grandaunt cursed and exclaimed and laughed nervously. Every bump in the road sent our seat up in the air a few inches, and before long everyone was feeling aches and pains from the jostling.

Our eyes eventually adjusted in the dark and we could at least make out each other and the space. Thankfully it was a cold December morning, so we were spared from being cooked in the windowless steel box we were trapped in. Time lost all meaning, and no one was sure how long we had been in the van or how far we had driven when Khalid Mamu finally pulled over and let us out to breathe.

I felt nauseous and Nani Amma refused to get back in the van, so Khalid Mamu switched her seat with her sister's up front, and I squeezed in with my two grandaunts, who berated their nephew, furious about being transported like packaged goods to their niece's reception.

We finally pulled up and got out in front of a narrow passage on a wide street, the opening to the alley leading to the groom's house. The others had already arrived in the car and were waiting for us on the corner, so we looked somewhat like a cohesive group. From there we walked to the house, thankful for not having to disembark like animals from the cargo van in front of the guests.

Tents stretched out behind Uncle Israr's house and we were just in time to eat. Which they insisted we do first, though Nani Amma wanted desperately to see her daughter, who was in fact nowhere to be seen. Unfortunately, they hadn't made any arrangements for a stage or platform, where the couple could be seated together and greet their guests. Instead the groom was hanging around outside, mingling with the men, while Zuby Aunty sat in a bedroom inside the house the entire time, and the women rotated through to see her.

Nani Amma was already upset when we finally made our way into Zuby Aunty's bedroom, and now even more so. Her daughter sat, draped in a pink outfit, on a bed, surrounded by women and girls. Her hair poked out in frizzled bunches from underneath the embroidered veil, and her makeup looked like she had done it with her eyes closed. She was swaying slightly, as if she was going to pass out. We nudged the others out of the way so we could sit on the bed with Zuby Aunty, who explained she hadn't slept or eaten since before the henna party, not even that morning, though Khan Gul Mamu had shown up bright and early with bags and bags of breakfast. She was too shy to eat in front of her new in-laws, like a girl on the longest first date of her life.

Too shy to eat? What did that even mean? I couldn't imagine.

Nani Amma asked for a glass of milk and a plate of sweets, and we finally got some calories into Zuby Aunty. Before we left, Nani Amma had one of my uncles fetch some dry fruit and biscuits from a little shop around the corner and quietly tucked them into a drawer in Zuby Aunty's bedroom. She knew her daughter, and she knew she would end up starving herself if she didn't have some snacks to eat privately. She would have to get through a few weeks of this before finally moving out with her husband to the military base where he was stationed.

We returned home under a cloud of sadness, having left behind a loved one to fend for herself among strangers. That's when I understood why Zuby Aunty never seemed excited in the weeks before her wedding, and why everyone shed so many tears the night she was given away. She no longer belonged to us, she no longer got to spend her days sleeping or shopping or doing whatever she felt like. Now, she would have responsibilities and have to learn to love strangers like family, which seemed an impossible task.

I couldn't understand why everyone was so worried about whether I'd get married or not. It didn't seem like weddings were much to be happy about.

"CHEW EVERYTHING TWENTY-FIVE times and eat daal and fruit to help control weight, and consume lots of milk and yogurt, it is good for the complexion. Don't eat cakes and cookies. If you desire something sweet, have a piece of jaggery."

These were some of the last words Dada Abu said to me before we left Pakistan, a month after Zuby Aunty's wedding. It seemed that word about my weight and complexion had gotten to him, though he offered the advice casually, as if he just gave these tips to everyone.

By the time we landed back in America, back to Abu after many months, there was a definite shift in my parent's perspective about my weight. It went from a casual concern, baby fat they had to keep an eye on but something I'd likely grow out of, to an urgent problem that had to be addressed as soon as possible. Ami had heard earfuls from both sides of the family, who scolded her for not controlling my diet and not seeing that I was headed for fat adulthood, and thus nonmarriageability. Sad affair or not, marriage was nonnegotiable, a quest above all others that must be fulfilled. No desi parent can die in peace unless and until their kids are married.

"Larki-zaat hai! She's a girl! Not a boy, who can just look like anything!" she heard over and over. And all of it, she passed on to Abu.

But my parent's concern didn't stop Ami from embarking on a months-long marathon of making Pakistani sweets called mithai, which she had suddenly developed a tooth for during our stay in Pakistan.

"I *hate* mithai," she used to remark, noting that it was her father's love of chum-chum—juicy, pillowy balls of milk solids cooked in pure syrup—that killed him. But since having my brother, the same uncontrollable urge for sweets that drove her father to a diabetic deathbed finally got ahold of her, too.

Her poison of choice was laddu, little yellow treats made of chickpea batter passed through a fine mesh strainer and fried in millions of tiny droplets, mixed with syrup, and finally pressed together into balls. Every week, for months, she made batches and batches and batches, and we had hundreds of laddus lined up on trays and in Tupperware stacked all over the kitchen and dining room. She and Abu ate a few at a time with every cup of chai, and after every meal. Our home constantly smelled like sticky cardamom syrup and fried besan.

I was never a fan of mithai, but I also was prone to eating whatever happened to be in front of my face, whether or not I really liked it or whether or not I was really hungry. That was a bad sign, a sign I wish I'd recognized as such back then. I popped laddu into my maw every time I wandered through the kitchen, and of course, I grew.

I was still haunted by that voice that called out that I should have done an Anjuman dance, and I thought "No." No, I am not Anjuman. I am Rekha. Or rather, a few pounds down, I will be. After all, there's always room for improvement.

There was a huge open field behind our row of townhouses and every day after school I began running laps around it, convinced a few months of jogging would solve the problems my family had with my weight. I felt pretty fancy jogging, it was the kind of thing white people did. And while Ami and Abu were thrilled that I was finally taking my size seriously, I'd never in my life seen my parents work out, much less jog. They didn't even own sweats or sneakers.

"Praying five times a day, standing up, bowing down, that's all the exercise I need," Ami said. I wasn't convinced, seeing as she had never stopped looking pregnant after having Saad.

Just like my parents, I'd never exercised, at least not on purpose. I started off with two laps, alternating between walking and jogging, until I could run the entire way. Then I added another lap, and another, and by the time I started seventh grade, I could do ten laps without stopping.

I was running to get skinny enough to everyone's satisfaction, but I never anticipated the exhilaration that came with it. I'd never heard of a runner's high, but I was feeling it, and I started to look forward to those thirty, forty minutes alone out on the field every day. I would run to a beat that only I could hear, a song in my head that I hummed on the inside, and I felt stronger with every stride.

Until the day I got chased all the way home, thinking all the while I was going to die. I was in the middle of a lap, humming to myself, when I heard a faint call that got louder with every second. "Look out! Look out! Stop! Stop! Turn around!"

By the time I turned around and saw the woman screaming from about a half a football field away, the dog she was chasing had nearly caught up to me. It was a large chocolate-brown Doberman and it was running like a bat out of hell, laser focused on its unsuspecting bouncy target. A leash flew behind it, still attached to its collar.

I froze for a split second and then ran for my life, shrieking, which only made the dog even more intent on capturing and killing me, or at least that's what I thought it was going to do. The woman kept yelling "STOP!" But I didn't realize that she was actually telling me to stop so her dog would stop chasing me, though I still probably wouldn't have stopped.

The entire chase likely took a minute or two, but it felt like slow motion. When I made it to our back-porch door and rushed into the house, I slammed the glass door shut right in the dog's face. The lady finally caught up and stood heaving on our porch, waving her hands and repeating, "Sorry, sorry, he just got away," as her dog paced around, wagging its tail. "You shouldn't have run, if you'd just stopped running, he would've stopped chasing you!" she said, and then grabbed the dog by the leash and pulled it away.

I stood shaking, pretty sure I had wet my pants, humiliated. I hoped no one had seen the mortifying incident. On the other hand, I was rather proud that I had outrun the beast. Working out had paid off. But working out had also turned me into a moving snack for that dog, so that was the end of my nascent running career.

Surprisingly, I missed it. It was my first taste of real, purposeful exercise, and it had made me feel good in a way I never had. It hadn't made me skinny, not by a long shot. My clothes had gotten a bit looser, but my cheeks were still fleshy, and my body still fluffy. I had already been dreading seventh grade, not wanting to return to a school where I had no friends. Now I had failed at my shot of transforming into a beautiful, popular girl over the summer.

The dread was short-lived, though, because soon after school began, I experienced the first real loss of my life, one that made my middle school woes diminish. One night, as we sat watching television, we got a call from Pakistan. There were certain times you would expect an overseas call—holidays, the birth of a baby—but a random call was never good news. Dada Abu had suffered a heart attack. He was calling us himself from the hospital, just a day after being admitted, to say he was weak but had survived and was okay.

Abu told him he would come immediately; he hadn't seen Dada Abu in eight years. Dada Abu reassured him that he was fine. Don't spend the money, he said. Your family needs you, you can't just leave them alone. He repeated that he was *fine*.

He spoke to me briefly as well, saying, "Puttar, puttar, it's okay, there's nothing wrong with me," as I sobbed and choked on every word I tried to get out of my mouth. I immediately felt like shit, remembering how many times I had left him alone in his room while I scampered around with my cousins or spent weeks at a time at Nani Amma's house.

When we hung up, it was clear that Abu was not going to take a chance. He began looking for his passport, calling friends to ask about ticket prices and schedules, checking the family bank account to make sure he could afford it. I retreated to the kitchen and sat alone in the dark at the table, flooded with endless hot tears.

I kept hearing Dada Abu's voice telling me to chew my food twenty-five times. Why the hell couldn't I manage to do it, I'd seen him do it at every meal. I could do it, *I would do it.* I would drink more milk and stop eating fried food, I would eat daal with a spoon and skip the butter and rice, I would eat stalks of cilantro after every meal, I would do everything he told me to do because he loved me so much, if only he would get better. I vowed this to myself.

With my eyes squeezed shut to stop the tears, I tried to remember every detail about him, his quavering yet authoritative voice, his shockingly white hair, his unseeing blue eyes, his deeply veined hands, the way he felt around his tray to eat, the way he shuffled to the shower and back, the way he took long, gurgling draws of his hookah as he reclined in the sun.

I was afraid I would forget it all, and I was certain in that moment that I would never see Dada Abu again.

I was right.

Abu scrambled to get to Pakistan to get to his father before something more serious happened. But by the time he reached Lahore four days later, Dada Abu had already been buried.

NOT LONG AFTER Abu returned from Pakistan, he received the transfer he had applied for months earlier so we could join the tiny Pakistani community that we visited every Friday in Hagerstown, Maryland. True to form, we never moved during summer break. Abu's transfers in the Department of Agriculture always happened in the middle of the school year, making every move even harder.

Hagerstown was almost a big city compared to Chambersburg. There was a proper mall and half a dozen strip malls, a decent public library, and multiple elementary, middle, and high schools. We bought a modest yellow split foyer in a middle-class suburb, the very first house we ever owned, with a backyard of nearly an acre. We all had our own bedrooms, and the house had a laundry room, two full bathrooms, a living room upstairs, and a family room downstairs. We had never had so much space before, space that actually belonged to us—we had finally achieved the American dream.

I ended up at E. Russell Hicks Middle School, a school at least three times bigger than Chambersburg Middle. There were enough students to divide each grade up into different levels, according to academic strength, and I tested into the top level. The student body was white, black, and even brown. There was an Indian girl in my class, which meant we *had* to become good friends. Or at least I secretly hoped we would. There were extracurricular activities like chorus and drama club and sports teams that played other schools—it felt like being in a Sweet Valley High book, though I actually never read those.

And outside of school, suddenly we had a real social life. There were five other Pakistani families already living in Hagerstown, every one of them doctor's families whose kids all went to private Catholic schools. Abu may have been a veterinarian, but our socioeconomic stature was clearly lower than the others. We couldn't even dream of affording private schools.

Every Friday, come hell or high water, we met our new friends at a local community center, which each family chipped in to rent, hauling glass pans, ceramic bowls, and aluminum trays full of food for a potluck. We weren't actually gathering to eat, though that may have been the highlight for some of us. The real purpose was a weekly Quran study, during which we sat in a circle as the fathers took turns leading us through the scripture and discussions about it. No one was a religious scholar, but it was the best the parents could do to keep their kids connected to the faith. It was a very long-seeming hour of study, followed by praying in congregation and finally feasting at the end of the evening.

There was a set rotation for the potluck, which the mothers took turns at: rice, chicken dish, vegetable dish, salad and naan, dessert. Every time Ami was responsible for dessert, she cooked the exact same thing, zarda. It was the easiest thing, she said, a big pot of basmati rice cooked with saffron, raisins and nuts, and sweetened with syrup. Those weeks, we started and ended the meals with rice.

Everyone's favorite dessert maker was an aunty I'll just call Aunty T., the always-blinged-out wife of one of the most prominent doctors in the entire town. She made cherry cheesecake and brownies and a pineapple cream cheese dessert that I would have sold my siblings for. She introduced our palates to baklava, and to basbousa: an Arabic semolina cake, both sweet and tangy, that was positively addictive. As far as I was concerned, she was so very fancy, while Ami was so very . . . basic.

What I didn't realize at the time was that the cooking I thought was so ordinary was the talk of the town with the others. Ami was, it seemed, the best cook of all the wives. She had perfected creamy, buttery saag, tender koftay, meatballs the size of my fist, seekh kabab, shaami kabab, haleem, kadhi, shorba, each one spot on and distinctive in taste. She knew which combination and quantities of spices created the signature flavor of iconic dishes found in restaurants, the Achilles heel for many home cooks, who just threw all the same seasonings into everything they made.

Some stews required whole spices, others needed ground spices, some needed aromatics, others needed tempering. She never, ever worked from a recipe or measured ingredients. She grabbed pinches and handfuls, or sprinkled spices straight from the jar right into a bubbling pot.

She beamed when guests wobbled their heads side to side and licked their fingers, but as proud as it made her to be known as a master in the kitchen, she didn't actually enjoy cooking. As far as she was concerned, working women shouldn't have to slave over the stove every day, but in America, who was going to do it if not her? Abu never worked less than two jobs and didn't have the time if he wanted to, but also, why would he want to when his wife was not only an excellent cook, but also a speedy one.

Ami cooked efficiently but always with a tinge of indignation at the menial task before her. That stuff they say about food tasting better if you cook with love? Utter nonsense. My mother cooked with grim determination and little joy, getting meals on the table as quickly as possible.

For the most part, we were on our own for breakfast and lunch, grabbing what we could and running out the door in the mornings, but we returned to a fresh, home-cooked dinner every single evening. It was usually shorba, meat or vegetable pulao (basmati rice cooked in heavily seasoned broth), a variety of daal and white rice, and saag, okra, or koftay. There was always a chopped salad, and afterward sliced fruit, watermelon, cantaloupe, or oranges.

There was a difference between everyday home cooking, and the special dishes that only got made when we had guests. The aunties would gently prod Ami to divulge her recipes, but alas, she didn't have any. Besides, as far as Ami was concerned, the taste in food came from the hands making the meals, not from any ingredients on a list. "Haath ki baath hai," she would say ("It's all in the hands"), and everyone would nod along because they knew it was true, but also, what else could they do?

It was just as well, according to Ami. Since nearly all the other women were Punjabi, no point in teaching them her refined dishes. "Punjabis are daal-khoor," daal-eaters, she would sniff, "mostly from villages. They load up on lentils and beans and don't know how to cook the finer things like goat meat," she'd continue, while ironically topping a pot of bubbling yellow daal with thinly sliced garlic sizzling in oil.

After all, she was raised in Punjab, married to a Punjabi man, and raising three Punjabi kids, so at least thrice a week we happily ate like villagers, filling up on masoor, maash, chana, and moong daals, always served with oily jars of hot mango, green chili, lemon, and garlic pickles. Some daals were creamy and porridgelike, others swam in a dark, tomatoey broth or were cooked nearly dry, bursting with slivers of ginger and paper-thin slices of green chili.

I never forgot Dada Abu's advice to stick to lentils and beans, but maybe he had forgotten to tell me not to eat them poured over mounds of soft steamed white rice. I could easily eat two or three plates of this ultimate comfort meal, daal chawal, at any one sitting. Those plates made their presence known when one day, as I leaned on the wall of the shower, enjoying a stream of hot water on my shoulders, the wall completely gave way. I fell clean through it, ceramic tiles in a pile both inside and outside the two-foot hole in the wall. I turned off the water and stood for a few minutes in shock, then burst into sobs. There was no way to cover this up, no way to wiggle out of *what it looked like*—that I was so fat, I broke an actual wall. Surely, though, I couldn't be. Not that fat. Chubby, sure. But not *fat*.

That was a tipping point for Ami and Abu. Something had to be done. One day Abu called me into the living room, alone. "Beta," he said tenderly, "I will give you three dollars for every pound you lose. I know you can do it, just twenty pounds and you'll be in the right place."

I quickly did the math in my head. That was a lot of money for a kid with no job and no allowance. But how did Abu know I needed to lose twenty pounds? I didn't even know how much I weighed. It had been years since I outweighed all my classmates in elementary school, but I didn't think I looked much bigger than I had then.

Maybe I was fat. But I wasn't *that fat*.

Abu bought a scale for the challenge, so we could all keep track of my progress together. After avoiding it for a week, I finally gave in to

Abu's repeated questions of whether I'd weighed myself yet and brought the scale into my bedroom. I stepped on it, and then stepped back off. I stepped on it again, and bent slightly over to watch, praying for the numbered disk to stop rotating.

I stepped off to make sure it was calibrated correctly. Yup, it lined up to the zero.

Then I removed all my clothes and stepped back on, sucking in my breath. It made a difference of a pound.

I weighed 148 pounds. I had gained 48 pounds in three years. That seemed like an awful lot of pounds put on, awful fast. Lilly had weighed herself earlier and reported in at 75 pounds. I weighed almost twice as much as her, and I was fairly certain I should *not* weigh twice as much as my sister. I couldn't do the challenge without telling my parents what I weighed, but there was absolutely no way I was going to tell them, they would lose their minds. Maybe they'd cut off my food altogether, starve me. I would just have to reject the challenge altogether.

I stared for a long time at the mirror. I just didn't get it. The scale didn't lie. It pretty much backed up everyone who thought I was fat. But when I looked at myself, I *just didn't see it.* I saw a pudgy brown girl, not attractive in any way but also not fat. I didn't feel *FAT.*

Was I delusional? Why did I see myself differently from how others saw me? Did I look like I weighed nearly 150 pounds?

I couldn't possibly look it. If I did, my parents would have wired my jaw shut by now. I decided to test my hopeful theory that I hid the 148 pounds very well. The next day I went to school and whispered to the boy who sat in front of me in math class, Chet. Chet had blue eyes and wavy, longish blond hair and a mouthful of braces. He played in the school band and was a total sweetheart. I had had a crush on him for at least two days, because I had a crush on every boy in my classes for at least two days. He was also one of the many boys I could easily defeat in arm wrestling, a trick I somehow thought would make me popular with the boys, but which shockingly did not.

"Chet, Chet, turn around." Chet turned to face me, wide-eyed and grinning as usual.

"I'm trying to test something. How much do you think I weigh?"

"You want me to guess your weight?"

"Yes, guess my weight."

Chet leaned back and tilted his head, narrowing his eyes as he examined me for a few seconds.

"A hundred and forty-eight pounds," he said, then turned around and went back to whatever he was doing.

I froze, thinking, wait, who told him??

But no one could have told him; no one knew how much I weighed except for me.

I guess . . . I guess I did look my weight then.

Around this time other girls in my class started thinning out in the waist, and getting curves in the hips, but not me. I had already done myself no favors by setting myself up as *the girl to beat* in arm wrestling, and lately my voice had started changing in a way I thought only boy's voices did. "When you open your mouth, it's like four voices come out," Ami said every time she heard my voice break into this new, deeper timbre. I was horrified. Why was my voice getting lower and huskier instead of more feminine like the women who crooned in Bollywood movies? I was supposed to be turning into a woman, not James Earl Jones.

This shift wasn't missed by the school chorus director either. About a month before the annual Christmas musical program, she made an executive decision. None of the boys could intone "These three kings of Orient are" in the commanding, sonorous way that I managed, and they were already outnumbered two to one by the girls. In an unprecedented move, the director shifted me from the girls' section to the boys' section.

If the girls and boys stood together, maybe that wouldn't have been such a big deal, but we stood on two completely different sets of risers, so there was no way for me to blend in. She also positioned me on the very top step of the riser, towering above the boys, so my voice would project over all of the others.

This left me very conflicted. On one hand, I felt rather proud that my voice was powerful enough to carry the boys' section, that I was the strongest bass in the chorus. On the other hand, I was mortified that I had a deeper voice than every boy that sang with us, and that this would actually be highlighted in front of the entire school.

Every winter, right before break, there were two Christmas concerts on the same day. One during the day for the student body and faculty, and one in the evening for parents. It was always an exciting day because if you were in chorus, you didn't have to go to class all day, instead you could run around feeling special, dressed up to dazzle at the concerts. We all felt a smidge like celebrities, because everyone knew we were part of the chorus, thanks to our uniforms.

The girls' chorus wore long black skirts, red belts, and white blouses, and the boys wore black pants with white button-down shirts and red bow ties. I had a black skirt that I'd managed to get Ami to buy me, which was exciting in and of itself, because I didn't own any other skirts or dresses. I had only a single pair of jeans, a pair of black pants, and a pair of khakis for school.

A week before the concert, the chorus director made another executive decision. It wouldn't look right, she thought, if I didn't match the boys. She wanted both sections to look uniform. So instead of a skirt, I had to wear what the other boys were wearing, red bow tie and all. She had a bow tie I could borrow, lucky for me.

I wore black pants, a white button-down shirt, and a red bow tie all day in school, confusing and amusing the other kids. My teachers mercifully pretended not to notice, and I pretended not to notice the other girls swishing around in black skirts and penny loafers. When I took my place behind the boys on the stage, I realized that no one in the audience would even be able to tell that I was actually a girl. After all, I was standing behind the row of boys and I had short hair and thick plastic glasses that obscured much of my face.

Maybe it was better that way. If they thought I was a boy, I'd be the best damn boy singer up there, and I'd do everything to make the director proud. So I straightened my bow tie, took a deep breath, and let loose with the deepest bass I could muster.

SIX

Kabab May Haddi: A Bone in the Kabab

"Jab se saal solwan laga,
Tera ang ang hai jaaga"
(Ever since your sixteenth year began,
Every part of your body has awakened)
—"O Ballo Sooch Ke Mele Jana,"
from 1965 Bollywood film *Khandaan*

I hoped against hope that when I turned sixteen, it would be the year I magically transformed from a blocky, boyish dumpling into a lithe siren, my body filling out in the right places, my skin aglow, flush with the hot blood of jawani—burgeoning, unbridled puberty. This was the year that boys, unbeckoned, would begin hovering around me, powerless against my innocent charms. At least that's what innumerable Bollywood songs told me.

All that really happened was I got a bit hairier in the one place I couldn't use a jhanwan, my face, and it became clear that I wasn't growing any taller. Ami, who stood a whopping five foot six, looked down at Lilly and me, both a full two to three inches shorter than her, with deep disappointment. We had turned out short like Abu, who was five foot seven on a good day, and Ami was sure two inches of that height was his thick, enviable hair.

Everyone thought Lilly was taller than me, because she was thin and lanky, but it was an optical illusion. I was a smidge taller but it was lost on my frame, thanks to the many pounds I also had on her.

The Hagerstown Pakistani community had grown since we'd moved there a few years earlier, more doctors and more doctor's wives. It might seem strange that all these Pakistani doctors were converging in the boonies of Maryland, but not if you understood that foreign medical graduates had better chances of getting residencies and jobs in rural towns, where there was always a dearth of health professionals. Kids who grew up in rural communities and went on to medical school rarely returned, so Arab, South Asian, Asian, and African physicians were often courted in medical deserts.

That's why a place as unlikely as Hagerstown—just up Route 40 from Frederick, the headquarters of the Invisible Empire of the Knights of the Ku Klux Klan—had over a dozen Muslim families, and attracted more every year.

The new doctors' wives were often young, fresh from Pakistan, bringing with them the latest shalwaar kameez, jewelry, and hairstyle fashions. I would stare at them every Friday, as I filled up my plate with mounds of potluck rice and roast chicken, watching as they nibbled on cucumbers and refused desserts. Being figure conscious was very fashionable in Pakistan, and they were determined to look great in the latest designs, long flowing gowns gathered under the bust or short, straight shirts with Patiala-style shalwaar that looked a lot like MC Hammer pants.

Neither of these styles suited me, and it wasn't for lack of Ami's efforts. One room in our house was dedicated to her sewing battle station, and the sound of her electric Singer buzzing nonstop was the veritable soundtrack of those years. This was well before the time when you could order Pakistani clothes online or visit an aunty who had a "boutique" set up in her garage, so we had to either rely on our relatives to send us clothes from Pakistan (they didn't), or on Ami's sewing skills.

There were a few fancy Korean fabric stores in Montgomery County, and she could sometimes find useful discounted cottons at the local Kmart, so she collected what she could when she had the money. There was always a stack of random pieces in a corner of the sewing room, and Royal Dansk biscuit tins held spools of thread, bits of sequined borders or lace, buttons, hundreds of needles, and lengths of elastic.

She would take apart and put back together old outfits with new swatches of material, trying to lengthen them or shorten them according to what the movies, or the doctors' wives, told us the latest fashions were. She'd cut up old saris, which would give her nine yards of fabric to work with, to make matching outfits for Lilly and me. Of course, they ended up looking very different on each of us.

"I could put a garbage bag on Lilly and she would look fine, but with you, it's so hard to make anything flattering," she would say, pulling down a shirt hitched above my hip, squeezing my arms through sleeves that clearly weren't wide enough. "You took the worst of both me and your Abu. His height and my arms. It's a curse, these huge arms of ours. They make us look bigger than we are, but you know what, it's still better than being bottom heavy. I feel worse for those women, with all those extra pounds on their rears and thighs. So much harder to get around."

Maybe it was harder to get around, but I would have preferred that over our bodies—square and blocky, broader on top than on bottom. Ami was shaped like a football player, and it looked like I was doomed to be shaped the same way. I knew exactly who she was talking about, though, when she talked about bottom-heavy women. She meant Aunty T., who was shaped like a pear, a lovely, curvy pear that I wished I was shaped like. Wasn't that how women were supposed to look?

No matter what, though, she always managed to make sure we had new outfits on Eid, the holiday that we celebrated twice a year. This particular year, gold lamé was all the rage. Ami found an entire bolt of patterned gold lamé fabric, from God knows where, and set about making our Eid clothes. The morning of Eid, I slipped on the stretchy gold shirt and the shiny hammer pants, feeling fancier than I ever had in my life. Ami had outdone herself.

Lilly and I narrowly escaped Ami's makeup clutches, avoiding that last-minute pounce before we headed out the door to the Eid events. Ami had only used three beauty products her entire life: Pond's Cold Cream, the holiest of face creams to the old-school desi aunty; Revlon liquid foundation, because Revlon was *the* prestige makeup company back home; and a single Revlon lipstick, in a reddish-brown shade. That one lipstick, which got replaced annually, sufficed to add color to her lips, cheeks, nose, and eyelids. And ours, too.

This, Ami believed, was the secret of movie stars. Or some movie star she had read about somewhere, who used lipstick, and no other makeup product, for her entire face.

I must have been around ten when I started being subjected to this makeup treatment before every function. Ami would pat waxy red smudges on her fingers from the tube and rub it onto the apples of our cheeks vigorously with her sturdy thumbs, pulling the skin back and forth until it turned red less from the lipstick and more from the friction. We got a dab of color on the bridge of our noses to try and create a flushed, youthful look, because apparently we didn't flush or blush on our own. Every part of our faces was brown, mine more so than Lilly's, one uniform chestnut canvas, including my lips.

Which is why I ended up with Revlon lipstick everywhere on my face but for my actual lips. Ami believed lipstick was bad for your lips and turned brown lips browner. So while my cheeks and nose bloomed red after her thirty-second makeover, my lips stayed cocoa.

At sixteen, though, I was finally allowed to have and do my own makeup, as long as it didn't actually look like I had makeup on, and I was excited about owning one maroon-colored lipstick and one jet-black pencil eyeliner. I patted the lipstick across my mouth and face, careful not to overdo it, and slid the pencil across the top of my eyelid. Eyeliner could be dangerous in the wrong, unsteady hand—mess it up before an event and you'd never quite get it off cleanly. At least I couldn't, because I didn't have any makeup remover, and instead used lotion and tissue to remove the black smudges after practicing in my room at night. But I had gotten enough practice to be able to create a fine, straight, clean line at the base of my eyelashes, with a slight upturn at the edges to make my eyes look even bigger and more almond shaped. That day, I felt rather pretty.

We bundled into the car in our Eid finery, gold lamé flashing, and headed to the community center to pray with the others and, of course, eat potluck. Then we would head to Rockville to see Iffi Mamu, Ami's third youngest brother, who had been living there for a number of years in a townhouse that served as a way station for scores of friends and relatives newly arrived in the country from Pakistan.

The community center was buzzing as we all checked out each other's clothes and bangles and henna, because the night before Eid, chaand raat, "the night of the moon," was when the celebrations really began. It's a Pakistani tradition to hold parties on chaand raat just for women, who gather, eat, dance, sing, and get hennaed. Unfortunately no one in Hagerstown held these celebratory parties, so we were on our own.

Every chaand raat went exactly the same way in our home. Lilly and I would mix the green powdered henna Abu fetched from the halal grocer with some water to make a thick paste, and then come up with innovative ways to apply it. Toothpicks, plastic syringes, sandwich bags cut and taped into cones like pastry frosting bags. We were forever trying something new, and Ami was no help. She hated henna, hated the smell, and hated the way it looked. I'll never forget the one year we asked her to do our designs, and she drew goats on our hands. That was the last time we asked for her motherly assistance with henna.

Lilly and I would spend hours trying to copy designs we saw in a magazine or a movie, or ones we drew from our own imaginations, lines and dots and paisleys and flowers, and then hours more waiting for the henna to dry, our hands frozen from the paste (henna has a cooling quality, like eucalyptus, and back home it's often applied on the soles of the feet to cool them off). We couldn't sleep until it dried completely, because we had both experienced the horror of waking up with orange stains on our cheeks and necks that lasted for days.

Inevitably, we would both be exhausted the morning of Eid, and 100 percent of the time the henna turned out terrible in both design and vibrancy. From the looks of our Cheeto-orange hands, it didn't seem like Lilly or I would end up with husbands who were crazy about us. This Eid was no different, so I threw on a bunch of bangles to distract and deflect, envious of the splendid intricate maroon designs some of the aunties had managed. There were two new wives in town, not aunties because they were only six or seven years older than me, so I called them baaji, "big sister," instead. They were both fair and slender, one of them green-eyed and doll-faced, as sweet as she looked, the other built like a model, tall and lean with angular features and a spitfire spirit. Her spirit, unfortunately, had no filter. She poked fun at everyone for a laugh, always the center of attention, and I was an easy target.

Baaji One, as I'll call the latter, sauntered over to me as I stood pouring a drink. "Eid mubarak!" she chimed cheerfully, looking down from her five-foot-nine frame. I braced myself for whatever insult was coming my way. Just a few months earlier Ami had complimented a new wool coat Baaji One had been sporting and had asked if I could try it on, so that she could buy me one, too, if it "suited me." Baaji One had laughed and said, in front of everyone, "No way, I don't want her to split my coat open!"

"Eid mubarak," I mumbled back, my mouth still full of naan.

"I have to ask," she continued, "did your mom use tin foil to make your outfit, and if so, how many rolls did that take?"

One of the boys, a doctor's son around my age, stood nearby and guffawed.

"It's true, it looks like you're wrapped in foil."

I turned and walked away—across the wide room, past the rows of aunties and uncles eating at long tables, past kids playing hopscotch and tag, tears hot behind my eyelids—heading directly into the ladies' bathroom. Once alone, I couldn't hold back anymore, and they fell loose, streams of fat drops plinking into the sink.

Suddenly I heard a flush and Baaji Two walked out of a stall. She had already begun washing her hands when she realized I was trying to wipe away snotty tears from my cheeks. "What happened?" She leaned close and put a hand on my back. She was flawless, cheeks flushed peach, her perfectly manicured hands delicate, a body shaped like an hourglass, dressed to the nines in designer clothes, gold and diamonds dripping from her ears and fingers. She was positively *chikni*: skin buttery, glowing and smooth, without a hint of peach fuzz. Her toes were polished an iridescent hot pink, and she smelled like heaven. Why, why God, couldn't I be like her?

I stayed quiet, not wanting to embarrass myself further. I was dressed in gold lamé from head to toe. Of course I looked like an engorged roll of tin foil. Where was the lie?

Then another aunty walked into the bathroom and came straight over. She was polished and dignified, not because she was the wife of a doctor, but because she was a doctor herself. She was the only female doctor in the community, commanding a level of respect well above the other ladies.

Doctor Aunty had seen Baaji One say something to me and witnessed my hasty exit from the area and had guessed what this was about.

Doctor Aunty rubbed my arm, looking at me in the bathroom mirror, and said, "I don't know what she said to you but I want you to know this, you are the prettiest girl in our community. No one has your features, look at yourself, at your big eyes, and your round face. You're so much more beautiful than that woman."

I sniffed, staring at my brown and orange hands.

"This is true!" Baaji Two said enthusiastically. "And the next time you come over, I'll share my beauty secrets with you! We all have to have a few tricks to help us look our best!"

Doctor Aunty nodded. "That would be great, but really you don't even need any beauty tips! All you have to do is lose a few pounds."

I DIDN'T JUST have to lose a few pounds though. The weight was only part of my problem. My forehead was too small, my neck too short, my hands too thick, my fingers too stubby and unattractive with dark joints and knuckles, my knees and elbows dark and scabby, my feet too small, my big toe shorter than the others, my hair too stick-straight and oily. And I was dark, dark, dark.

"But," said Ami, "you have perfect ears."

Ami's solution to problem areas was to make sure not to call attention to any of them. No necklaces, especially chokers, because they drew attention to the heft of my neck. No rings or nail polish, to avoid people noticing how unladylike my hands were. No big hoop earrings, because they exaggerated my large, round face. No wearing my hair up, because that would reveal the hump of fat on the base of my neck. No short sleeves, best to cover up those elbows and chunky upper arms. No sandals or open-toe shoes, so no one would ever see that chubby little big toe having fallen behind its comrades.

Ami had been particularly concerned about the hyperpigmentation on the joints of my every finger, something no one else in the family had. Not my siblings, not my parents, not my parents' siblings. It wasn't just an unattractive condition, though, it could also be painful. The tips of my fingers, all around my nails, were slightly bulbous, and a few times a year they would swell further and the skin would peel in thin, painful strips. Years earlier Ami had asked a doctor during a routine checkup what it could possibly be. The doctor, an elderly white man who likely had almost no other patients of color, peered at my fingers and said maybe it was arthritis.

A twelve-year-old with arthritis? As if I didn't have enough wrong with me.

He told Ami he didn't have any treatment for it and to just moisturize as best as possible to keep the skin from peeling, so Ami bought me a surplus-size tub of petroleum jelly and instructed me to rub it into the tips of my fingers, and also onto my elbows and knees, and scrub them daily with the jhanwan I'd brought back from Pakistan.

I did scrub and scrub and scrub my knees and elbows until some of the skin actually just came off, leaving it looking spotted, and definitely not improving it any. The fingers, though: nothing would stop the painful peeling. I was convinced, for no discernible reason, that whatever it was that was wrong with my fingers was eventually going to kill me.

"I'll probably be dead by the time I'm nineteen," I told Shubnum solemnly and repeatedly. She was shocked and sad at this revelation and carried the knowledge like a heavy burden for years. By the time I turned sixteen, though, Shubnum and I had both realized that I would survive the peeling fingers just fine.

Up until now, Ami had also believed in another unfortunate fairytale, the one that Taya Abu told her: that by the time I turned sixteen, everything about me would fall into place. But none of it had come to pass, and now she was becoming panicked. This was the age at which people started taking notice of the girls in a community and kept an eye on them for future marriage proposals. Was it too late to course-correct for me? She hadn't ever spent much time on beautification and skin care herself, but maybe she should have taught me a thing or two, because it seemed I really needed it.

One day Ami pulled me into the bathroom I shared with Lilly in the bottom level of our split foyer and popped open a Tupperware container. "This," she said "is besan and turmeric. Back in our day we didn't use fancy store-bought washes, or soap on our face. The lather is bad for your skin. We used besan. The chickpea flour makes a perfect scrub, and the turmeric brightens the skin and prevents breakouts, it's an antiseptic."

I watched as she took a handful of the dry yellow powder from the plastic tub and added a few drops of water from the faucet. "Just mix it together, you want the paste to be thick, rub in circles on your face, and then wash off. Rubbing it in circles also helps remove all the little peach fuzz."

Not long after, she started sharing what she read in Pakistani magazine beauty columns, suggesting tips she remembered from her aunts and cousins, or from other aunties. Yogurt was great for your scalp, she advised. All the chemicals in the water in America were awful for your hair, see how hers had thinned out, she said. My hair may have been thick but it was oily, and my scalp was dry, like Abu's. We both suffered dandruff, but a weekly, vigorous oil scalp massage, and conditioning with full-fat yogurt every time I washed my hair, would keep my hair soft, strong, and shiny and my scalp clean.

She demonstrated how to do the scalp massage, heating a bit of olive oil in a bowl, and then rubbing handfuls onto my scalp with such ferocity it felt like she was trying to set it on fire. She pulled and scraped with her strong fingers, rubbed the heel of her palm in circles, and dragged a comb over and over my follicles so hard I was sure my head was bleeding by the time she was done. I wasn't bleeding though, the heat and rush

I felt was the blood circulating through my scalp. That circulation was what would give me great hair and squelch the dandruff forever. Now that I knew how to do it, I was on my own.

"Squeeze a lemon in milk," she read to me from an Urdu column, "and when it splits take the clumpy part and rub it on your face and let it dry. Then wash it and rub the lemon halves on your face to help lighten the skin, and rinse. Do this every day."

"I don't know what a mask is," she told me on another day, "but it says here to mix honey and lemon and rose water and use it once a week as a face mask. You should try it."

Our bathroom was turning into a pantry filled with besan, yogurt, oil, lemons, and honey.

Abu, on the other hand, was still working on the weight part. He had long ago given up trying to bribe me per pound and had moved on to trying to guide me by example. "See, I now start all my meals by filling up on salad, and then eating only half a roti. I didn't even have to try that hard and I lost twenty pounds."

"Just touch your toes a hundred times every day," he would tell me. "It's the best exercise. Stand up, raise your hands above your head, and bend down and touch your toes. Do it as fast as possible a hundred times. You'll be winded, but it will totally flatten your stomach."

"Jumping rope is better," Ami interjected. "I used to jump rope at your age and I had a waist the span of a single hand." She bought me a Hula-Hoop, because some woman she worked with who had a tiny waist told her it was the best way to work off tummy fat.

Finally, they decided they had to make a financial investment in my weight loss, though their budget could barely allow for it. They signed me up for Weight Watchers. Ami handed me some cash as we pulled up at a nondescript strip mall, pointing to a storefront that men and women, mostly women, all heavy, all older, were filing into. "Go check in there, sign in, and give them the weekly fee. I'll be back in an hour."

I got out of the car and dragged myself inside as she watched until the glass door closed behind me. Rows of folding chairs were set up, and about thirty people sat scattered around. There wasn't a single kid in the room, it was all grown-ups.

"I am an aunty too now," I thought. I handed over the twenty Ami had given me to a woman who signed me in, handed me two dollars in change, and gave me a folder of materials. I have a vague recollection of some slides being shown, and then people in the room talking about the kind of week they'd had, mostly about their failures and cravings and self-doubts.

Finally, there was a weigh-in. I had no idea we would be weighed in front of everyone and froze until I realized that, while we would get on a scale in front of the group, there would be no calling out of numbers like there had been in fifth grade. Instead, a woman standing with a binder was the only person to see the weight. She would then write it down in her black book, preserved forever like a diary of shame.

I removed my shoes and got on the scale: 159 pounds.

I wasn't sure if I should be horrified or thrilled. Just a week earlier a girl who sat next to me in biology class had looked up from a magazine and said, "I would rather *die* than be fat. Like, totally *die*." She pointed to the story of a teenager who once weighed 220 pounds but had dieted and exercised a hundred pounds off. Other girls leaned in to take a look at the before and after pictures, and so did I, hoping I looked nothing like the before picture.

"Two hundred pounds! Jesus, can you imagine being *two hundred pounds*?!" someone said, giggling.

I shook my head along with them and said, "If I ever weigh two hundred pounds, please someone just shoot me. Shoot me right between the eyes and take me out of my misery."

They all laughed, and I laughed, relieved that I was laughing with them, and not being laughed at. Also relieved that I didn't weigh 200 pounds, because if I did, then that meant I was fat like the girl we were all laughing at.

On the other hand if I wasn't fat, why was I at a Weight Watchers meeting and why were Ami and Abu willing to spend eighteen whole dollars a week for this?

I went home with the materials and tried to understand the point system and the journaling and the free foods and realized that this program was going to require a whole lot of headspace and actual work. I couldn't imagine having to stop every time I wanted to put something in my mouth to first look up how many points it had and then calculate if I could have it, and if I could, then write it down, day after day after day.

I was a good forty pounds away from two hundred, and most of the others in that Weight Watchers room looked well over it. Ami and Abu had made a mistake, I decided. I didn't need Weight Watchers. I wasn't anywhere close to being "obese," a word I had just learned at the meeting. For the next two months, Ami dropped me off at the meetings, but instead of going inside, I walked right past the storefront and wandered the plaza for an hour, eighteen dollars richer, and much less stressed out than the people who were stuck inside the meeting.

After having spent a couple of hundred dollars, my parents realized I looked exactly the same. Every couple of weeks they asked how the weigh-in went, and I told them "Good, I lost a pound or so," and they accepted it, though they didn't see evidence of it.

Two months later, they let me quit the program because it actually looked like I had put on weight. Maybe that was the trick, that Weight Watchers made money by keeping people fat, keeping them coming back to collect fees week after week.

The real reason I was gaining weight was because I finally had cash every week to buy junk food and had recently discovered kettle-cooked chips and fatty, creamy ranch dip at the 7-Eleven down the block from the Weight Watchers meeting. I stuffed my jacket pockets with tuna-can-size tins of the dip and little bags of chips, and king-size Snickers bars, eighteen dollars' worth of empty calories, before Ami arrived to pick me up. When we drove home together, I sat as still as possible so nothing would rustle. I felt like a drug-smuggling mule with a single buyer, me.

I ate the chips and dip in bed, late at night, as I read from the stack of books next to me. There was an added deliciousness to eating in secret, it enhanced the flavor of the contraband. I could take my time, and not shovel food in fast like I did at the dinner table so that no could see how much I was actually eating.

Eating in secret became easier, and habitual, when I finally got my own car, a six-hundred-dollar beater that Abu bought me, a proud moment in furthering our American dream. Kids back home, especially girls, couldn't imagine having their own cars. Most families in Pakistan were lucky to own a single car, but in America a family had as many cars as it did family members over sixteen. Therefore, as an American teenager, I had to have a car, as Abu's thinking went.

Now I could hit up every drive-thru, stop at any fast-food joint, swing by any convenience store, to get my fixes without anyone ever knowing, and could eat all the junk in the world in the privacy of my own car. No prying eyes to stop me. Other kids branched out into drugs and alcohol and sex when they got a car, I branched out into KFC and Dairy Queen.

The back of my car was nearly always littered with empty fast-food wrappers, half-eaten bags of chips shoved under the seats, and boxes of Pillsbury soft-batch cookies hidden under a pile of papers and books. I had a car and a source of income now, because Abu had recently opened up his own veterinary clinic, where on weekends and evenings he put in another thirty hours a week besides his full-time job with the USDA and where I had started working part-time, too.

He had signed a lease on a commercial space in a small, newly built strip plaza down the street from our house, and we spent two weeks putting up drywall ourselves to split the space into two halves, one side a clinic and the other a pet goods store, painting the concrete floors and installing shelves. Even more walls created a reception area, an examination room, a surgery, and all the way in the back, a room with a grooming station and stainless steel cages where animals could recover after surgery or wait to be picked up after getting groomed.

I gave the haircuts and baths, with literally no experience or training in animal grooming, but I loved animals and Abu figured that was qualification enough. He hung a huge poster with pictures of every breed of dog so I could try and copy their different hairstyles with my new-found clients.

Cats, I discovered, were hell to groom. They were terrified of everything, from running water to the buzz of clippers, from the harness used to tether them to the counter next to the stainless steel tub to the other animals watching quietly from cages. I'd spend half the time trying to untangle them from the harness leash after they'd gotten stuck in it, spinning and flopping around to escape what surely seemed like certain death to them.

Dogs were great, even the very tiny, yappy nervous ones. They nearly never flinched when I slid the clippers across their fur, or snipped straight lines under their chins with scissors, and they all pretty much loved the water. I could even clip their nails, which I wasn't ever going to attempt to do with a cat.

We had a special line of pet shampoo and conditioners, fur-freshening sprays, and little elastic bows to pretty them up so when their owners came to retrieve them, they would ooh and aah with delight at their sparkling little girl or boy, now free of tangles and knots and smelling good. I gave flea baths and removed ticks, and cleaned gunk out of eyes and ears, and proudly dried and fluffed the animals at the end of every session.

I became more and more confident in my skills with every passing month and could make a hundred bucks in a weekend as my take of the grooming fees—big money for a teenager. But then, a giant poodle came along.

The two men who brought in the gorgeous, cream-colored, knee-high poodle explained that she was a show dog and was extremely well behaved. She needed a bath and a fresh cut. Not a problem, I told them. I had groomed dozens of poodles by then, I knew the haircut exactly. Their girl was in good hands. I took her back and got to work, using the lowest clipper setting to trim the fur close on her body and limbs, and leaving puffs of fur around her feet, tail, head, and ears. Then I whipped out my scissors and shaped the tufts into fluffy balls, cutting out stragglers and rounding out the edges of the ears perfectly.

She wagged her tail the entire time, happily compliant when I lathered and hosed her down with warm water and then dried the decorative tufts of fur into even fluffier heights. I secured two pink bows around her ears, gave her a treat, and led her to a cage to wait for her people.

Only one of the men returned to pick her up a few hours later and I bounced back to retrieve the dog. As I led her down the hall toward the man, his mouth fell open.

"What . . . what did you do to her?"

I looked at the poodle, who looked absolutely adorable and deliriously happy, with the huge pillows of fur on her butt, head, paws and ears. She looked great. What was he talking about?

"She is a *giant poodle*. Not a toy poodle. You groomed her like a toy. She isn't supposed to have these ridiculous balls of fur and be nearly bald everywhere else!" His voice reached a high pitch, and Abu came running out of the exam room.

"Is anything wrong, how can I help you sir??"

As the man began explaining, I quietly backed away and headed straight for the dog poster. Poodle, poodle, poodle. Standard poodle. There she was. And, oh . . . oh God.

The dog in the picture looked almost like a bear, uniformly furry all around. I had turned what was supposed to be an elegant, graceful animal into a poodle nightmare.

I returned reluctantly, mortified, as Abu was telling the customer that we wouldn't take any money, and that he was so very sorry, and in the future we would groom his girl for free. My eyes had begun tearing and before I knew it, the dam burst into salty, hot rivers.

Seeing how upset I was, the customer suddenly stopped and shook his head. He pulled three twenties out of his wallet and handed them to Ami, at the cash register. "It's okay, just . . . It's fine. Nothing to worry about," he said, and quickly left with the adorable monstrosity I had created.

Ami shook her head and handed me thirty dollars.

"Crying, again?" she muttered. "Get yourself together, baat baat pay rona." (You cry at the drop of a hat.)

I stuffed the bills into my pocket and walked out the front of the clinic, heading next door to Rocky's Pizza and, still smelling of wet dog, bought two slices of cheese pizza and a soda for $2.15, as I did at least four times a week.

A COUPLE OF slices and a drink for $2.15 was a great deal, but not a better deal than I could get at McDonald's, because by then Lilly had gotten her first job in my favorite fast food joint. It was the year that McDonald's answered a call the nation never made, for larger, glutton-ous portions that put international serving sizes to shame. "Super Size Me!" was the catchy new motto, and the Large Extra Value Meal was born. Now your entree could come with nearly a half a pound of fries and more than a quart of soda.

I learned very quickly that I could eat two Super Size meals in a sit-ting, and my twelve-year-old brother could easily eat one. We were both on our way to becoming Super Sized ourselves. Lilly, despite working in the belly of the beast with access to all the free leftover Big Macs and fries she could ask for, wasn't at all tempted. I still chalk that up to better early eating habits when she lived in Pakistan. After her first weekend on the job, Lilly described how her manager threw away whatever sandwiches and fries were sitting in the warmer for too long and my heart leapt into my throat. A travesty, so much wasted food. And not just any food, but McDonald's food, the *absolutely best fast food*.

We didn't often eat McDonald's because, though they had experimented with many fast-food restaurants, there really was only one American restaurant our parents thought worthy of their hard-earned money: Pizza Hut. Pizza Hut was the gold standard of pizza for my parents, thanks to their thick pan crust, greasy and baked until deep brown, just like Abu liked it. No floppy, half-cooked dough would pass his lips. Pizza Hut was also so popular among our little desi community that every single doctor's kid had every single birthday at the Pizza Hut party room, a luxury my parents couldn't afford when it came to our birthdays. Those were the good old days, when Pizza Hut had a salad bar and was slightly more respectable, and in Hagerstown it was maybe one of the nicest places to eat. One dinner for our family could run nearly forty dollars, though, so it was a rare treat.

Luckily I got my fill for years by milking the Pizza Hut BOOK IT! reading program, earning a precious pan pizza for every five books read. I was getting rewarded for something I did anyway. I checked out ten books at a time from the local library and earned at least three tiny pizzas a month.

Lilly's new job meant eating all the McDonald's goodies we were normally denied, because if Ami and Abu ever made a trip there, they only ever bought Filet-O-Fish sandwiches. My parents weren't quite sold on burger patties that seemed to have absolutely no seasoning.

"You can taste the beef," said Abu. "Who wants to taste the beef? You want the meat to be flavored with enough spices so you *don't* taste the beef."

Useless, gray, flabby kababs, that's what my folks thought of fast-food burgers. If they wanted burgers, they made them much better at home, seasoning the ground beef with at least a dozen spices before frying or grilling patties. Okay, maybe they were actually kababs, but once you put them inside a sesame bun, they were officially burgers. Comparing kabab burgers and McDonald's burgers, though, was like comparing fried chicken and tandoori chicken, if you asked me. Both winners in their own leagues.

The year Lilly started working at that magic fast-food window, McDonald's had also unveiled a brand-new item that I couldn't get enough of—the chicken fajita. I had never actually had a proper fajita in my life, which explains why their version was revelatory. And at ninety-nine cents each, I could stuff myself for under three bucks.

Thanks to Lilly though, I didn't even have to spend those three bucks. We had worked out a system. I would strap Saad, who was lately turning into a butterball himself, into the back seat of my car and head down Route 40 every Friday evening, when Lilly was scheduled to work. She knew in advance that we'd arrive about an hour before her shift was over and was waiting for us to pull up to the window, without having placed an order.

I already had both the driver's-side windows down, giving her not one but two chances to chuck in as many bags as possible as I very slowly cruised past her. Lilly had the bags ready, full of the burgers and fries and fajitas and apple pies she knew were close to being thrown out by the manager. It was a win–win situation as I saw it. In effect, we were saving the very soul of the manager, who otherwise would definitely go to hell for throwing away perfectly good food.

I would drive back around to the other side of the lot and park, and then Saad and I would dig in, tearing open the brown bags like it was Christmas. We ate and burped, and ate again, until it was time for Lilly to get off work, and then the three of us would head home together, making sure we left no evidence for Ami and Abu to find.

If Abu, who had an unbendable code of ethics and honor, knew what we were up to, I wasn't sure he wouldn't call the police himself. Once I had asked him to borrow a pen. He pulled out a black government-issued pen stamped with USDA on the side in white letters from his shirt pocket. He had dozens of these pens in his car, his briefcase, and always one in his pockets.

"These pens," he said, "they're given to us to use for government business only. We are entrusted with these pens, trusted to use them for official business, and not to spend the ink on things they haven't been authorized for."

It seemed like overkill, I couldn't imagine him actually getting in trouble because his kid used his pen to write a letter, just once, and I shared my opinion.

"It's not about getting in trouble. It's about the principle of the matter. The government will never know, and maybe they won't care. But God will know, and I care."

He wouldn't let me use the pen, and therefore Abu could never know about the purloined burgers.

Ami was less stringent about enforcing rules, not that she would ever swipe anything herself. I had witnessed her return to stores multiple times to pay back extra change a clerk had mistakenly given her. But she certainly wasn't going to lose sleep over multinational corporations losing a few bucks here and there to the little man.

She was, however, much more principled than her family. The sibling immigration petitions Ami had filed had started getting approved one by one, and that meant almost every year, having been nearly bereft of relatives until now, we finally started getting visitors from Pakistan.

Iffi Mamu had already been living in the US for a number of years, having gotten married here. The marriage was short-lived, but he had settled in Maryland and worked as an architect for the University of Maryland system. Quiet and reserved, he was the outlier among his four other brothers. Years later Khalid Mamu arrived, tall, dark and handsome, with a questionable Pakistani law degree, full of frenetic energy, cuss words, and hustles. Pummy Mamu came to visit every so often, still fighting his dad bod, still the most sentimental, and not yet ready to settle down in the US. He had a great career as a flight engineer with Pakistan International Airlines, and he wasn't about to give that up to drive a cab in America, like so many of his friends ended up doing when they moved here. Zuby Aunty's green card was next, and she came a few years after her wedding, pregnant, her trip timed perfectly for her to give birth to an American-citizen baby.

The uncles crashed together at Iffi Mamu's place, but Zuby Aunty stayed with us up until she had a daughter, and then returned home when the baby was a few months old.

Ami and her siblings got together nearly every other weekend, every gathering a whirlwind of food and fighting. I loved going over to Iffi Mamu's home. I had made it a habit to explore the musty corners of the rooms at Iffi Mamu's, especially examining the kitchen cabinets and fridge to see what goodies I could find.

There were always oddities. Iffi Mamu was absolutely unable to drive past a junk heap of broken old furniture and household goods on a curb without stopping to comb through it. He had thus collected nearly a dozen PC units and monitors, none that turned on; busted-up, unmatched furniture; pots and pans and dishes; strange sculptures; and fake plants. You name it. Nothing was irredeemable and thrift was king. He bought discounted fruit and vegetables and bread that had begun going bad, collected thousands of packets of condiments and pilfered napkins from fast-food restaurants and 7-Elevens.

One day I found cans of infant formula in his kitchen. There was no baby in the house, there never had been. He explained that a neighbor was getting rid of them, samples from the hospital, since she was breast-feeding and didn't need formula. Milk is milk, he figured. So he brought it home to use as creamer in his chai. He insisted we all try it in our tea and it was as awful as you'd imagine.

The second she got a chance, Zuby Aunty threw the formula into a trashcan outside his house. But by that evening, Iffi Mamu had fished them out and brought them right back into the kitchen.

Another time when we visited, I opened the freezer to find three huge plastic bags of chicken nuggets stacked one upon another.

Pummy Mamu grinned.

"Those are McDonald's nuggets, moti, want some?"

It was a gold mine of nuggets, hundreds of them. How do you buy McDonald's nuggets in bulk, I asked?

Wrong question. One of his friends had worked his way up to manager at the local McDonald's and he always gave any new Pakistani arrival a job at his store. He also let them take home bags of fries and nuggets as long as none of the American employees found out.

Pummy Mamu had begun doing some shifts at the store, so every time we saw him after that, he had bulk bags of McDonalds nuggets and fries for us.

I delighted in Ami's crazy family.

Until Ami's youngest brother finally made it to America, that is. Khan Gul Mamu was a captain in the Pakistani army and built like a Mack truck. He was only to going to be around for a month or so and then head back—no way was he going to leave military service. He stayed with us during the week and headed to Iffi Mamu's on the weekends. I loved having him around. He was funny, irreverent, and had an insatiable appetite, just like me.

Every day after school I rushed home to hang out with Khan Gul Mamu, along with two other new additions to the house. Someone had abandoned a pair of giant French Lop bunnies at Abu's clinic. For a couple of weeks Abu had let them lounge around the clinic, like bodega cats, while he built a pen in our backyard. Now they'd finally come home, and it was my job to clean the pen and fill their water bottles and food bowls every day. The bunnies were huge, four times the size of our fat gray cat, Moto, named for her chunk. Moto would sit on top of the pen, peering down through the chicken wire, hoping for some action, but she wasn't getting any. Both bunnies were older and spent their days dozing in the sun, as active as a pair of beanbag chairs, usually snuggled together in some corner or another. I could lay my head on them and they wouldn't budge.

One day, I got home, threw my bookbag into my room, and headed out the basement door into the backyard. The house was quiet. Ami was usually home from work by now, but there wasn't any sign of her, and Khan Gul Mamu was nowhere to be seen, either. I walked up the slight incline in our yard, staring intently at the bunny pen. It was empty. My breath caught in my throat and I had flashbacks of Bonnie and Bill. What if an animal had gotten to them, too?

But there was no sign of any bunny carnage, and Moto was calmly sleeping on top of the pen. Had they escaped? The pen was securely latched, so unless they got out, turned around, and latched the door themselves, that wasn't a possibility. Besides they were too lazy to run away.

Maybe Abu had taken them to the clinic, I thought. But it was only four o'clock in the afternoon. Abu didn't get home for another thirty minutes from his day job and didn't head over to the clinic until five-thirty. Khan Gul Mamu had been the only one home all day. I turned back to the house and went upstairs, calling out to Ami and Khan Gul Mamu. No one answered. Maybe they had gone shopping.

I shrugged and opened the fridge to grab a snack. Three shelves were filled with trays and bowls of meat—raw, pink chicken meat. What was going on? Were we having a barbeque or something? That was a lot of chicken just for our dinner. I reached around the meat for some juice and made myself a cheese sandwich.

I was still munching as I read a book at the dining table, when the front door opened and Ami came inside alone, looking sheepish.

"Where is Khan Gul Mamu?" I asked.

"Uh . . . he left. I told him to leave."

"Why?" I figured they'd had a fight. Abu said Ami and her siblings couldn't digest a meal without fighting first.

"I told him to leave after I realized what he did. Did you see the meat?"

I blinked once, twice, and slowly, a tiny alarm beginning to sound from an ancient part of my brain.

"The chicken?"

"No. It's not . . . chicken."

Khan Gul Mamu had slaughtered, skinned, gutted, and butchered the bunnies into tikka-size pieces to grill. He wanted to make enough bunny kababs to take to the Friday potluck.

I howled in disbelief and rage.

He killed our bunnies to EAT THEM??? Who the hell ATE BUNNIES???

Ami explained that Khan Gul Mamu had military training that included killing and eating rabbits and squirrels and whatever else they might have to in order to survive in a combat situation.

But he didn't have to kill to survive here in America, here in our house! We had a freezer full of meat, and cupboards full of food, and counters full of fruit and bread, *why my bunnies??*

Because, said Ami, he said they are delicious.

I ran to my room, enraged and sobbing, and refused to come up for dinner. I wanted to kill Khan Gul Mamu with my bare hands. Ami knew it would not go well for him and told him to get out of Dodge before we all got home.

All night I imagined the carnage of the slaughter. I wondered if they had struggled or cried, I wondered if the neighbors had noticed this huge man, a stranger they hadn't seen before, killing the bunnies, and they'd scuttled back inside, terrified. Where was the rest of the bunnies, their skin, their heads?

Oh God, where were their heads??

The next morning I emerged, face swollen from crying, but stomach empty and gurgling. As much as I did not want to go to the kitchen, staying hungry seemed like an even greater horror, so I decided to face my fears. There was no sign of bunny meat anywhere: not marinating in the fridge; not on the stove, where I was afraid to find a pot of bunny stew; not roasting in the oven or cooking on the grill outside.

Ami and Abu sat at the dining table looking glum.

"We threw away the meat," said Ami.

Abu shook his head slowly. "What kind of animal does something like . . ." He stopped to glance at Ami before finishing emphatically, "We don't eat our pets."

We never mentioned the bunnies again, and Khan Gul Mamu never returned.

SEVEN

Ghaans Phoos: Rabbit Food

There were a few more weeks left in my senior year of high school, and for the past three months all the seniors in my level were acting as if they'd already graduated. Skipping classes, skipping school altogether—and no one, not even the teachers, really cared. Probably because we were already a group of overachieving nerds, most having earned early college admission, with our class rank firmly in place.

I had applied to a single university, the only one I dared apply to, the University of Maryland in Baltimore County. It was the closest state university to Hagerstown, but far away enough that I'd have to live on campus, which seemed like a dream. It had almost been an impossible dream because Ami said, "Absolutely not, you are not leaving home," a reaction I fully expected from her. On the surface, she was a pretty hands-off mother, not one to micromanage, or even manage at all, but she still wanted her brood at home, where she could keep an eye on us as needed.

Just because she was no helicopter parent, though, didn't mean we were entitled to privacy. Privacy is not a thing in the desi household, and it was certainly unheard of in my parents' generation for kids to have rooms of their own, which, however, each of us did. Back home there were always other siblings and cousins sharing a room, and oftentimes a mother slept in the same room as her kids until they were well past grown.

Ami never slept with us, but she did walk into our rooms, which were always expected to stay unlocked, anytime she wanted, at all hours of the day and night. She kept odd hours, sleeping from 10 p.m. to 3 a.m., up until after the sun rose, and then back down for another few hours. In those predawn hours, she would wander the dark house like a phantom, draped in a scarf, prayer beads in hand, as she recited some prayer or another thousands of times. At least thrice weekly she barged right into our bedrooms at around 4 a.m., to take a look around our dressers and closets and riffle through our books and papers in the dim glow of the hallway light.

Every visit ended with her leaning down close and blowing hearty gusts of prayer-filled breath, *phook phook*, right into our faces. There. That would protect us for the rest of the week, or at least the day. Sometimes we woke up, terrified, and sometimes we didn't, and either way, she didn't care.

Abu, on the other hand, never entered our rooms, not even once. He had a much stronger sense of boundaries and decorum and believed in the fatherly tradition of keeping a distant, though watchful, eye. He was also pragmatic and that included my on-campus college plans. He realized there was no other affordable university or college, other than community college, within driving range. And if I was going to be a doctor, then I couldn't very well go to community college. So, Abu told me, where I studied was my life and my decision. *What* I studied, not so much. There was no question but that I would study medicine.

Besides, I had the costs covered. I had worked up the courage to apply for and get enough scholarships and loans to cover two years of tuition and board, and after that I'd figure it out. So while I wanted their blessing, I didn't need their permission or financial support to go away for college. It was my first act of defiance against either of them, maybe my only act of defiance, ever, in my almost eighteen years of existence.

I had never been to a party, or a concert, or tried drugs, or alcohol, never snuck out at night, never had a boyfriend, never so much as touched a boy. I decided one day that I couldn't very well graduate without having committed a single teenage sin, so I planned a daring bunk day. I would skip school for one whole day, a thought both terrifying and exciting. Lilly and I both had our own cars by then, and we drove to school separately. She would have no idea if I actually went to school or not.

I just had to figure out what I wanted to do with my day off. I didn't have any friends that I could hang out with, my only friend was still Shubnum, all the way in Delaware. The local mall was dead even on Saturday nights, and during the week it would be full of retired seniors taking strolls.

I could go see a movie, or lots of movies, but I had never, ever been to a movie theater because . . . well, I'd never been to a movie theater. Back in Chambersburg almost a decade earlier, Abu had taken us to a drive-in theater to see *Gremlins* and that was the only movie I ever watched outside of the house. I didn't even know how to find out what movies were playing and when and where.

After thinking about it for days, I decided it wasn't safe to go anywhere in my car because I could be spotted anywhere, by any aunty or uncle, in our sleepy town. I decided the best place for me to bunk school would be at home. I could have the entire house to myself, a luxury I had never experienced: watch some Indian movies, rummage around in the fridge, read in bed, blast music on my tape recorder.

Abu left for work by 6 a.m., Lilly and I headed out around seven-thirty, and Ami and Saad left for work and school by eight. After Lilly left I told Ami I was going to take the bus that day because my car didn't have gas. Ami sat where she always did every morning, perched on her prayer mat in the living room, looking down at the front door. She nodded silently, fingering prayer beads and loudly whispering her daily devotions.

The game was afoot. All I had to do was walk right past the bus stop, walk around the neighborhood some, and return after the house was empty. I was giddy with exhilaration and also wracked with fear and guilt at this truly delinquent thing I was about to do. But I deserved it, just one day of breaking loose. I had stocked up the day before on chips and cookies and soda, stashed them in my room, so I could have a truly hedonistic day at home.

I walked deep into our subdivision, swinging back toward our house about thirty minutes later. As I got close to our little yellow split foyer, my breath caught in my throat. Ami's car was still there. What was she doing home?? It was almost 8:15 a.m. Maybe she was going to work late. That was okay. I would wait. I had a place I could hide out until she left.

I snuck into the backyard. Right outside the window that led into Lilly's bedroom was a shed where Abu kept the lawnmower and cans of gas and random boxes of tools. There were some folding chairs in there and I would just hang out until Ami left, no big deal.

I carefully opened the shed door and closed it behind me. It was dark and dusty, and because it was the end of May the shed was already beginning to warm up. No worries, I'd doze in a chair. An hour went by. I quietly opened the shed door and stuck my head out. I could hear Ami talking loudly on the phone through the kitchen window right above the deck. Crap, she still wasn't gone.

I checked every hour, at eleven, then at noon, as the sun rose higher and the shed got hotter. I was burning up, sweating, suffocating. I was well and truly stuck. I couldn't pretend to return home early because how would I explain how I actually got home? I spent the rest of the day roasting, hungry and dehydrated, in the shed, waiting for my watch to hit 3:30 p.m. I didn't even have a book to read, having stacked them neatly on my bed, to wait for me.

When it was finally safe to pretend to return home, I dragged myself out of the shed quietly and walked around to the front of the house. I unlocked the door and stepped inside, beet red and exhausted. Ami stood in the kitchen, again chatting away on the phone as she chopped cauliflower. I nodded to her and went downstairs to wash up and crawl into bed. A little while later, I heard her call to me.

"Bobbi? Bob*beeeee*?"

I went halfway up the stairs and stopped. She was standing with her hands on her hips. "The school called. They said you were absent and asked why."

I hadn't even thought of that because I hadn't even thought anyone would be home to take the call. I stammered. "Oh, that's strange. Must be a mistake. Maybe they missed me in homeroom. I was there all day, where else would I be?"

Ami looked at me for a few seconds and shrugged. Of course, where else could I be? I didn't even have my car all day.

Every single thing about that day made me feel like the worst person alive. That I had skipped school, and that I had lied to Ami, and that she had believed it because she trusted me.

She didn't, however, trust the rest of the world. In a matter of months I would be moving onto campus at UMBC and she needed a plan to keep me safe in the big, bad world outside her nest. She couldn't be there to protect me, but someone had to, because I was not at all ready, too innocent, inexperienced, and naïve to be on my own.

Her chance came during freshman orientation that summer, a weekend-long event that meant I would be away from home, away from my little desi Muslim bubble, for the first time ever in my life. Ami, Abu, and I drove to the small, contained campus in the suburbs of Baltimore that Friday afternoon, and I grew more terrified as we got closer.

No one was outright cruel to me in high school, but no one paid any attention to me either. I wanted to be a somebody and get involved in things that would make me relevant, so I joined the student newspaper and soon became its editor, chief photographer, and for about year, the writer of nearly every story in it. That gave me an excuse to attend all school events, like homecoming and prom, and every football, basketball, softball game, every tennis match, and every track meet. I was everywhere, but I may as well have not been. Despite all the trying, I was still a nonentity.

I was chubby, unpopular, and a square inside and out. Lilly was popular and pretty, had friends, and boys were tripping over themselves around her, so even she could not endure hanging out with me.

I can't blame her. If I were her, I wouldn't have wanted to hang out with me either. I wasn't exactly the life of any party. And now, after all those years in Hagerstown, I would be leaving without having a single friend to miss. Technically, I had made one friend—tall, lanky, sweet Doug. Ami at one point had high hopes that maybe Doug would marry me, but Doug, thankfully unaware of Ami's hopes, would have had to miraculously change his sexual orientation for that to be a possibility. Also, we'd had a huge fight our senior year and no longer spoke.

I was excited to be going away to college, but what if I didn't make any friends there, either? What if everyone avoided me, ignored me, and I spent the next four years a ghost on campus, a nonentity like I was in high school, which was almost worse than being hated.

Or maybe, just maybe, I could reinvent myself. No one had to know that I wasn't ever cool before college.

Orientation weekend, we gathered with hundreds of other eager, pimply incoming freshmen and their tired-looking parents in the quad and from there took a leisurely tour of the campus. I spent the entire time scanning the crowd for a potentially friendly face. We were handed packets of information, our assigned room keys for the weekend, and then the parents were told to head off so we students could start the evening's icebreaker events.

I stood on the sidewalk with Ami and Abu outside the dorm building I was assigned, waiting for them to leave, but Ami showed no sign of budging. She was looking around, frantically—for what, I wasn't sure. And then suddenly, she grabbed my hand and dragged me with her, stopping in front of a brown family—parents and two kids, a brother and sister.

If there was anyone who was more out of place than me in the entire UMBC freshman class of 1992, it was that girl. Her hair was pulled back in a single tight French braid, and she wore a white button-down cotton shirt, a long plaid skirt, and leather flats. Though she was dressed a bit odd, she was lovely. Tall, with smooth mocha skin, raven eyes and hair, a tiny little nose, and a full little mouth like a doll's, she stared at her feet, painfully shy, as Ami tried to communicate with them in Urdu.

It turned out they were Sri Lankan and didn't speak Urdu. Well, they were close enough to Pakistani, and this was exactly the kind of girl—innocent, shy, clearly never seen a party in her life—that Ami was comfortable leaving me with. Ami was further thrilled to learn the family had only recently immigrated, and their daughter had attended a Catholic convent in Sri Lanka. Adding to the excitement was that she, like me, like probably every desi kid there, was pursuing a premed degree. And once Ami learned they lived in Frederick, just miles down the road from Hagerstown, it became clear that this meeting was divine intervention of the highest order.

Ten minutes later, our parents had managed to make us promise them that we would stick together all weekend, though we hadn't actually said a word to each other. Only then was Ami okay with leaving her firstborn behind, in the hands of what appeared to be the least worldly girl I'd ever met.

HER NAME WAS Upeksha, and no I could not call her Upi though I tried, because Upeksha was a beautiful Sinhalese name that she would not let me corrupt. We did stick together all that weekend, and then called each other the rest of the summer, waiting for the fall semester to start. While I continued to work at Abu's clinic, Upeksha worked at her family's Mexican restaurant, both of us saving up for our great transition into adulthood.

Upeksha was so shy she made me look relatively outgoing, but it didn't take long for us to connect in our shared social awkwardness, our love of reading, and our traditional families, though hers was Buddhist and I'd never met a Buddhist in my life. Befriending one was exciting. I'd always had a fascination for what other people believed in. When we visited Aunty Kaushi and Uncle Ramesh, our only Hindu friends, I'd hide away in their son's room and read the illustrated Hinduism-for-kids books, memorizing the names of the deities and their stories. I was engrossed by the brightly colored, multilimbed deities, part human and part animal, like Hanuman and Ganesha, the ravishing blue Krishna, and the terrifying Kali.

At Shubnum's I'd stare at the reproduction of the Final Supper and a painting of a mournful-looking Jesus, eyes turned upward, hands together in prayer. I studied the embroidered, framed Bible passages they had on their walls, and snuck peeks into their Bibles, delighted when I recognized the name of a Prophet. I didn't understand what it was like to worship a God you could see, one you could paint, one that seemed more human than God to me. But I heard echoes of the same tales across Christianity and Islam—stories of a great flood, of a holy child set afloat to escape a murderous king, of evil beings bent on destroying mankind—and on some level it all felt very connected to me.

Upeksha patiently explained the different kinds of Buddhism to me, the philosophy of the Buddha, the virtue of suffering, reincarnation based on your deeds, but unlike Hinduism and Christianity, much of it seemed amorphous, a spiritual system I couldn't quite grasp. Islam was so much more cut-and-dry, things were right, things were wrong, halal or haraam, you prayed five times a day, gave charity, fasted in Ramadan, went to Mecca, and then ended up in either Heaven or Hell. Pretty straightforward.

Buddhism, in contrast, seemed like a lifelong commitment to the Golden Rule, without many actual rules. That part, I liked.

That first weekend Upeksha and I swapped confessions about our complete lack of interaction with and interest from the opposite sex, our crushes, and our insecurities.

"I think I'm too boyish for boys to like me," I told her. "Ami always said I should have been a boy, and that I sound like a boy, and would have looked better as a boy."

Lilly had said once, in that offhand way someone says something without realizing the other person will remember it forever, that I looked like a Native American man. Much more specific than Ami. My broad, flat face and stick-straight black hair made me look like a tribal chieftain, she said.

Why not a chieftain's daughter, I wondered?

Upeksha's face scrunched up when I shared my lament about being manly looking.

"You are," she said casually, though it stuck with me forever, "the most feminine looking girl I've ever met. Everything about you is feminine. Your eyes and dimples and round face and long, straight hair are like those statues on temples, haven't you seen them?"

I hadn't, but I looked them up later. They were sensuous and curvy, with tiny waists and fleshy, plump bottoms, hips jutting out in one seductive way or another. Maybe, I thought, if I stood like that, I would look voluptuous and not like a linebacker. It didn't work, but neck up, I guess Upeksha had a point. And if I was going to reinvent myself, it was time to lean into whatever I had to work with.

I would become as feminine as I possibly could in this new incarnation of college Bobbi. The day of the big move onto campus, I pulled on the UMBC sweatshirt I had bought over the summer and stacked my bags in the back of Abu's pickup truck, taking along with me freshly purchased makeup, clothes, and hot curlers. Upeksha and I hadn't been able to get a room together, freshmen weren't allowed to pick roommates, and I'd been assigned to someone named Nakia.

Between Abu and me, we managed to drag everything I had in one trip up to the fourth floor of Potomac Hall, a brand-new dorm building that just opened up that year. The fourth floor of Potomac was the only floor in any building on the entire campus that was a girls-only floor, a concession that my parents demanded and, frankly, one that I was relieved to oblige. Boys scared me.

We got to my room, and I unlocked the door and swung it open. Half the room looked like it had been lived in for months already, though I knew no one had moved in until that day. Nakia sat on a bed on her side doing her nails and watching the small color television she had perched on a shelf. Her towels were hung, books set in a row on her desk, posters taped above her bed, her sheets and pillows and matching comforter all in place.

I stood heaving, musty and sweaty in my sweatshirt, while Nakia was in a tank top and shorts, her deep brown legs long and shiny.

Oh my God, I thought, *Abu has never been around a girl showing this much skin.*

Abu stood at the threshold of the room and, without stepping a foot over it, flung my bags inside and said, "Okay Bobbi, call your mother, khuda haafiz," and left.

Nakia watched me without blinking, nail file never skipping a beat as it zipped back and forth across her acrylic tips, as I stumbled over my bags and mumbled my hellos. "Are you okay?" she asked.

I wasn't sure what she meant by that question then, but in hindsight she was definitely concerned that she had gotten stuck with a bumbling numpty. The rotary phone, sitting on the windowsill between our beds, suddenly rang and Nakia picked it up. "It's for you," she said.

How . . . how was it for me? Oh, it was probably Upeksha. I took the phone and chirped, "Hiiiiiiii Upeksha!"

It was Ami. She began interrogating me about my roommate, right in front of my roommate, and I tried my best to answer in Urdu, which likely only confirmed to Nakia that we were talking about her. Finally, Ami said, "Give her the phone, I want to talk to her."

I sheepishly stood up and offered Nakia the phone. "I'm sorry, my mom wants to talk to you."

Nakia took the receiver and listened, nodded, said, "Yes . . . yes . . . yes I know . . . okay yes I will," and then hung up. Then she looked at me pointedly and said, "Your mom asked me to wake you up every morning for your morning prayers. I told her I would. Where's your prayer mat?"

I wanted my big, funky sweatshirt to swallow me whole. But Nakia was as nonchalant as if Ami had told her she was sending a care package of cookies.

"I'm so sorry, no you don't have to, let me explain, see, we're Muslim," I started, and she stopped me.

"Listen. I'm Black. Every Black person in this country has some family members who are Muslim. Doesn't freak me out at all. And no problem for me to remind you to pray."

She flashed me a big, red smile and went back to her nails and her TV show, and I got to work unpacking and planning my wardrobe for the week.

I had never cared much about my clothes because it had been drilled into my head that my body sabotaged virtually anything I wore. But tomorrow would be the first day of the rest of my life as "Rabia reinvented," and I had to plan ahead. That included getting heated curlers in my hair that night, so the next day my hair would be bouncy and voluminous, if only for a short while. It was so straight the curls rarely ever took.

I lay on my face, the only way I could with a head full of curlers, and listened to Nakia snore all night. I didn't catch a wink.

The next day I dragged myself out of bed at 7 a.m. when Nakia nudged me to get up and pray. I prayed, and then pulled the curlers out of my hair. It was an unruly, hideous mess that didn't at all look like the bouncy waves I had hoped for. My head looked huge. I skipped breakfast trying to frantically brush it out, which just made it worse, and finally just quickly washed my hair. Hair still wet, I met Upeksha in our 9-a.m. Biology 101 class, along with approximately four hundred other students. While we couldn't live together, we had tried to coordinate as many classes together as possible.

She still had her hair in a French braid and wore a long, modest, matronly skirt and a cotton cross-body bag. She looked kind of cute, I thought, in a hippie way. But between the two of us, surrounded by girls with teased hair, crop tops, heeled booties, and lip gloss, neither was getting invited to any parties. We spent the morning hopping from one building to another until it was lunchtime.

I had been able to purchase a meal plan for the year, which meant I could eat all my meals, three times a day, at the dining hall, and never have to worry about food. No starving for me, like some college students I had heard about. We had seen the dining hall during orientation, but most of it had been closed, and we had been given boxed meals and pizza over that weekend. So the first time I stepped into the dining hall as an official student that afternoon, I knew I was screwed.

There were permanent food stations that served pizza and burgers and fries and Chinese, one station that had a new special every day, a salad bar, a soup bar, a bread and roll selection, an ice cream and dessert station, and soda on tap. There was no limit to how much you could eat, how many times you could go back for more, how many glasses of Coca-Cola you could down, or how much you could stuff into your pockets and backpacks and take with you. It was the stuff of both my dreams and my nightmares.

Self-regulation had always been my biggest challenge. I didn't really know when to stop eating because feeling full was relative to feeling hungry, and I frankly never felt either. I ate food not because I needed the fuel, but because it was in front of me. And I ate until there was nothing left, not on my plate, and if possible, not on the table. I saw people who left food on their plates, who packed up half to take home, who actually had leftovers after a meal, and I didn't understand it. What are you saving it for, I wanted to ask?

Upeksha and I grabbed our trays and our lunches and stood looking around. Hundreds of students buzzed around us and past us, joining others, friends, and groups of friends. We needed two seats together, but at a couple of tables we tried, we were told, "Sorry, these are taken." Then I spied two desi girls sitting across from each other, eating silently. There were two open seats next to them. They sat sullenly, two brown girls who were the least threatening prospects in the huge buzzing space, and I approached them with Upeksha trailing behind me.

We stood next to their table, unsure and nervous, clutching our lunch trays, as they stared at us, curious. I finally said, "Hi, can we sit here, with you?"

One of the girls rolled her eyes and went back to eating. I was already scared of her. The other nodded and said, "Sure."

It felt like we were interrupting a standoff, but with no options, we put down our trays and joined them. I'm sure we introduced ourselves to each other, but beyond that, I have no idea what we talked about. What none of us knew at the time was that, in that moment, we had just become a posse, a clique that would spend the rest of our college years together, and the following thirty years as best friends.

Anu and Veena had known each other from well before college, they were family friends and had grown up in Montgomery County, one of the chicest, wealthiest, most diverse counties in Maryland. Veena, the magnificent eye-roller, was tiny, not even five feet tall, but mighty and intimidating, with a head of the blackest, most captivating curls, eyes that could pierce your soul, and a perfect, brilliant smile that was always a bit shocking because it had to be earned.

Anu had short, highlighted, stylish hair, stylish clothing, and stylish shoes. She was branded from head to toe and smelled of pricey perfume. She was giggly and a little high strung but sweet, a people pleaser who, unlike Veena, definitely cared about what others thought.

They were both from South India, and ethnically Tamil. I had no idea what that even meant. I didn't know there was a difference between North India and South India and that not all Indians understood Hindi. What about Bollywood, I asked? If they didn't understand Hindi, how did they watch Bollywood films?? Who needed Bollywood, said Anu, when they had Tollywood, a rich Tamil film industry with incredible actors and musicians and singers.

My mind was blown. Anu and Veena's language, clothing, music, and even their film industry were completely different than anything I associated with India. They were both Hindu and I felt a bit of pride at my Hindu self-education, so at least I wasn't completely ignorant on that front.

But this delusion came to a screeching halt the first time Veena invited me to her dorm to share some food her mother had dropped off. She had a row of pictures of deities taped to a shelf, and a few small figurines above it. I leaned closer, trying to recognize them so I could wow her by throwing around my limited Hindu knowledge. But I didn't know who any of them were.

Veena saw me peering closely at a picture of a deity with six heads and ten arms, perched on a giant peacock, and said, "This is the god Murugan, and his different incarnations."

"Murugan?" I asked. I thought I had heard wrong.

"Yep."

"Oh haha, that's funny, it sounds like murgi, which means 'chicken' in Urdu. Is he a chicken god? Does he have something to do with chickens?"

Veena's eyes went cold.

"That . . . is really rude. No, he has nothing to do with chickens."

My face grew red and I stammered, "I'm sorry, I just thought because Ganesha is part elephant and Hanuman . . ."

Veena turned around and said, "Anyway, let's eat."

She handed me a Ziploc bag filled with what looked like crunchy yellowish pinwheels dotted with whole spices. Try it, she commanded. They were crispy and savory. This was some kind of nimko, a fried snack that seemed to be made with besan or lentils, but I couldn't place the flavors.

Then Veena popped open a series of Tupperware containers and the room suddenly smelled heady and nutty and herbal. I've always had a nose like a bloodhound and can smell and distinguish different aromas, good and bad, from dozens of feet away. But I had never smelled anything like the smells that were floating out of the three little plastic boxes.

Veena handed me a puffy, spongy white disk a few inches in diameter, shaped like a UFO. Sweet, savory? I had no idea. "That," she said, "is an idli." She told me it was made from rice ground into a batter, fermented, and steamed. I thought hard but couldn't think of a single steamed Pakistani dish. Fascinating.

She held out two containers to dip the idli in, explaining that the creamy white sauce was coconut chutney and the other was sambar, a soupy, tamarind-based broth with lentils and vegetables. None of it was like anything I'd ever eaten before, the sambar tangy and spicy, the chutney creamy and cooling, and the notes and scents I couldn't put my finger on turned out to be curry leaves. I knew Ami used bay leaves, but curry leaves? Never.

I professed my love of idli to Anu soon after and she told me her favorite way to eat them was smeared with chili oil and sprinkled with a spice blend called milagai podi. I had to try it, so she took me to her house one day and I ate them as fast as her mother could scoop them out of the steamer.

Anu and her family were vegetarians, the first vegetarians I had ever met in my life. Though I had heard about it, I couldn't really wrap my brain around an entire cuisine based on vegetables. Vegetables were hardly ever more than a side dish in our home, and Ami's rotation was pretty limited: there was saag, the creamy mustard green dish we ate with cornmeal flatbreads, which could kind of be considered a meal on its own. Otherwise, Ami made palak or bhindi or gobi—spinach or okra or cauliflower—with potatoes or often, because she couldn't help herself, with meat. Baingan, eggplant, was probably cooked half a dozen times a year, but it was never the star of the show, just an accompaniment to whatever main meat dish we were having.

I couldn't imagine eating these same five vegetable dishes over and over, day in and day out, forever, and I definitely couldn't imagine them being the main event. It turned out, of course, I didn't quite understand what it meant to be vegetarian. There were at least a dozen vegetables Anu and Veena's families ate that we never did, but also they combined lentils and daals into a hundred different combinations, made thin savory crepes called dosa in dozens of varieties with as many different stuffings, and cooked rice in so many ways that I'd never heard of: lemon rice, coconut rice, tamarind rice, tomato rice, porridges, besi bela baath, and what seemed like a thousand different kinds of fried, pakoralike dumplings eaten dry or in a sauce. They even made a "meatball" curry, malai koftay, out of vegetables and paneer.

Upeksha wasn't a vegetarian but she introduced me to one of the most satisfying, delicious vegan dishes I've ever eaten—steamed white rice with pol sambol, a simple, spicy coconut relish. Upeksha was a deft cook in her own right, having been responsible, as the only daughter of the family, to cook for them every day. My first Sri Lankan meal was a spread that Upeksha told me was customary. One rice, one meat dish, one daal, something crisp and crunchy, and one sambol.

Everything was delicious and fiery, but the sambol was a revelation. Upeksha mixed desiccated, unsweetened coconut with grated onion, finely chopped green chili, salt, and enough lemon juice to hydrate the coconut but not make the relish wet.

"Eat this with the rice alone," Upeksha commanded.

Frankly, we didn't use coconut in any of our home cooking, so I wasn't sure what to expect, but I certainly didn't expect the savory, spicy, tangy *meatiness* of the coconut. It transformed plain white rice into a complete meal. I could see now how you could live your life with an incredibly rich variety of vegetarian food. But then what I couldn't understand was why Anu and Veena were both like me, struggling to lose weight.

I thought being vegetarian necessarily meant you were lean and healthy—and I also wondered what the point was if you still weren't skinny. That misunderstanding was put to rest when I got into a heated argument with Anu about how to cook vegetable curries. She said that her mother didn't use any water all, she just stewed them with onions and tomatoes and enough oil to cook them through, even vegetables like potatoes. That was *impossible*, I argued. How could you cook things like potatoes or carrots or even leafy veggies without water? Nope, she responded, water diluted the flavor.

Okay, I thought, if they're eating vegetables made purely in oil, then no wonder they have weight problems like me.

But that wasn't it. It wasn't the homemade food that was making any of us heavy, even if it was cooked purely in oil. It was things like pizza and pasta and chips and ramen and a world of desserts. All of which I ate mostly with Anu, in copious amounts in our freshman year. Of the four of us, Anu was the only one who had a car, mine having given up the ghost over the summer. She knew all the best spots to eat in the area, had a credit card, and was entirely too generous with her broke friends. There was a Chinese buffet close by, just $9.99, full of saucy, greasy noodles and vegetables, where we shoveled platefuls of fried rice into our faces with abandon. Anu introduced me to the swanky Bombay Tandoor in downtown Baltimore, where we dished out $13.99 each to treat ourselves, as often as possible, to their mostly vegetarian lunch buffet, topping every meal off with three or four of their house-made gulab jamun, deep-fried balls of a milk-solid dough swimming in saffron and cardamom-scented syrup. A few times a month we hit up the American Cafe, perched atop the Baltimore harbor, which had the best vegetarian chili around and unlimited sourdough bread, *unlimited* being the operative word. And there was no place like the Olive Garden to get stuffed to the gills with pasta and breadsticks, all the while assuring ourselves that those three bowls of salad we started the meal with, rich with dressing and extra parmesan cheese, balanced it all out.

Anu introduced me to frozen bean-and-cheese burritos and Mama Celeste pizzas, both foods cheap, filling, and tasty, and even when she wasn't around I could walk to the local grocery store and buy as many as I could fit into my dorm mini fridge. And of course, late at night when the munchies hit, there were the always-reliable twenty-five-cent packets of ramen that I could make in my electric kettle, soothing, filling, and utterly fattening.

It turned out there was really a lot of awful-for-you vegetarian food out there, and between the dining hall and Anu's easy transport, by the end of freshman year, when others gained the infamous fifteen, I had gained the terrible twenty-five.

THE FIRST SUMMER back at home, Ami and Abu were simply not having it anymore. They had seen me grow, slowly but surely, throughout the course of the year, noting my fuller face and wider hips every weekend that I was home.

Ami looked at me carefully and said, "You don't even know what you really look like anymore, that's how much weight you've put on. Your face, it's not really your face. It's hidden in fat. Don't you want to know what you really look like, what your face is really like?"

She couldn't see my face anymore, but clearly saw my freshman gluttony. I now weighed 175 pounds. Abu weighed 165 pounds. I was almost nineteen and, as far as my parents were concerned, these were the seminal years that could make or break a young woman's future. These were the years the proposals should start coming in, and they weren't; if they didn't, before we knew it, I could be near thirty and then virtually unmarriageable for life.

Anu and Veena's parents were thinking along the same lines. Sure, they wanted their daughters educated and professionally successful, but if we didn't get married, it was all for naught. The hunt for all three of us was on.

Upeksha's parents weren't worried about any of that. First of all, the whole arranged-proposal thing wasn't the way they operated. But also, while I had turned from a dumpling into a full-on bao during my first year in college, Upeksha had transformed from a plain convent girl who passed by unnoticed into a stunner who made all the "hottest girls on campus" lists.

To be fair, it didn't take much. She was already tall and slender, built like a model, and she had stopped wearing her hair in a braid and had gotten rid of the long, pleated skirts. A simple pair of jeans and a knit top, her curly dark hair cascading past her shoulders, was all it took to suddenly catch the eye of every boy on campus, even though she didn't want to. All the new attention was killing her, she was still so shy.

Upeksha would shrink when the shyness overtook her. She'd pull up her legs into a little knot in a corner of a couch or cross them in a way that seemed impossible, over and around and around again, one foot hooked behind the slender ankle of the other. It made me realize how little my body could even express—it couldn't twist and turn like hers, it couldn't shrink, I couldn't even cross a leg over the other.

I was determined to drop some weight before sophomore year, as much of the twenty-five pounds I'd piled on as possible. The internet was this new thing, and I could find all kinds of information at my fingertips, a miracle really, so I spent hours searching for diets and weight-loss plans. I learned about something called a Body Mass Index, and that my BMI was 30. I was first unbelieving, and then cried when I realized I was in the "obese" category. I discovered anorexia and bulimia and considered if I could make those work for me. Anorexia required actual starvation, and I wasn't capable of that. Bulimia seemed promising. I could eat as much as I wanted and then just throw it up.

I tried once, twice, three times to vomit up after gorging but it didn't work. I stuck my finger down my throat, then a pencil, then a toothbrush. I gagged and coughed over the toilet but I just wouldn't throw up. It was like my body would not let go of the food. I moved on. I tried laxatives, the waxy chocolate kind, but after a week or so I couldn't even look at them, they made me so nauseous.

I could try a fad diet. Yes, they were fads, but they were also diets, which meant I would lose weight. There was the cabbage soup diet, the six-bananas-a-day diet, the four-eggs-a-day diet. Upeksha told me how her brother's girlfriend lost fifty pounds in two months by having only fruit for breakfast, lunch, and dinner. I tried them all, each for four, five, six days, feeling starved all the while, and then losing complete control and binging until I was sick.

Lilly had told me more than a few times: "Just stop eating, losing weight is not rocket science." Anytime she'd want to lose five pounds (because she never had to lose more than that), she ate soup for a week and was done. But I was so hungry, all the time, famished, unable to think about anything but what I wanted to avoid—food. I tried fen-phen to suppress my appetite and found my heart racing, palpitating in my chest so hard I thought I was having a heart attack.

Fast twice a week, said Ami. That was the Prophetic tradition, fast Mondays and Thursdays, it's impossible to stay fat if you just do what the Prophet Muhammad did. Drink hot lemon in water first thing in the morning. Boil caraway seeds in a pot of water, strain and cool it, and drink it all day, the weight will flush out with your urine. Drink only hot liquids, it will melt the fat that's stuck to your organs and inside your skin, like butter in a broiler. Chew ginger, all day, it will kill your hunger. Take a spoon of apple cider vinegar morning, noon, and night, it's *guaranteed* to boost metabolism. Black seed cures everything, even death, so surely it would cure me.

Cure me of fat.

The avalanche of advice was steady and forceful, from all sides. For the first time in my life, I realized they had all been right, my family, all these years, but I hadn't seen it.

I had spent a year on a college campus surrounded by young men, thousands of them, and not caught the interest of a single one. Until now, I had thought, "I'm not that fat," but now it was clear as day that I was definitely *that fat*. Whatever force field had prevented me until then from realizing I was as fat as everyone said suddenly disappeared.

And my relatives back in Pakistan were right, no one would ever marry me.

I struggled all summer and managed to lose twenty pounds before returning to college. I had grown my hair down past my waist and was able to squeeze back into the cuter clothes I had bought a year earlier. No one noticed.

Not until one night when Anu and I took Veena out because she had had a difficult week. I had only been "out" once before, tagging along with a group to a club on a Friday evening and instantly regretting it. I sat in a corner watching people get drunk and fall over each other as jarring rave music played to flashing lights, and I was fairly certain I was in hell. Or at least on my way there. Two hours away, in Hagerstown, my parents and siblings would be at the weekly Quran study potluck, and here I was, in a pit of sin.

My conscience couldn't take it and I didn't enjoy it either, so I refused to go to a club that night but agreed to go with my friends to a lounge, instead, which I was told was much tamer. That night we ran into two young Pakistani guys and chatted and exchanged numbers. They were foreign students in graduate programs at American University and wanted to hang out again sometime.

We said sure, why not, and a couple of weeks later we met them at a diner. To my amazement, they both were clearly interested in me, but there was only one I was interested in, the little guy. The tall one had wide green eyes and an earnest look, but he was geeky and awkward and kept telling me my face was as round and beautiful as the moon. I knew he was complimenting me, but after fighting so hard not to have a round, fat face, it just wasn't landing.

The little guy was different. He was sharp, fast-talking and funny, and smirked with his head tilted down and a corner of his mouth curled up as he stared right at me, as if we both shared a secret no one else knew. He was as light-skinned as Pakistanis come, virtually glowing, had big, droopy, dark bedroom eyes, and a swagger like he owned every place he walked into. Everything about him made my pulse race.

When they dropped us back off on campus, the tall guy tried to put his scarf around me to keep me warm, and I slid it right back off and handed it to him, looking at his friend. I'd made my choice clear, and a week later the little one came to see me, alone.

It was my first date, though I refused to acknowledge it was a date. It was dinner, just dinner. That night he told me about his family, their business in the Gulf, his world travels, his career aspirations. I could barely look at him. He wasn't like the boys at UMBC, because he wasn't a boy. He was a man, twenty-four years old. He had beard stubble and had on real cologne, not shitty Axe body spray, I could smell it. He wore a blazer, and had his own car, and a wallet full of credit cards. I had no idea what he saw in me.

"You know, you look like Rekha," he said, and my heart twirled like Umrao Jaan. "Dusky like her, big eyes, small mouth. Just a little rounder though, fuller. But still, like Rekha."

It was the closest any person of the male persuasion had come to calling me beautiful, and in that moment I actually believed that maybe I was. He asked me question after question over dinner: What part of Pakistan was my family from, where was I raised, what were my siblings like, what did I want to do in my life, and what was my romantic history.

I had no romantic history, I told him.

"No boyfriend? Ever?"

"None," I responded.

"Okay but maybe not a boyfriend, but what about guys you've fooled around with?"

"I haven't. Ever. Fooled around with a guy."

He sat back and stared at me, rubbing the back of his neck.

"You must be the only virgin in this entire country," he finally said.

The blood rushed to my face and I kept spinning my lo mein, refusing to answer.

A week later my future ex-husband called me and asked if he could speak to my parents. He wanted to visit Ami and Abu and extend a formal marriage proposal. He had met me thrice and wanted to marry me. I couldn't believe it. This fun, handsome, smart, ambitious man wanted to marry me. *Me!* The girl no one wanted to marry, the girl whose family said would never get married. He wanted to marry me despite my weight. He wanted to marry me even though I was a dozen shades darker than him.

That didn't happen, that never happened. Fair desi men didn't marry dark girls. Only dark desi men married dark girls, but if they could avoid it, they'd marry a fair girl, too. After all, they had to think about the next generation. These were the unwritten rules of our racist culture.

Was it all too fast? Yes, but wasn't that how it happened in Bollywood movies? The leading hero and heroines didn't even have to talk to each other, they'd fall in love in passing glances, and then run away together, defying their parents, and society, and God, and whatever else stood in the way of their passion.

I couldn't wait to tell Ami. When I first went away to college, Ami had said casually, laying a trap for me, that I was free to meet a young, marriageable man and to let her know if I did. But until now no young man at college really cared to meet me. Anu, Veena, and I would day-dream about various guys, crushing on them from afar, playing Mariah Carey's "Dreamlover" on repeat, but it got us nowhere. Ami would now be so proud of me, having beaten the odds all my relatives believed I was up against. I couldn't wait to tell Lilly and Saad. See, someone wants to marry your big sister! And I couldn't wait for Abu to find out, so he could finally breathe a sigh of relief, having tried so hard for the past ten years to help me lose weight for exactly this purpose. Their worries would be over now.

Their actual reaction wasn't even close. They were aghast. I was nine-teen years old, a sophomore in college, had I completely lost my mind?

And who was this guy, what was his family background, how could we trust anything about him?

Ami and Abu said no. Their daughter, who was headed toward medical school, was not going to throw her life away by getting married at nineteen. If he wanted to marry me, he would have to wait until I graduated from college and got into med school, and until his parents could come from Pakistan and ask for my hand in marriage themselves.

A year later, they did.

EIGHT

Gosht Khor: Meat Eaters

There's something to be said about the fitness motivation a budding romance can propel, though I use the word *fitness* loosely. Okay, maybe completely inaccurately.

AK, which is how I'll refer to my future ex-husband, wasn't completely alone in America as a student. His two younger brothers were also here, studying at university, and he had a cousin and his cousin's family, who in fact were the people who came with him when he unsuccessfully asked for my hand in marriage.

Ami and Abu did not reject AK out of hand. They kept open the possibility of a yes, hoping perhaps in the next couple of years a better proposal would show up or that things would fizzle out between us. Maybe AK would move on, find another girl, and get tired of waiting for me. But he didn't. He remained firm in wanting to marry the only virgin left in the United States, and we continued to meet surreptitiously every so often, and now he wanted me to meet his brothers.

This was a previously unknown stress to me, the stress of wondering if the family of the man you had fallen head over heels for would approve of you. All signs up until now indicated this was unlikely. There was an awkward situation in the proposal department in our home. It was rude to both send, and entertain, proposals for a younger child when an older one was still unmarried, which meant Lilly was kind of stuck until I got out of the way. The problem was the grapevine only brought inquiries about Lilly to my mother, skipping directly over me. People would send messages of their interest in Lilly, poking around without sending a direct proposal, knowing I was as yet unmarried, but hoping maybe something was already in the works for me.

Nothing ever was. No one, said Ami, asked about me.

And if no mother, sister, cousin, or aunt was interested in me for their son, brother, or nephew, that meant meeting AK's family was risky. They could do the entire thing in. I had to lose weight.

By that point I had developed what was likely an actual addiction to Coca-Cola. My body was otherwise a temple, undefiled by drugs and alcohol, so maybe it was particularly susceptible to sugar and caffeine. I didn't know at the time I may as well have been snorting coke. I could skip meals if compelled to, but I couldn't give up my cola, and my addiction grew from a few cans a day, to a liter a day, to a few liters a day. Diet Coke didn't cut it, I had to have the real thing. I hadn't been raised drinking soda, it almost never came into our house, with a few exceptions: parties, holidays, and during Ramadan, when we made a drink that I'm reticent to divulge but is too delicious not to: Coke-doodh. Coca-Cola mixed with milk.

In case you're having an unpleasant visceral reaction to this idea, stay with me here. After all, it's not a great leap from a Coke float. Half Coca-Cola, half whole milk, sugar to further sweeten, and as much ice as you can fit in a vessel is the simple formula. Other desi households, I learned later in life, make a version of the drink with 7 Up or Sprite instead of Coke, but the brown stuff is exponentially better. This was one of those Ramadan-only foods that we forgot about the minute the month was over, so it wasn't really until college, and the soda fountain at the dining hall, that my enslavement to Coke truly took hold.

Luckily, I thought, if weight loss and gain were about calories in and calories out, which is what the internet told me, I could have all the soda I wanted as long as I had a calorie deficit. A two-liter bottle of soda has less than 800 calories. That meant I could have up to four liters a day and still lose weight as long as I didn't eat much of anything else. Which was the hard part, because I couldn't really avoid the dining hall. It was the one place where I regularly met up with the small group of friends I now had—Veena and Upeksha, and Upeksha's brother and his friends, and my roommate Nakia, and a few others—because for the rest of the day most of our class schedules had pretty much diverged.

One day, the answer came by mistake. I was salting my pizza, the only food hack Nakia ever taught me, and suddenly the cap came off the salt container and spilled all over the two slices. By this point my salt and sugar addictions were likely neck in neck, but still, there's only so much salt you can take. I picked up the slices and brushed them off, not wanting to get back in line for more, and tried to eat them. I couldn't. They were like poison.

Every day I watched as Upeksha stopped eating when she was full, a feeling I didn't recognize, and then pushed her plate away and was done, but that pizza must have been the first time in my life I had thrown food away. The next day, I began salting my food but didn't stop at a few shakes. I kept going, going until I knew I had made the food inedible. I picked at it but couldn't eat it. Then I threw it away. Every day, instead of simply not getting any food, I started oversalting it, which satisfied my emotional need to have a plate full of food in front of me. I didn't feel deprived this way, and I got my calories from the liters of soda in my dorm.

I had also recently discovered the school gym. I knew one existed because I often saw lithe, toned guys and girls dressed in athletic gear headed up campus with gym bags. I would stare at the girls more than the boys, with a mix of envy and depression and fascination. What was it like to wear short shorts and tanks and sports bras in public, so confident in your body, so unaware of its smooth perfection? From the time I was in middle school, I had stopped raising my hand to solve problems on the chalkboard, not wanting to stand up and let the class stare at my chubby backside. I had started to develop a pouch on my lower tummy by high school and never wore shirts tucked in or short enough to see it. When waves of self-consciousness hit, I would stretch out sweaters and knit shirts by hand to loosen them up more, wear bigger and baggier jackets to cover myself up, tug my tops and jeans this way and that, conscious of the angle anyone nearby had of my body. How I wished I could have the ease of moving without feeling like the eyes of the world were judging my body.

I had never actually worked out in a gym and felt intimidated to even go. Where to start? Would people stare? What do I wear? Veena and I teamed up for the endeavor, and we hit the gym together. I chose the StairMaster as my torture device, put it on the easiest setting, and casually climbed the stairs at the slowest pace possible. Fifteen minutes seemed good enough to me, that had to burn some calories. It was for sure more than what my new roommate, a sixteen-year-old child prodigy from Russia, was doing.

Elena was a freshman, five foot eight, heavy boned and heavy faced, intensely awkward, with a thick Russian accent. There was no doubt in my mind she would one day soon run a nuclear fission program some-where. We didn't talk much because we didn't see each other much, and because I didn't know what to talk to her about. I think we were both a bit weirded out by the other. Every day, three times a day, she would smuggle fruit and dinner rolls back from the dining hall and thus amassed a small hill of consumables on her desk, which she worked her way through in the evenings as she studied. She was in bed and asleep by 9 p.m. and up bright and early at 5 a.m. She ironed her jeans and washed her underwear and bras by hand and hung them up all around her side of the room. She had forceful, early-morning conversations in

Russian on our shared phone and I was only half joking when I told my friends she had to be a Russian intelligence plant. She collected the hair from her hairbrush and added it to a growing ball of brown fluff on the shelf above her bed and wore strappy flat sandals with socks when it was freezing outside.

One time, after she left for class, a jacket fell out of her wardrobe, so I opened it to hang it back up and saw for the first time that nothing was hung up. All her clothes were wadded up in balls and shoved in a pile. But that wasn't the part that freaked me out. There was a clear plastic bag hanging from a hook inside the wardrobe door with what looked like . . . was it . . . yes it was . . . used sanitary pads.

To this day, I still sometimes wonder about what she did with the hair balls and used pads.

When the spring semester began, the freshman fifteen having found her, Elena decided to start working out. One day I walked out of our dorm building and stood at the top of the steps leading down to the sidewalk and campus road we were situated on. Out of the corner of my eye, I caught a slow-moving object come around the right side of the building. It was Elena. I watched in amazement as she jogged in what I can only describe as slow motion.

She didn't see me standing on the steps as she plodded by at the pace of a hobbled zombie, if zombies could jog. Students passed around her, staring, as she huffed and puffed, her face red with exertion. Approaching her from the back as she put one lead foot in front of the other, I walked right past her. I kept walking until I was about ten feet in front of her, but thought it was rude I hadn't acknowledged her. I turned and said, "Hi, Elena, I didn't know you'd taken up . . . jogging."

She smiled, still moving through invisible tar, and replied, "It's the best way to reduce the hips!"

Every morning Elena went out for her slo-mo jog, which I both marveled and laughed at, until I saw her after the summer. She had geriatric-jogged her way to half her previous size.

My efforts at the gym might have been much more vigorous than Elena's version of exercise, but ultimately it was her persistence and consistency that gave her superior results. I went to the gym less than half a dozen times, and then just couldn't do it anymore. When I say I couldn't, I mean that literally. I had grown so weak living only on Coca-Cola for weeks on end that my hands would shake all day, and my knees gave out more than once on the StairMaster. But though my results were not as lasting as Elena's, I did end up losing nineteen pounds in a month and I was ready to impress AK's brothers. I was lighter than I had been in years, under 160 pounds, but as they say, easy go, easy come.

Once I started eating again, because I had to start eating again—living exclusively on soda, I couldn't even function in class anymore—the weight came back, plus an extra five for good measure, within a couple of months. By then I had met AK's brothers, who were friendly, but the real test, his mother and sisters, was yet to come.

AK's parents and younger sister arrived from Pakistan toward the end of my junior year and immediately set out to get their son what he wanted—me. AK had never sent them any photographs of me, but I assumed that they assumed the girl who swept their son off his feet had to be attractive by Pakistani standards—tall, thin, and fair. I had seen pictures of them and was braced for the worst. His family was Punjabi but hailed from Kashmir, which any Pakistani could have guessed, given how *white* they were. They were whiter than white people.

By this time, Abu had shut down the clinic and my parents had moved to Baltimore. Lilly had joined me at UMBC and also lived in a dorm, and my parents saw no point in being all the way in Hagerstown while we were in Baltimore. They had moved into an apartment as they hunted for a house, and one weekend, AK's parents arrived at the apartment door with a box of sweets and a gold ring.

I was in a bedroom and heard murmurs coming from the living room for nearly an hour before Ami and AK's mother finally entered the room. I sat on the bed, frozen. His small, chubby, white-as-cream mother sat down next to me. I stared at the ground as she stared at me, more intently than anyone had ever looked at me in my life. I glanced her way a few times and each time her gaze was fixed on a different part of me. I twisted my hands inside my scarf and curled my toes, hoping she didn't see how awful-looking they were.

Finally, she spoke. "Your big toe is shorter than your second toe. That means you are stubborn and will want to control your husband. And you have two dimples. That means both your mother-in-law and father-in-law will die soon after your marriage."

This was not a good sign.

But then she sighed and slid a simple gold band over the ring finger of my right hand. And just like that, I was engaged.

AK'S PARENTS INSISTED that the wedding take place that summer because they had to return to Pakistan. Except that I had one more year of college, and my parents had been firm that I wasn't getting married until I graduated. Their firmness gave way, though, worn down by repeated calls and visits from AK's family, who convinced Ami and Abu that they couldn't return the following year for the wedding. (It turned out that none of them planned to leave anyway.)

The wedding date was agreed upon, but even then, Ami was adamantly against the marriage. This match would be a disaster, she believed.

"Urdu-speaking people say a daughter-in-law is like a crown you wear on your head. She's lifted up and respected. She's not allowed in the kitchen for months, not allowed to do any domestic work at least until her henna fades completely away. Punjabis say a daughter-in-law is like the bottom of your shoe, to be kept down, in her place, crushed. They'll put you in the kitchen the day after your wedding."

I rolled my eyes. Surely, all the mother and daughter-in-law drama they showed in Pakistani drama serials and Bollywood movies was exaggerated. Besides, AK had confided in me that his mother had been physically abused and mistreated by her husband and mother-in-law all through her marriage. A woman who had suffered like that would make sure not to do the same to her own daughter-in-law.

The wedding lasted three days, back-to-back: the henna party on Friday, the nikkah ceremony on Saturday, and the groom's reception on Sunday. It's hard to be a happy bride when your own mother is miserable and refuses to participate in actually celebrating the marriage, but in hindsight she could see the things I couldn't, and she knew things I didn't. I could never have anticipated the deep differences in the culture of our two families and how it would impact my life, starting with the fact that not only did my in-laws have no intention of returning to Pakistan, but also that they expected us all to live together as a joint family.

I knew about "joint family" setups but had never actually seen one in America. It didn't really work here. Those of us raised with an American sensibility couldn't fathom it, and I could have never imagined that I would end up in one. I moved into the three-bedroom apartment where my new husband lived with his two younger brothers, his parents, and his little sister. I can't say I hadn't been warned about what was coming.

The day after the wedding, I was summoned into the kitchen, which was strangely outfitted with a large oriental-style rug. My mother-in-law stood cutting vegetables and looked me up and down. "Where are your bangles? Your jewelry? You just got married, you have to look like it for at least the first year. Go put it all on."

I went to my room, slipped on my eight 22-karat gold bangles, a few of the gold rings I had been gifted, and a small gold necklace and earring set, and returned to the kitchen.

"Acha, okay, so tell me what do you know how to cook?"

Ramen, I thought in my head. "I don't really cook, Ami cooks at home or I eat from the dining hall at school."

"Did your mother teach you how to cook anything?"

No. No my mother had not. She was raising her daughters to be educated professionals, not domestic help. Her logic was that if she taught my sister and me how to cook, our husbands and in-laws would expect us to cook. She should have known that they would expect you to cook anyway.

"Okay," said my mother-in-law, "let's start with roti. First, make the dough." They had been in America for a few months and were tired of eating the store-bought, mass-produced naan that came twenty to a bag. Now that I was there, the family could have homemade roti. She dumped a few cups of whole wheat flour into a bowl and instructed me as I added water in increments and mixed it by hand.

My father-in-law walked into the kitchen, nodding his head in approval. "Your mother-in-law has cooked and cleaned for six people for thirty years. You are now here to help relieve her burden."

I thought about their own daughter, having chai and potato chips in the living room and laughing at a movie with her brothers. My mother's voice, telling me I'd forever be the bottom of a shoe to this family, echoed in my head.

"When you're done, let me know, and I'll show you how to make the roti and you can fry the eggs," said my mother-in-law. Then they left me to continue kneading the dough, and the tears that dripped quietly out of my eyes made it into that first batch.

In the early weeks of marriage, friends and family hosted us for dawaats, dinner parties for the new couple, and "new couple" meant the groom's whole family as well. Every few days we got dressed in our finery and had awkward dinners with family friends of theirs. I would sit quietly among the women, who carefully examined and interrogated me. The jewelry I was wearing, was it from my family's side or from AK's side? The clothing I had on, did it come from my dowry or was it part of the bridal gift from AK's family? How old was I? How many siblings did I have? Where in Pakistan was my family from?

The nights were never complete, though, without a conversation about my physical appearance. Funny, they said. I didn't look Punjabi, but I also didn't look like an Urdu-speaking Pakistani. Punjabis were fair, tall, and well built. Urdu-speaking people were dark and petite. Here I was, the worst of both worlds. Short, dark, and overweight.

I had lovely long hair, nice features, they agreed. "Yes," said my mother-in-law, "she looks like that Indian actress Aishwarya Rai, but dark and fat." No worries, the ladies had lots of advice on how I could address these pressing problems. They went down the list of home remedies I had been hearing for years, but also there were new beauty innovations. Did I know of Pearl Cream? It was from China, all the rage in Pakistan, and in salons they mixed it with bleach to give women whitening facials that left you glowing.

Did I get a whitening facial before the wedding?

I certainly did not.

If I didn't bleach my face, how come they couldn't see any hair on it?

AK's mother had an interesting theory. The hair on my face was hidden for two reasons. First, it had been sucked into the fat on my cheeks. The fat, she believed, would grow around hair follicles, and eventually they'd drown in it, never to be seen again.

Second, because I was dark, the hair and peach fuzz was harder to see. They were all so fair-skinned, their body hair stood out everywhere. On their faces and necks and chests and arms and legs and stomachs and backs. They had to wax everywhere, twice a month. But because I was so brown, you could barely see any hair on my face or body.

I thought to myself, no it's because I've been using that redbrick jhanwan my aunt had given me since childhood, and also because my family was less hairy than the average desi. Abu barely had any hair on his chest, Ami didn't have a hair on her entire body or her face. It was as if none of these people had heard of genetics.

I hated those dinners.

The first time my parents hosted us, and again by "us" I mean all seven of us, Ami came to me and said, "Your mother-in-law is asking what's going on."

"What do you mean, what's going on?"

"Meaning, do you have any news?"

"News of what?"

"Are you expecting yet?"

We had been married less than a month, and I still had to finish college. I hoped to God I wasn't expecting.

"Well she's worried that you won't be able to have a baby because of your weight. Fat girls have trouble getting pregnant. If you don't conceive, they'll think it's your fault."

AK and I spent the night at my parents' while everyone else left after dinner. I had begun taking birth control shortly after the wedding, and that night I threw away the pills.

When we returned home bearing more gifts from my parents, I went to stack them into my bedroom closet where our other wedding gifts were. I was saving them for when we would eventually have our own place, which had to happen at some point. This couldn't be a permanent situation.

The closet was nearly empty. All the boxes and gift bags were gone. I thought we had been robbed. I panicked and ran out and told the family. AK's mother sucked her teeth, watching me carefully, and then left the room. Everyone else ignored me. That's when I understood—the family had taken them.

That was the first in a series of events that made me see that those Pakistani serial dramas and Bollywood movies weren't exaggerating. I found pictures of AK's mother and sister wearing my clothes, learned they had slept in the bedroom set my parents had gifted us, which had been delivered weeks before I moved in. I realized the hard way that if I accidentally left a ring or bangles in the kitchen while cooking (gold, I learned after getting arms and hands scorched, is an incredible heat conductor), I risked losing them.

By the third month, I had managed to prove my mother-in-law

wrong. I was pregnant. Shortly after I found out about the pregnancy, AK beat me for the first time.

His family heard every sound coming from our bedroom, but no one came. When I emerged the next day, desperate for water and a painkiller, his mother said, "If I had my way, he would beat you every day."

Clearly I was completely on my own for my survival. I couldn't tell my family or friends what happened, and I couldn't go back home, the shame of having been beaten, of returning home pregnant after only months, was unfathomable. Abu had never laid a hand on my mother, I had never seen domestic violence up close and personal, but I had always held the conviction that I would never stay in a relationship if a man hit me.

But I stayed. I stayed, knowing my only shot at life was to get through college and get into graduate school so I could support myself, and this baby, one day. I just had to get through these years.

During my final semester I spent nearly twelve hours a day out of the house. I had twenty-one credits to complete, and I had to finish them before the baby came. I drove from Virginia to UMBC early in the mornings, lumbering around campus as my belly, and the rest of me, grew bigger and bigger. By this time it was abundantly obvious that I was not going to be getting into medical school. I didn't have the grades and I simply couldn't wrap my head around chemistry.

It seemed like the end of the world because I had no alternate plan, but in hindsight I should have known there was no way I could stomach medicine. In my time working at the clinic, Abu would often call me into the surgery room to help, regulations be damned. He couldn't afford a veterinary assistant and he usually needed me to quickly position and secure a patient's legs to the surgery table as the anesthesia kicked in. Other times he needed me to hold open an incision as he dug around looking for a cat or dog's fallopian tubes. The metallic smell of blood combined with the heat from the surgical lamps left me dizzy and nauseous. I'd stumble out of the room, certain I was going to pass out, while Abu shook his head in disappointment.

I wasn't the only one nearing the end of college with no idea what to do next. My best friend, Shubnum, was on a similar trajectory, it having dawned on her that medical school was not in the cards for her, either. What were we going to do? She told me she was going to take a shot at the LSAT and see if she could get into law school, so I registered for the test, too, out of desperation for any path forward.

Less than two weeks after walking across the graduation stage, I gave birth to a daughter. I had stayed at my parents' those last few weeks, knowing she could come at any time, knowing I would need to be with my family and not AK's when it happened.

By the time AK arrived at the hospital from Virginia, I had already delivered her, squeezing her out with all my might, determined not to let him share the experience. That night, as I stared at the perfect pink bundle in my arms, it felt like falling in love for the first time. I would not let my baby down.

AK's family arrived the next day to see the baby. They hadn't seen me in weeks and the first thing his mother said was, "Ooof, you have gotten even fatter."

I had finally crossed the threshold over two hundred pounds by the end of the pregnancy, so yes, I had gotten even fatter.

Two weeks later I took the LSAT, as breast milk leaked through my bra and dribbled down my shirt for hours. It was the first time I had been away from the baby for that long. I scored in the 92nd percentile and was offered admission to two different law schools without even applying.

I hadn't really chosen the profession of law. But it had chosen me.

LAW SCHOOL WAS a blur that I survived only by having a strict daily schedule. My in-laws didn't object to me continuing to study, as long as I took care of the household duties, which included preparing lunch and dinner every day, for everyone. I made a curry for lunch in the mornings before leaving for the part-time internship I had managed to snag at a local law firm, and dinner in the two-hour break I had between work and my classes in the evening. I returned home from class every night around 9 p.m., spent time with my daughter and the family, and then studied and did my classwork after everyone went to sleep. I took advantage of the one boon of a joint-family system, that the children of the family are raised by everyone. I never had to worry about my daughter when I was at work or school, thanks to a house full of in-laws.

I had managed to master the dishes my in-laws ate, learning to make them fast and tasty, after a year of painful failures cooking for them. The problem wasn't that cooking was beyond my skill set, I knew what each dish my mother made tasted like and had figured out how to approximate it, or when all else failed, to call Ami and just ask. The problem was that my in-laws cooked nearly all their meat dishes completely differently than Ami did. AK's mother stewed every meat dish in the same oily, thick gravy without any of the brothy shorba I was used to. When I made koftay and bhindi gosht (meat with okra), I made them like Ami. In an aromatic but rich broth. We were raised on shorba, and most of the time it was goat shorba.

"The Prophet Muhammad's favorite meat was goat," Ami told us as kids, "it's the healthiest, tastiest meat in the world." I had no idea whether the Prophet Muhammad loved goat or not, but he couldn't have loved it more than my mother. There was always either a pot of goat shorba bubbling on the stove or sitting in the fridge, garlicky and gingery, and flecked with cilantro. Ami, like her own mother, ate it almost every day. She cooked the goat with all the bones, so the broth pulled flavor from the marrow, the most delicious part, according to her.

Ami always got the marrow bone, and she was welcome to it. We three grossed-out kids couldn't look away as Ami sucked hard on one end of the nalli and slurped up the gelatinous cylinder in one breath.

Yup, she could have it. That, and trotters and brain and organ meats, too.

The shorba, though, *that* we would drink by the bowlful.

Even though Ami hadn't taught me how to cook before marriage, it turned out that whatever was in her hands, in the hands of the women in our family, I had luckily inherited. I could usually identify the spices and herbs in a dish and replicate it and know what was missing from something with only a few bites, and how to fix it.

I could make the dishes just like Ami, but my father-in-law or brother-in-law would pick up the broth with a ladle and let it fall back into the dish, laughing. Didn't I know how to make saalan?

Saalan is the word we use to describe what non-desis would call a curry, a word I didn't hear until high school, when a teacher asked me what kind of curries we made at home. AK and his family didn't think what I was making was either curry or saalan. That's soup, they joked.

No, you heathens, I wanted to say, it's shorba.

I eventually stopped cooking like Ami and instead started copying AK's mom's food. I added more oil, and more spices, and more tomatoes, and less water, and cooked chicken, beef, and goat all down into hearty, chunky stews. What did I care if that's how they liked it, if they couldn't appreciate the delicate nature of Ami's food, didn't differentiate between a yogurt-based korma and a tomato-based karhai and a brothy shorba?

Over the first couple of years I became the kind of home cook who didn't need a recipe, who never measured anything, and who could efficiently cook three dishes at a time. I had to, in order to get it all done. My mother-in-law was sufficiently impressed with my skills in the kitchen. I could, and did, cook for groups of fifty, a hundred, a hundred and fifty. I could stuff and fold hundreds of samosas and mix and shape dozens and dozens of seekh kabab in a matter of hours. I worked like djinn, she said.

It was true, I was working harder than I ever had. Which necessarily meant I had no time to take care of myself. I rarely ate the food I cooked every day, because that would require sitting still and eating. My car was the only place I had time to eat, as I drove from home to work and from work to home and then home to school and back. I had become a regular in the local drive-thru fast-food joints, picking up breakfast, lunch, and dinner daily, and stuffing the food, unthinkingly, into my mouth as I drove. I graduated from Egg McMuffins to McDonald's Steak, Egg & Cheese Bagels, with two orders of hash browns and a large orange juice. For lunch there was KFC and Subway. For dinner, I grabbed Taco Bell and sometimes had time to stop at Five Guys, a local burger place with the best burgers and fries I'd ever eaten. And with every meal there was soda or a milkshake full of chunks of Oreos, which gave me the sugar rush I needed to get through my classes. Sometimes, after my last law class at night, I'd stop at Ravi Kabob House, just around the corner from the school, and pick up a fourth meal to satisfy what felt like an endless hunger.

I would sit in the parking lot in the dark, wrap a hot, fresh naan around a couple of kababs, and eat it so fast that I would be surprised when it was all gone. I ate frantically, as if the food would escape. Minutes later I'd be left feeling stuffed but empty and ashamed. I'd loathe myself then, but these were moments of temporary self-soothing before I had to head back to a house I didn't belong in, full of people I was too embarrassed to eat around.

Having hit the weight at which teenage me hoped someone would just shoot me, I wanted to believe some of it would come off after the pregnancy. People told me breastfeeding would burn thousands of calories. For the first four months, I tried. I nursed my daughter in the early mornings and late evenings, and in the middle of the night, and pumped milk for when I was out of the house. Maybe it did burn calories, but it also left me ravenous. What I couldn't eat during the day when I was out of the house, I ate late at night when everyone slept, studying with a bag of chips and cans of soda and boxes of cookies by my side. My mother-in-law was baffled. She never saw me eat, how did I keep putting on weight?

No one knew that I ate when no one was watching, and that's when it clicked. I realized what Ami's late-night roamings had been about. Throughout my childhood she rarely sat down to eat with us, which made Abu crazy. He wanted more than anything for his family to gather together every evening, eat and talk together. But we almost never did. Ami would cook but instead of joining us at the table, she would busy herself with cleaning the kitchen, or she would watch television, or retreat to her room. We would put the leftovers in the fridge, but in the morning they'd be gone, because she ate them late at night, when no one was up.

I always thought her behavior was antisocial, or that she just did it to snub Abu, but it wasn't until I started eating in solitude that I realized maybe Ami also ate alone out of some sense of shame.

My older sister-in-law, a doctor, theorized that perhaps I had a thyroid issue. She had arrived with her husband and son from Pakistan a year earlier, also with no plans to ever go back. She was smart and competent, the kind of person who does exactly what they set their mind to do, and she arrived having set her mind to pass the US Medical License Exam and stay in the US to practice as a physician here, for good.

"You know," she said to me one day, "when you got married and AK sent us pictures of the wedding, I didn't show any of our friends or relatives in Pakistan."

I wasn't sure where this was going, but I should have known.

"I was too embarrassed for people to see who my brother married. They would be shocked that he picked a fat, dark girl. You know how many beautiful girls there are in Pakistan? He could have had his pick of tall, thin, gori gori—fair girls. But . . . he picked you. I just told everyone the pictures had gotten damaged."

No, I didn't know how many beautiful girls there were in Pakistan because I hadn't returned in thirteen years, not since my aunt's wedding. But I would find out soon because I decided it had been too long. It was time to go home.

I FINISHED MY law school credits in the fall of 2000, and since I wouldn't be graduating or taking the bar exam for five more months, I finally had time after years of nonstop study and work to visit Pakistan. This trip would be the first time I would get away from the ever-expanding joint family I lived in. Things had settled down in some ways—AK wasn't hitting me anymore. Not after the time I finally hit back. But this didn't mean our relationship was good; it was irrevocably broken, but we both still hung in there, keeping busy with everyone else around us. One of AK's brothers had also recently married and had a baby, and now there were ten of us living together. At least we had moved into a three-level house with more space to spread out in.

I was nervous about this trip, having grown up hearing stories of how my relatives reacted to my weight when I was a baby, and now I'd have to not only face them, but some of AK's relatives, too. "I'm telling you right now," said my mother-in-law, "don't be offended if someone calls you moti. You get offended too easily. We call a bald man bald, don't we? It's just like that. If you're moti, you're moti. Just stating a fact, don't take it personally."

Okay, then.

My three-year-old daughter and I landed in Lahore on a crisp December night. Two of my uncles, Pummy Mamu and Khan Gul Mamu, were there to receive us. I hadn't seen Khan Gul Mamu since he had slaughtered our bunnies and took off, but Pummy Mamu visited us in the US fairly frequently and had even come for my wedding. I reminded him then that he had told me when I was a kid that he'd salute the man I married, and that time had come. In fact, I had gotten married before he did, a feat I wasn't going to let him live down.

The day of our groom's reception, Pummy Mamu had come up to the stage and posed for a photo behind the sofa that I was sitting on with AK. Then he leaned down and whispered in my ear, "Moti, have some shame, stop grinning so much. I know you're thrilled you're getting married, and we all are because we never thought this would happen, but put a lid on it. Brides aren't supposed to be showing their teeth."

Here I was, a few years later, with very little about my marriage to smile about.

Nani Amma's old house still stood in Sham Nagar, but some things had changed. The neighborhood around it had grown furiously, the road it sat on now had dozens of new shop fronts, and the population had tripled as once-spacious homes had been subdivided and rented out to people who had moved from villages to the city for jobs.

Originally her small house used to be connected to her family home, Laal Kothi ("the Red Mansion"), by a shared yard, but it was now completely walled off. I vaguely recalled the mansion from my last visit, its interior courtyard dark from the four stories that rose up around it on every side, keeping it shady and cool in the summer months. During the Partition, my great-grandfather and his brothers had traded properties with a wealthy Sikh businessman. They swapped their property in Delhi and got Laal Kothi in Lahore in return. It had been the largest house in the neighborhood, hidden behind a massive yellow gate. Over the years, the brothers had died and their children had started their own families and moved out. Left mostly empty, it was eventually sold off in bits and pieces, until none of it belonged to us anymore.

When I looked up, I could still see the mansion's redbrick facade rise high above the dividing wall. Nothing about Nani Amma's house had changed though. It was exactly as I remembered it, and I remembered it like it was yesterday.

Neither of my uncles lived in the house and they hadn't in decades, but they rotated dropping by to check in on Nani Amma as did other neighbors and relatives. Once it became clear that she was too elderly to live alone, the brothers forced her to come live with them. She spent a few months at one son's home in Karachi, then a few months in the other son's house in Rawalpindi.

She hated it. She wanted to be in her little home, in the home her father had built and gifted to her when she was married. My visit gave her the chance to do that for a bit, and both of my uncles had taken time off to come hang out in Lahore with me, too.

It is hard to describe the feeling of returning to a place that has never been your home but feels more like home than any place you've ever lived. From the moment we touched down, the air, the sounds, the smells, the people, it all just seemed like mine, everything familiar, all of it a comfort. The only way to describe it is to say that a part of me had never left.

It took days for our bodies to adjust to a completely inverted sleep schedule, so my daughter and I found ourselves up much of the night and sleeping much of the day for at least the first week. We'd rise late in the afternoon, and late at night Pummy Mamu and Khan Gul Mamu—my uncles and I being kindred fat spirits—would go fetch parathas stuffed with spicy mashed potatoes from the man who set up a stall every evening with a pan the size of a satellite perched precariously on top. The parathas were nearly two feet in diameter, glistening with ghee. Our tummies full of warm carbs, we'd finally start getting tired, but by the time our lids got heavy, we'd be jerked awake, terrified, by a booming, crackly voice.

It came from a truck owned by the neighborhood mosque, which roamed the streets beginning at 3 a.m., screaming at sinners to get the hell up and pray. It would stop every fifty feet, the voice beseeching us through an ancient megaphone and speaker system to get up for the sake of the beloved Prophet Muhammad, to answer the call of God, get up and cleanse our sinful limbs with ice cold water and pray.

The predawn prayer wasn't until 5 a.m., but the mosque made it their business to start harassing believers well beforehand. It was enough to turn you into an infidel. Khan Gul Mamu and Pummy Mamu snored through it, having been thoroughly conditioned all through childhood to zone it out, as it seemed had much of the neighborhood. How they kept from murdering the roaming devotee, I'll never know.

In our waking hours the three of us planned the coming day around food. Pummy Mamu had been fighting the battle of the bulge since he was a kid, staving off obesity over the years by alternating between binges and starvation, but Khan Gul Mamu had encountered the battle a bit later in life and had surrendered. He was huge. He had spent most of his career in the army, but years earlier had had a horrific car accident, his military jeep going over the side of a cliff. His driver died and he survived, but barely. He had broken ribs and legs, and one eye came clean out of his face. He spent over a year in recovery and therapy, putting on weight from lying in bed and from depression-eating when he realized he would never go any further up the officer ranks.

Now he stood at six foot two, around 350 pounds. His one good eye was still hazel and bright, and the other looked off to the side, dim and damaged. He had managed to get married after the accident, to a dentist who maintained a size zero figure by barely eating or cooking. That was okay, though, because he preferred to eat out. It suited his lifestyle (and tastebuds), since he'd become a security consultant after his early retirement and now spent most of his days on the road.

The three of us food addicts together determined to eat everything worth eating in the entire city. They knew where to get the best of the best, and they assured me it was almost never in the fancy restaurants. We would eat at the street-side stalls and holes in the wall, from wheeled carts pulled by donkeys.

"Some of these places may not look hygienic," said Pummy Mamu, "and they aren't. But if a vendor doesn't sweat into his pot of haleem or scratch his crotch before he chops vegetables, or flick his cigarette ash into his chutneys, it just doesn't taste as good."

There was a 100 percent chance I was going to get food poisoning or water-borne disease, but my uncles assured me the food would be worth the day or two of violent diarrhea and vomiting. I agreed. I wasn't going to pass up on this chance to eat Lahore. Every morning one of the uncles fetched fresh, buttered sesame kulchay—chewy and soft naan, quilted like a mattress—from the local bread tandoor. We tore them into pieces and dunked them into the chai Nana Amma made from milk that had been simmering for over an hour. For lunch we never strayed far, sampling food from the surrounding neighborhoods and starting most expeditions with a stop at a stand selling the best dhai bhalla I've ever eaten.

Dhai bhalla is another one of those dishes, like chaat, that even non-desis who love our food likely haven't tried. Essentially, it's savory dumplings, pakoray made from either besan or daal, in a tangy, spicy yogurt sauce, topped with various garnishes. It is, I admit, an acquired taste for palettes that are only used to eating sweetened yogurt. I had never tried sweet yogurt, strawberry, banana, all the flavors I'd see in the supermarkets, until college, because we exclusively ate our yogurt savory: either plain or with a salaan to temper the spice, or as a raita with crushed cucumber or zucchini or tiny fried crunchy goodies called boondi, or in dhai bhalla.

Every day at around 2 p.m., the dhai bhalla man would set up his cart on the corner, with a dozen different bowls and containers. He worked fast as lightning, throwing a couple of dumplings in a clear plastic bag, ladling the seasoned yogurt sauce on top, and topping that with a handful of boiled potatoes and chickpeas, two kinds of chutney, chopped onions and cilantro, and a generous punch of chaat masala. It was the perfect appetizer, costing the equivalent of about a quarter, before we scoured the local streets for whatever we happened to be in the mood for. One day, Pummy Mamu asked if I wanted to have seekh kabab and I remembered the tiny, thin kababs I had eaten by the dozen the last time I visited. Yes, absolutely. This time there was no motorcycle ride. I followed him on foot through a labyrinth of blocks and alleys until we reached an open storefront with a four-foot line of skewers sizzling over coals. They looked amazing.

There was seating behind the men who worked the grills, so we headed over and sat down. I watched as trays of skewers were carried from where the kababs were being shaped to where they were cooked.

And then. Then I saw the man who was mixing the meat. He sat on a high stool with a big plastic tub full of raw ground beef in front of him. I watched him add onions, green chilis, cilantro, and fistfuls of spices. Once the meat was thoroughly covered in all the mixings, he pulled up his pajama legs, lifted his feet into the tub, and began kneading it.

With his feet.

Pummy Mamu saw my face change.

"What's wrong, moti? So what if he's using his feet, they're clean, washed."

The meat squished up around the man's toes and ankles, clinging onto the hairs on his legs.

"No. Oh no no no. I will not eat here, let's go."

Pummy Mamu scowled. "I shouldn't have let you see it, the kabab are so good, and all the germs get cooked out over the grill anyway. The fire purifies everything!"

I wasn't convinced.

"Well, don't Europeans use their feet to make wine?"

I thought back to the *I Love Lucy* episode where Lucy pranced around with an Italian woman in a vat of grapes. He had a point. But no. I wanted to eat authentic Lahori food, but even I had lines I would not cross.

Since I'd last visited, Lahore had succumbed to the power and allure of Western foods and corporate brands. A lot had changed in those ten years. Now the city, and country, were dotted with McDonald's and KFCs, and even Pizza Hut.

My daughter perked up at the first mention of Pizza Hut. She hadn't had pizza in weeks, so one night we stuffed ourselves, along with Nani Amma, who ordinarily wasn't interested in any of our food adventures, into a rickshaw and headed to Gulberg, one of the fancier addresses in the city. It didn't look great to be rolling into a neighborhood full of corporate and designer headquarters in a cheap little rickshaw, but frankly my daughter and I couldn't get enough of them. They are simply an insane ride, three-wheeled and jaunty, most of the time missing doors, fast enough to cause some damage, but small enough to maneuver between cars and gutters and stray dogs and everything the city could throw at you. You felt every bump in the road, every rock, every crater, in every bone of your body. It was exhilarating.

Five of us fell out of the back of the rickshaw like clowns out of a tiny car and the doorman (yes, Pizza Hut is fancy over there) rolled his eyes at us and opened the door. I didn't realize until then that I had been missing some of the tastes of home, too, and the aroma of pan pizza was actually pretty exciting.

While American brands have made it overseas, every country they plant themselves in still adapts the menu to local tastes, and Pizza Hut was no different. We ordered a large cheese and a large chicken tikka pizza and, surprisingly, even Nani Amma enjoyed it. She had never returned to the US after her trip over two decades ago, but she had eaten pizza enough times in Pakistan to finally like it.

There were not very many foods I ever saw her relish eating. She had grown thinner and shrunk shorter than me, and she mostly pecked at food while her sons begged her to eat.

"STOP FORCING ME TO EAT IF I'M NOT HUNGRY" I heard her yell more than once when she couldn't take the badgering anymore.

"I can't eat like you three! A bird will eat like a bird, and an elephant will eat like an elephant."

We looked at each other and nodded. Couldn't argue with that.

We managed to convince her to accompany us to one more meal before I left to visit Zuby Aunty in Abbottabad, about three hundred miles north of Lahore.

"Get dressed nice, moti," Khan Gul Mamu told me. "We are taking you to a fancy place. Amma, you will have to go, too, no arguing!" he yelled at Nani Amma.

I got dressed in a shalwar kameez warm enough for the cold winter night, both my uncles put on proper button-down shirts and creased pants with belts, and Nani Amma wrapped herself in a rich, black, hand-embroidered wool shawl and swiped a light layer of pink lipstick on her lips. I had never seen her wear lipstick, and she looked radiant.

No rickshaws tonight, we were going to ride in style in a hired car.

Pummy Mamu handed Nani Amma a large purse to carry but she refused. She had her little clutch with a mirror and a lipstick and didn't need the big bag.

"Amma, samjha karo," he insisted, "try and understand."

She sighed and gave in, clearly getting the hint, but I didn't.

We arrived thirty minutes later at a beautifully appointed, proper sit-down Chinese restaurant, again in Gulberg. The staff and chef were all Chinese, some of the many tens of thousands of Chinese nationals who settled in Pakistan, thanks to our shared border, robust trade, and the many infrastructure projects that China was funding and overseeing in Pakistan. We settled around a cloth-covered round table, waiters in brocade vests hovering around us, taking our drink orders, but there was no menu. That was because this restaurant only offered a lavish twenty-five-dish buffet. Four kinds of soup, egg rolls, dumplings, scallion pancakes, a dozen Szechuan and Cantonese entrees, stir-fried noodles and rices, and a variety of desserts.

"Pace yourself," said Pummy Mamu, "it's going to be a long night."

At three hundred rupees per person, I knew he took the mission of getting his money's worth seriously.

We brought Nani Amma a bowl of soup and appetizers and made her an entree plate and then got down to business ourselves.

"Fill up your plate as much as possible," hissed Khan Gul Mamu.

"No, why? I can get seconds," I pointed out.

"Just do it, especially the stir-fried prawn and chicken lollipops. Get extra."

I did as told, piling up the prawn and six chicken lollipops, leg pieces in which the meat has been scraped up and stuffed with a filling, then battered and fried so they look like a lollipop. A waiter standing behind the buffet raised his eyebrows at me, and I returned to my seat quickly, embarrassed. No way was I going to eat all those chicken legs, but maybe my uncle wanted me to get them to share with the others. I looked around the table, and they both had their plates piled high, too.

Pummy Mamu leaned over and whispered to Nani Amma. She shook her head. Then he whispered again, urgently. She was sitting on my left and she leaned down into her purse on the ground between us and pulled out a Tupperware container and slipped it under her shawl.

Oh my God this was not happening. My face was burning up. They were going to get me arrested for stealing food from a buffet and I'd never get another visa to Pakistan. All for a few hundred rupees.

"No, Nani Amma, don't do it. I'll pay for dinner!" I softly begged.

But there was no going back. Slowly, ever so casually, my uncles spent the next fifteen minutes transferring prawn and chicken from their plates onto hers, which she would then slip into the container in her lap and put in her purse. Then they reached over to take the food I wasn't eating off my plate, and popped it onto hers, too. They tag teamed the effort, watching the waiters, who watched the patrons like hawks.

Or at least it felt like they were looking right into our souls, circling us like wardens, but that was probably me projecting my guilt. Every half hour or so my uncles would fill up their plates, eat some of the food, and disappear the rest, until four containers were packed away in Nani Amma's purse. Over two hours passed exacting this malfeasance.

I was convinced we would all be stopped on the way out and imagined my tiny little grandmother humiliated and handcuffed, just so my uncles could satisfy their gluttony. We paid the bill and left without incident, my uncles strutting out as if they had conducted the greatest heist of the twentieth century, me and my Nani quietly enraged.

"I will *never* go to a buffet with you again," she said the minute we got in the car.

The uncles laughed, and then Pummy Mamu twisted around in his seat and looked at me. "This is about justice. It's completely unjust for them to charge that much and we only eat a plate and leave. That's criminal. This evens the score. You'll be a lawyer soon, you should care about justice!"

All I cared about then was getting out of there. I turned away, angry.

A few hours later, though, I joined my uncles on the verandah around midnight, they in their undershirts and pajama bottoms, me in my long cotton nightgown. Together we sucked the sauce off big fat prawns and chewed on chicken lollipops until they were all gone.

ABBOTTABAD WAS BREATHTAKING. Tucked up in the north, it was one of many tiny hill stations that the families of colonizing British officers escaped to during the brutal subcontinent summers. It was also, in fact, named after one of those colonizers, Major James Abbott, the first British deputy commissioner of the region, who declared he fell in love with the place at first sight.

Two months after Pakistani independence, the country established the Pakistan Military Academy in Kakul, Abbottabad. And that's where I was headed, because that's where Zuby Aunty's husband, who was now a lieutenant colonel, taught cadets. A private van took me and my daughter up the winding roads from Islamabad, the capital, through picturesque mountain passes and past sheer, terrifying cliff drops until we reached a bus station in the middle of the town. There my uncle, in full dress uniform, greeted and escorted us to a car with a military driver. I was in awe as we approached the impressive gates of the Academy, and more than a bit proud at seeing my uncle saluted by everyone we passed by.

He dropped us off at a charming white bungalow with peacocks strutting in the yard, and there I reunited with Zuby Aunty, whom I hadn't seen in over a decade. They had three daughters now, the youngest just six and the eldest, the one who was born in America when Zuby Aunty lived with our family, now twelve.

Zuby Aunty was as stunningly attractive as I remembered her, but she was nothing like the quiet, shy little sister and new bride from all those years ago when she had stayed with us. She was now a seasoned officer's wife, hung out with the wives of generals, and had become accustomed to all the amenities afforded officers in the Pakistani military. They had drivers and gardeners and cleaners and, most important, a batman, a soldier assigned as a personal servant to every officer. The batman was a holdover relic from the British, and they were responsible for making sure their officer's uniforms were clean and pressed, their shoes polished, and they accompanied their officers anywhere they went, including to war.

Most of the time, though, and against all the rules and regulations, the batmen would end up becoming household servants, cooking for the family, washing the dishes, packing kids' lunches, ironing their clothes, and running general errands. And they were at your disposal 24/7 because they lived with the officer's family, usually in separate servant quarters.

Zuby Aunty had gotten used to being a well-taken-care-of officer's wife, which allowed her the time to have a robust social life. That included being the Academy's Food Secretary, an actual position that put her in charge of creating the menus and overseeing the catering for every Academy social event. She was now a social butterfly who loved to impress with her culinary skills, so it was a perfect role for her.

The best part, of course, was that she never had to actually do any of the prep, or cooking, or cleanup herself. But she did have to instruct and oversee the dozens of cooks and assistants, and teach them her techniques and recipes, and was rewarded by getting full credit for the lavish spreads. Continental, Chinese, Italian, Pakistani, she had it all covered, and had built quite the reputation.

Having never had the amenity of a servant my entire life, it was all a marvel to me. A life of privilege and prestige. Zuby Aunty didn't see it that way.

"You know how hard it is to get these servants to do their jobs? God forbid you accidentally insult one, they can completely turn on you, add too much salt or chili or whatever to completely ruin the food, ruin an entire party, and then who gets blamed? Me. Plus, I have to share my cooking secrets with them, then they go on and use them in other homes and restaurants, impressing people with *my tricks* and taking all the credit."

I understood her frustration but it didn't seem like such a bad tradeoff to me.

"And," she leaned in close, "there have been batmen who killed their officer's entire families as they slept, that's how much resentment and anger they can harbor. You have to be very careful with them."

I looked at the older, kind-looking man who stood over a stove much of the day, making and delivering fresh rotis to the table as we all sat around snarfing them down like entitled aristocrats. It wasn't hard to imagine how someone in his place could finally snap. He was from a remote village, where his family, elders, wife, children, lived without him, and he had enlisted in the army when he was young, thinking he would be a soldier and serve with honor. Becoming a domestic servant was never in his plans, but he carried out his duties with dignity, and frankly he was a fantastic cook.

"Of course he's a great cook, I taught him all my secrets," Zuby Aunty declared. And now she was going to teach a few to me. In a storeroom next to the kitchen, she showed me stacks of twenty-pound bags and I peered into one. It looked like bleached white flour.

"It's cornstarch," she grinned.

What on earth was she going to do with all that cornstarch, I asked her?

She had begun a side hustle of repackaging the bulk bags into smaller packets with her own label and selling them to vendors both inside and outside the Academy.

But why cornstarch, I asked.

She had discovered, over the years, how absolutely magical cornstarch was in cooking. No more having to roast besan or flour to thicken up sauces and gravies or bind meatballs and chappli kabab, when a few spoons of cornstarch would do. No more dipping cutlets and shaami kabab in beaten egg wash, when they could be dipped nice and clean into dry cornstarch and deliver the crispiest coatings ever. Chinese chicken soup? She could make it in an hour with some stock, leftover chicken, a few eggs, and cornstarch. Haleem was made silkier with cornstarch, nihari unctuous and lump-free with it.

She really, really loved cornstarch. But, I asked, unless you tell others how many ways you can use it, why would they buy it?

That, she admitted, had been a problem. The cornstarch wasn't moving like she hoped it would. But she preferred to take the loss rather than divulge her culinary secrets, for those were what elevated her above the other officer's wives.

It killed her to even have to share them with the batman, especially the secret of a masala blend she developed that she swore cut cooking time to a third and made every salaan taste amazing. She swore me to secrecy and then spread a countertop with fresh ingredients, spices, and herbs to make a jug full of her masala. After showing me the proportions and blending everything together, she took off the lid of the blender jug and held it out to me. I inhaled deeply. It smelled spectacular.

"You'll never have to fry onions again to make a saalan," she said. Just a few spoons of her masala made the perfect base for any meat or vegetable dish, and she demonstrated exactly how to use it. She was right. Every dish Zuby Aunty made with it tasted better than any other version I'd ever had. It was magic.

"You have to bottle and sell this, it's magic masala," I told her. "Please!" She never did though. It's been over twenty years now and still, every time I make her magic masala I think, "Someone needs to sell this."

My theory had always been that she didn't want other women to be able to compete with her cooking skills, but she later told me, no, it wasn't that. The masala was great, of course, a brilliant and tasty shortcut, but it was also a matter of haath ki baath—the flavor of the hands doing the cooking. She had it in her hands, like her mother and my mom. Her daughters, though young, had it in their hands. And she was certain my sister and I had it our hands. That's how it worked, passed down in our blood.

There was no doubt that Zuby Aunty had flavor in her hands, and also that she was a born food innovator. She loved to come up with unexpected dishes. She made me nut soup, no not a cream of nut soup, but a soup with actual whole roasted nuts, a recipe that she created just for a general's reception. She made naan pakoray, a brilliant use of leftover, stale naan that she coated with a thick besan batter, smeared with whole spices and chopped onions and cilantro, and then deep-fried. The first time I ever had chaat masala french fries was at her house. Stewed spinach with chicken meatballs? Why not. Every day I was there, she made me something unusual, something I'd never had. I begged her to stop feeding me, because I just didn't need to be fed so much, but she harumphed.

"Who says you're fat?" she said. "You're round and soft, just like men like women."

No, that was definitely not true. My own husband made it clear it wasn't true, and I told her about one of the many times he told me I was disgusting and fat, and that if I left him, no man would ever want me.

She was enraged to hear what AK and his family said about me. "LEAVE HIM!" she urged, repeatedly. "His village ass thinks you aren't good enough for him? He's short and bald and has a pakora for a nose! Are you kidding me, you're beautiful! Thousands of men would want to marry you, I can find you a new man right now, before you even leave Pakistan! Leave him before you end up with another baby!"

I couldn't believe what she was telling me, because nothing in my life had ever made me feel like any of that could be true. But Zuby Aunt's words planted a seed in me, and as the weeks went on, I did start feeling different about myself. We lounged and ate fresh fruit in the winter sun during the days, sometimes venturing out into the charming little bazaars of Abbottabad, and went for drives on the curving, scenic mountain roads. At night, after dinner, I would go on long walks throughout the perfectly manicured lanes of the Academy as the dark hills around me twinkled with tiny lights from the homes of locals.

One day, when it was raining, we piled into their little car—Zuby Aunty, her husband, her daughters, me and my daughter, all of us sitting on top of one another—and drove the twisting road to the famous Ilyasi Mosque, blasting music as we navigated the lanes filling with water. The historic mosque, white and gold, gleamed from a distance. It was built over a stream that brought crisp, sweet glacial water down from the mountains, said to have miraculous healing properties. But we weren't heading there for the curative waters or to pray. Instead, we joined dozens of others shivering in the cold to eat the famous pakoray served by the side of the mosque. The rain ignites pakora cravings in my people, and I was told that the pakoray made at the mosque were uniquely delicious because the batter was made with that glacier water.

Vats the size of kiddie pools bubbled with hot oil, and the pakora makers hand-dropped hundreds—no, *thousands* of pakoras into them, along with thick potato wedges drenched in batter. A fistful of both kinds of pakora was then stuffed in a fresh naan, topped with thinly sliced onions and chutney, and wrapped in newspaper for patiently waiting customers.

I'd never had a naan-pakora wrap, never even heard of it, a big fluffy carb stuffed with deep-fried carbs, a diet nightmare. But the experience was a dream, otherworldly, sitting in a car listening to old Bollywood classics, the rain pouring around us, laughing and dropping chutney-soaked bits all over ourselves. This was followed by cups of Kashmiri chai—pink, salty, sweet, full of pistachios—which we each balanced carefully in our cold hands as we drove back home.

I had never been so relaxed as I as was in those weeks, so aimless and serene. I ate what I felt like, as much as I felt like, and lost fifteen pounds.

When it was time to return home, I didn't want to.

NINE

Chawal Ki Bori: A Sack of Rice

My daughter and I loaded onto a small bus in Abbottabad's square, one that would take us down south to Rawalpindi, where Khan Gul Mamu would pick us up and drive us back to Lahore. We had passed through Rawalpindi two months earlier on our way to Abbottabad, having taken the fancy new Daewoo Express cross-nation bus service from Lahore to get there. The Daewoo wasn't like any bus I'd ever taken before. It had all the service you expect on an airplane, movies and television and uniformed young attendants, who served us snacks and boxed lunches and drinks.

The minibus taking us back to Rawalpindi wasn't like any bus I'd ever been on before, either. It was painted with murals and calligraphy in a hundred different colors, strung with tinsel and swags of block-printed fabric. It was a peacock of a vehicle, veritably crowned with spiky painted metalwork across the top of its windshield. Crates of chickens were secured to the roof, and on the inside it was painted in orange and red and yellow, and hundreds of psychedelic doodads and woven ornaments swayed from the ceiling.

I sat with my daughter in my lap, pressed between a window and two women covered in shawls, only their eyes showing. Every seat was packed and the bus smelled like the inside of a pickle jar, cumin, and sweat. We creaked and groaned down the mountains, and the sheer, rocky drops we had seen on the way up seemed much closer going down.

A couple of hours later, when others started breaking out their snacks and dinners, I was feeling nauseous, but it didn't stop me from unwrapping the stack of naan pakora that Zuby Aunty packed for the trip. If there was one thing I learned in Pakistan, it was that you can never go wrong deep-frying everything and anything in a besan batter.

The greasy naan pakoray were cut into wedges, slathered with a bit of green chutney, and wrapped in foil. The women next to me offered their paratha omelette rolls, samosay, and a thermos of chai. We shared our provisions, and clutched our paper cups of steaming hot chai, groaning "Allah" every time the little bus lurched and turned.

By the time we got to Rawalpindi, it was dusk and the bus terminal was chaotic. Hundreds of different buses from dozens of different bus lines, private vans, taxis, all converged in a cloud of dust. Khan Gul Mamu managed to find us and we crammed into his tiny car with our suitcases strapped to the top. It was too late to start driving to Lahore, another four hours away, so we would stay the night at his house and head out in the morning. But true to himself, he couldn't just take us home. He had to stop at one of the most famous restaurants in the busy city—Savour Foods.

I was tired and grimy and just wanted to get a bath and a bed, but he wasn't taking no for an answer.

"Look, moti, my wife is fit and skinny and doesn't realize some of us need to eat proper meals. She'll have some dinner made but I always have to eat before I get home. And you also haven't tried anything like this yet, so tonight, we eat Savour pulao."

I stopped protesting when I heard pulao. In the Chaudry home, pulao was always king, but we could never find it in Pakistani or Indian restaurants. Biryani—signature orange-and-white basmati grains mixed with spicy meat—was the only rice dish ever found on menus outside the house.

Abu hated biryani as if the dish itself was a personal affront to him. "You know what biryani is?" Abu has asked, not really asking, numerous times. "It's just leftovers layered with white rice, sprinkled with artificial food coloring, served up to idiots who think it's the best thing ever."

Pulao, on the other hand, pulao required true skill to master. The basmati had to be cooked to perfection in a deeply savory, aromatic bone broth. Too much broth and the rice would be mush. Too little, it would be raw. Just right, and you'd end up with fluffy, tender rice, a rich golden brown from the broth, each grain distinct and coated in a slight sheen of ghee.

I agreed with Abu, pulao was superior to biryani, and if Savour pulao was famous for it, we had to do it. Khan Gul Mamu drove us through foggy winter roads until we reached a large, well-lit, open restaurant with multiple levels. We headed upstairs to the family dining area, a common feature in many Pakistani establishments. The ground floor is usually occupied by groups of men, but more spacious and comfortable seating for families with kids, or women who wanted to sit away from the riffraff, is often separate. I was initially put off by the gender segregation of this arrangement throughout Pakistan, until I realized how much easier, faster, and safer it was for women to have their own lines and spaces at airports, movie theaters, buses, and the like. It actually felt a bit like royal treatment.

There was no menu to choose from because the restaurant served one single thing: chicken pulao with shaami kabab. It took all of three minutes for our plates to arrive, holding mounds of caramel-colored rice topped with a couple of chicken pieces and two shaami kabab patties each. Salad, raita, and water were unceremoniously plunked down to share, and we dug in.

It was the best pulao I'd ever had, every plump kernel of rice standing apart from its brethren, fragrant from cardamom, cloves, and cinnamon, tangy with tomatoes and a kick of green chili, and shiny and rich from the fatty broth it was cooked in. It was the star of the show—the chicken and kabab, while tasty, were just afterthoughts.

Khan Gul Mamu and I tucked in, finishing our plates embarrassingly quickly. He motioned for two more. We polished them off, too, as he loosened his belt. I was thankful for the elastic-band shalwar I was wearing.

I was still burping pulao when we got to his home, and despite the nice dinner his wife had made, I went straight to bed, praying my intestinal tract could digest the cups and cups of rice I'd inhaled. The next morning Khan Gul Mamu whispered for me to skip breakfast because he was going to take me somewhere before we set off for Lahore. I once again insulted his wife by just nibbling on a biscuit with my chai and leaving a table full of fried eggs and parathay untouched.

An hour later I was standing with my uncle and my daughter at one of the most sublime, ornate shrines I'd ever seen. It was the shrine of Shah Abdul Latif Kazmi, the seventeenth-century patron saint of Islamabad, also known as Bari Imam. Khan Gul Mamu pulled out a handkerchief and tied it around his head, covering it out of respect. We bought bags of rose petals from a vendor and joined a few dozen others, pilgrims and beggars, lighting candles, saying a prayer, and scattering scarlet bits of rose around the mausoleum of the saint.

I had no idea Khan Gul Mamu was a sufi, or even spiritual or religious, so I was equal parts impressed and surprised by this early morning act of devotion. That was until he ripped off the handkerchief and led me to a small stone building in one corner of the shrine's courtyard. Inside the structure, a couple of men stood over huge aluminum caldrons. Khan Gul Mamu leaned inside, said something to them, and a few minutes later they brought out plates to us.

"Wait, what is this?" I asked.

"It's langar. Free food they give to all the devotees."

I looked around and saw a line of impoverished-looking people, raggedy children and bone-thin ancient elders, congregated off to the side, watching us and waiting to get their food.

"This . . . this is for poor people, isn't it? Wait, did you cut the line? Look there's an entire line!"

Khan Gul Mamu leaned down and hissed, "Moti, just eat, I gave them a nice little donation and they can tell by looking at us that we aren't meant to be standing in line with the others."

He was dressed in a suit and tie, and I was carrying a designer bag with matching heels, sunglasses perched pretentiously on my head. My daughter pranced around in jeans, light-up sneakers, and a cute, very imported-looking sweater. I looked at my full plate of mutton pulao on one side and zarda, sweetened, saffron colored rice with nuts and raisins, on the other, and flames of entitlement burned my cheeks red. Khan Gul Mamu was already shoveling small mounds of rice into his face with his fingers, a shit-eating grin stretched ear to ear.

My brain was caught in a vicious cycle of mortification at the optics of it all—two clearly indulged, well-dressed fatties holding plates piled high with food meant for the needy people, *needy people who were watching us*—and also worry about eating from a plate that may have never seen dishwashing detergent in its entire existence, a concern that just added to my elitist shame.

One of the cooks saw me standing there without having taken a bite and ran out, holding a spoon. Ah, I was probably not used to eating with my fingers, he said, triumphantly handing me yet another implement that could send me to the toilet or the hospital for days.

Khan Gul Mamu had had enough of my spoiled American hesitation.

"EAT," he barked.

So I did. But I did it wrong.

"Mix the pulao and zarda together," he said.

I thought, "Okay, that will just ruin them both," but I did as he said.

I expected it to be a revolting combination, meaty rice and sweet rice, but it was one of the best meals I'd had in my life. Both of the rices on their own were delicious, but eating them together somehow enhanced them both. My very recent shame was immediately buried under waves of savory and sweet, tender hunks of mutton, and plump sultanas. Within minutes we cleaned up. I politely dabbed the grease from the corners of my mouth, my back turned to the line of people still waiting for their portions, put the plate down on a peeling wooden stool outside the kitchen, and walked away, head held straight.

I had three days before, sadly, I was to return to America. Months of eating and laughing and traveling and shopping and mostly doing absolutely nothing in Pakistan had been a balm for my soul. I had stayed longer than I had originally planned and had not only missed my own law school graduation, but also missed taking the bar exam. But my diploma would come in the mail, and the exam happened every six months, and this trip would never happen again.

I wasn't about to get a moment's rest those last few days. We had to make goodbye rounds of all the relatives in Lahore one last time, pack up half a storeroom's worth of shopping into the four international-size suitcases, and pick up what was still outstanding from some of the shops.

Two months earlier I had ordered nearly a dozen outfits for myself from vendors in Ichra Bazaar. Tailormade clothing is customary in Pakistan, and every neighborhood has its local darzi, usually a highly skilled but frazzled male tailor draped in measuring tape and thread, operating out of a tiny open-face shop. But the trend for "readymade" clothing had begun fairly recently, which meant you could now buy shalwar-kameez suits right off the rack.

Apparently I couldn't, though. On at least three occasions, as I browsed through racks of readymade tunics and suits in a boutique, the store clerk felt it necessary to stop me. "Those won't fit you! You are too big. Readymade doesn't come in your size, sister."

Each time, aflame with embarrassment, I snapped back, "They're not for me, they're gifts!" and huffed out.

I would have to get my clothing custom made, given my size.

A cousin had insisted on taking me to Ichra Bazaar after seeing how I was getting fleeced in some of the more upscale bazaars in town. The vendors could tell I was not local, and that I likely had American dollars or British pounds at my disposal. How, I wondered? Every time I went shopping, I dressed in the simplest suit possible and wrapped myself in a shawl, aunty-style.

"It's the way you walk, the way you look people in the eye when you talk. People can just tell. Also, your purse and shoes look foreign-made," my cousins revealed to me.

I was game to check out Ichra Bazaar, keen on saving some bucks. The bazaar was old, tight, crowded, and brimming with clothing and jewelry shops. Much of it wasn't great quality, but a few shops did in fact have remarkable things.

Since I placed my orders, my cousin had made multiple rounds to pick them up but was waved off every time, being told the clothes were still not ready. The day of my flight Khan Gul and Pummy Mamu said, "Okay, let's go get your stuff."

There is no way to drive into the narrow lane that runs through the bazaar, so we walked in, my uncles following me, until I reached the large shop where most of my clothes were being held hostage. There was a row of customer seats at chest level with a platform where the portly, mustachioed shop owner lounged on stuffed bolster pillows. Surrounding him were shelves reaching the ceiling stacked with embroidered and embellished chiffons, silks, and cottons. He sat up when he saw the three of us file in, suddenly getting a serious look on his face. Signaling for us to sit, he waved to a young man to go fetch chai and coke bottles.

Pummy Mamu leaned forward with a smile. "Brother, we have made multiple trips to get her order. Do you know who she is?"

The shop owner looked at me and nodded. "Haanh, I know this sister gave us some orders a few weeks ago and they still aren't ready. It's busy you know, busy wedding season. No need to worry, we will deliver them to the house when they're ready!"

The scrawny shop helper returned with a tray of drinks and samosay. I took a cold bottle and started sipping the soda through a straw. Khan Gul Mamu picked up a samosa.

"No," said Pummy Mamu. "It wasn't a few weeks ago. It was two months ago. You said it would take a month. She's paid you tens of thousands of rupees. Again, I ask you, DO YOU KNOW WHO SHE IS?"

The owner was still smiling but his tone was definitely not friendly anymore. He crossed his arms and responded, "No I don't know and it doesn't matter. The clothes aren't ready."

Both my uncles leapt up onto the platform simultaneously, as if they'd planned it.

"She is the NIECE OF GENERAL PERVAIZ MUSHARRAF!" Pummy Mamu roared.

What in the holy crap, I thought.

General Pervaiz Musharraf was not just the top-ranking general in the Pakistan military, he had also recently deposed the government in a successful coup. I had seen the annual "passing out" ceremony at the Pakistan Military Academy weeks earlier with my aunt and her family. The highest-ranking military officers, as well as General Musharraf, were in attendance as the cadets graduated.

In what felt like my most surreal moment in Pakistan, I chatted with the general for a few minutes at the reception. But apparently it wasn't the most surreal moment, because now here I was, frozen in horror as my uncles wreaked havoc on some poor man's clothing shop, screaming, "You insult the niece of General Musharraf?!"

To be clear: I am most definitely not the niece of General Musharraf.

Pummy Mamu grabbed the owner by the collar and slapped him twice. The shop helpers who had been stocking the shelves tried to scatter and run, but my uncles caught them, too, smacking them around as I yelled for them to stop.

A few hundred men gathered at the front of the shop, watching the mayhem, until a young patrol officer broke through and climbed up on the platform. My uncles turned, both of them towering over him, and Khan Gul Mamu barked, "What station are you from? I'm Colonel Rehan Ali Khan. We are madame's guards. Get out of here, son, go call your senior, he knows us."

The kid in the uniform saluted my uncle, pivoted and left, shaking.

My uncles sat back down, one on each side of me, and Pummy Mamu menaced, "Now. Do you know who she is?"

I was raging inside, humiliated by the shop owner's treatment and by the absolute ludicrousness of the lie. Why in the hell would the niece of General Musharraf be shopping at a bazaar like Ichra?

The owner pulled out a metal box and began counting rupees. He didn't have enough. He sent a kid to other shops nearby and collected the money he owed me as my uncles sipped chai and ate the samosay that hadn't been knocked off the tray. After the owner handed over the money, my uncles got up and asked me, "Okay, where's the other shop?"

The other shop, just a few blocks down, had already gotten the news of the carnage. As we walked there, the sea of people parted, watching for what would happen next. Nothing happened because the shop owner already had an envelope of cash waiting for me, my refund. He silently handed it to Pummy Mamu, and we walked back out of the bazaar, which had fallen totally silent.

We got in the car and my uncles high-fived each other, laughing at what they'd just pulled off. I was livid and didn't say a word, refusing to talk to them.

Khan Gul Mamu turned around. "What, why the face, moti? We got back sixty thousand rupees for you, you better treat us to the best dinner ever tonight!"

And I did. We feasted one last time on fried fish and seekh kabab before I boarded the Pakistan International Airline flight back to the life I hated.

SIX MONTHS LATER I was no longer with my husband.

A marriage doesn't break in an instant. It takes hundreds of instances, of words said and unsaid, of grief and resentment, disappointment and heartache. Our marriage didn't even have a chance to build, much less break. When AK hit me the first time, just weeks after I left my family's home to join his, he shattered any foundation our relationship could have had. You cannot build on rubble, but for five years, for the sake of our daughter, I had tried. Ultimately, I wasn't even the one who ended it, AK did.

Ami knew exactly why he wanted out, and she explained it to me. It was because I was fat, and in America AK was surrounded by thin, attractive, half-dressed women everywhere. In the streets, at work, in the movies. Ami was a solid two hundred pounds herself, with an ever-pregnant-looking belly for the past thirty years. Things had worked out for her, I thought to myself quietly.

She wasn't completely wrong, though. All throughout the marriage AK and his family made my weight the butt of jokes and torment. You would think the most painful thing AK ever did to me was hit me, but it wasn't. The most painful thing, the thing that buried itself deep inside me and stays inside me, was the time I threatened to leave him after he hit me, and he responded, "Where will you go? Who will take you? You couldn't even support yourself hooking because no man would pay ten bucks for you."

The thing he loathed became the thing I loathed, my body. My body didn't shrink from the loathing, rather it grew. His disgust fed my body like fertilizer, and I became heavier and heavier, expanding with the pain, bloated with my own self-loathing and humiliation. Six months after I returned from Pakistan, weighing more than I ever had at two hundred and ten pounds, I moved back in with my parents in Baltimore, but not with my daughter. My daughter was still with AK, and I was just at the beginning of a custody battle to get her back. But for the first time in years, I had more time to myself than I knew what to do with. I was working full time and studying for the bar exam, but I didn't have to cook and clean, I didn't have a child to look after, and every evening I had a few hours of complete freedom.

I decided to join a gym. The day I signed up, the manager asked, "So what's your goal?"

"I want to lose weight, at least fifty pounds. I had a baby and put on a lot."

He smiled and said, "Oh well of course, that's expected. How old is your baby now?"

"Uh. Well, she's almost four."

"Four months old? Wow, well you're getting right back at it then."

"No," I said, "she's almost four years old." As the words left my mouth, I realized how long I'd taken to get there.

For the next year, as the divorce proceeded and my custody battle continued, I saw my daughter once a week. The other six days I spent every evening in the gym, reliving the euphoria I'd experienced as a kid when I ran laps in Chambersburg. I'd already lost a hundred and sixty pounds of baggage and regret the night I left AK's house, and each week a few more melted off as I pounded away on the treadmill, keeping the beat to bhangra, R & B, and Sufi folk music.

It started with thirty minutes in the gym, then an hour, and then two hours. Time flew as I listened to audiobooks, wandered from machine to machine, hung out in the sauna, and struck up friendships with the faces I saw every night. It didn't feel like work, it felt like freedom, and the stronger my body got, the more my spirit healed. By the time I won custody of my daughter eight months later, I was down twenty-five pounds, and I looked and felt like I'd turned back the clock ten years.

I couldn't keep living with my parents though, if for no other reason than because every time someone in the aunty network asked why I was there, Ami lied and told them I was staying in Baltimore for work. She persisted in the lie that I was still married, but it got harder to do so when I was as up-front as possible that I definitely wasn't.

I can't say I'm a pioneer in our community when it comes to divorce, certainly there were those who came before me, but at the time I knew only one solitary divorcée in my entire social network. Whatever shame it was supposed to bring me never came.

"Stop telling everyone you're divorced," Ami begged. "Why are you insisting on cutting off our noses in all of society?"

Zuby Aunty, on the other hand, was thrilled to find out I was single again.

"Thank God you got rid of that short, bald loser. He never deserved you. There are so many tall, handsome young men here, military cadets and officers and the sons of officers, you'll have your pick! Just . . . well just don't tell anyone about your daughter. And say you're twenty-three years old, not twenty-eight."

She began plotting potential marks but getting remarried was the farthest thing from my mind. I had just begun tasting independence and I wanted more. So I took the big step, as big as "going away" to college, of moving into my own place with my little girl. I needed to get far from the aunties in Baltimore who still thought I was married or were scandalized that I was divorced, and I missed Virginia, so I moved back across the state line.

The plan, when I started law school, was to practice corporate law eventually. A comfortable, stable financial future was priority number one. We all know what happens to best-laid plans. Two events forever changed the course of my career: first, a young man from Baltimore by the name of Adnan Syed was arrested and charged with murder, and second, nineteen terrorists had hijacked four planes, targeting the World Trade Center and Pentagon.

Adnan Syed was seventeen when he was arrested in 1999, and I had known him since he was twelve. He was my little brother Saad's best friend. I had seen repeated local news stories about the disappearance of a high school student named Hae Min Lee but had no idea Adnan had any connection to her. Not until the day I saw a live broadcast announcing his arrest for her murder.

Impossible, I thought. Of all the boys in the Baltimore Muslim community, Adnan was the gentlest, most respectful, decent young man I'd ever met. I warned my brother not to corrupt Adnan because he was such a good kid. Without knowing a thing about the case, I thought he must be innocent. Once I learned about the particulars, I was convinced of his innocence.

I was still in law school and still married to AK when Adnan was arrested, and from the beginning of that ordeal I did my best to support him and his family as they navigated the trial, his conviction, and subsequent appeals. What I saw in the courtroom put me off criminal law, and broke my heart, forever. I continued to advocate for his exoneration, but at the time none of us knew it would be a fight that we would still be embroiled in decades later.

When I took the bar exam for the first time in the summer of 2001, months before 9/11, I failed by 3 percentage points. That was okay, I reassured myself, I still did well, considering that most of my peers didn't have kids, were able to take time off work to study for the test, and could afford a three-thousand-dollar preparatory course. I was barely getting by on my part-time law firm intern wages, and I didn't have more than a few hundred bucks in my bank account.

I waited a year to take the test again, long enough to save the money for it, and to get enough weekends in to do some nominal studying. In the meantime, though, the US was still reeling from the worst domestic terrorist attack it had ever experienced, and tens of thousands of Muslims here were being rounded up by the newly formed Department of Homeland Security. Our community needed lawyers to help. We had to find out where they were being detained, figure out if they were being deported, and sometimes help them actually get deported after being held for months in prison with general populations.

"I'll get back to corporate law," I thought. "This needs attention now." I spent that year, as I readied to retake the bar exam, doing low-paid and pro bono immigration assistance work.

I took the bar exam a second time and failed by two points. I had to wait another six months before I could try again. I supported myself and my daughter by doing menial contract-litigation support work. It was a struggle. Five days a week, for ten hours a day and not much pay, I sat in a naval warehouse, alone, stamping thousands and thousands of documents with a Bates stamper.

The third time was the charm, however, and when I finally passed the exam, I had a job waiting for me at a tiny immigration firm run by two Argentinian attorneys. I still didn't plan on actually making immigration law my career, but for the moment they had the hours I needed, and I had the experience they needed. It also helped that I had the potential to bring in clients from a base they couldn't tap—Muslims and South Asians.

Being a single working mom, while also trying to pass the bar exam, had squelched my self-care routine. No more time for the gym, very little time for good, home-cooked meals. I reverted to fast food and

Mama Celeste pizzas, and by the time I could put "Esquire" after my name, I had gone back up a couple of sizes. And frankly, I had also reverted to not caring so much. Survival was key, by whatever means necessary, including cheap boxes of Kraft Macaroni & Cheese, ramen, and McDonald's multiple times a week.

The poor food choices I had been making for the previous year, though, didn't feel so good from the first day I stepped into the new firm. Seated at the reception desk was an Argentinian woman, nay, a goddess, shaped like an hourglass and dressed to show every curve she was blessed with. I don't think I'd ever seen a woman with such proportions.

Our secretary was Jessica Rabbit. I clomped past her every day in my stodgy flats, boxy blazer, and pleated pants, my face ashy and defeated. I'd given up on makeup long ago. Who had time for it while trying to get breakfast and lunch ready and hustle a first grader awake and delivered to before-school care? I'd started wearing a Muslim headscarf a year earlier, hoping to look chic like Grace Kelly, but ended up looking more Russian-grandmotherish.

Jessica Rabbit never had a single long, wavy brown hair out of place, her face was perfectly powdered and rouged, and her lips glistened with eternal gloss. She exclusively wore dresses molded to her frame, and four-inch heels. Every single day. When we bumped elbows in the little employee kitchen, I stared at her impossibly small waist as I popped a Coke and waited for my Mama Celeste pizza to ding in the microwave. How is there enough space inside that body for her organs, I wondered.

Jessica Rabbit ate the same lunch, day after day, which she prepared fresh in the kitchen. She sliced one large tomato, drizzled it with balsamic vinegar, and sprinkled it with salt and pepper. Then she strode on her heels back to her desk and ate the tomato with great enthusiasm, carving up bits with a knife and fork, as if it was a steak. Equal parts shame and inspiration from watching her drove me to try and get back to better eating, so I started bringing Weight Watcher frozen entrees and low-calorie yogurt for lunch. At first, I needed to eat two frozen meals and two yogurts to feel even remotely full. And dinnertime was still a free-for-all.

I lost a few pounds, but otherwise remained a solid size sixteen and squarely registered as "obese" on the BMI calculator. One day I worked up the nerve to ask Jessica what she ate for her other meals and if she worked out.

"Black coffee for breakfast and usually steamed vegetables with protein—tuna or boiled eggs, or tofu, whatever I have on hand, something I can make fast—for dinner," she responded. She liked her curves and wanted to keep them, so no running for her. She alternated resistance training and yoga a few days a week, which kept her exactly in the shape she preferred.

Boiled eggs? Not a problem. Tofu? I had no idea where to even start. I had some experience with tuna but like so many other otherwise healthy ingredients, my family had figured out how to make it terrible for you. Iffi Mamu was a tuna master. It was a cheap protein that he always kept stockpiled in his pantry. He made desi tuna subs by frying the tuna in butter with sliced onions, green chilies, cumin seeds, red chili powder, ginger, and garlic, which he loaded on whatever nearly expired bread he bought at discount that week. Topped with lettuce, sriracha, and gobs of mayonnaise, there was nothing remotely healthy about it.

His more inspired take on tuna was turning it into "tuna biryani" right in the microwave. He kept cans of tuna, dry basmati rice, and boxes of biryani seasoning at his desk at work. When the craving hit, he combined them with some water and zapped the whole thing in the microwave for twenty minutes. Voila. Tuna biryani. Given how that had to smell, I cannot imagine why his colleagues at the architectural division at the University of Maryland did not ban him from the kitchen for life.

I wrote down Jessica's suggestions and then did absolutely nothing with them. Not until I was finally, and predictably, motivated by a new romantic prospect.

HE CALLED ME Baaji at first, as a sign of respect for someone who could have been his big sister. Irfan was five years younger than me. We met at a chance encounter at a Muslim convention where I was wandering around with flyers about Adnan's case and a box to collect donations for an appeal. My email address was on the flyers, one of which ended up in Irfan's hands, and a couple of weeks later he emailed.

He was from Toronto, though "back home" his family was from Karachi. They were Urdu-speaking muhajirs, not Punjabis, though he was mostly just Canadian. Our emails turned to instant messages, where we chatted about Adnan's case, music, religion, and food, and fat. If we bonded over anything, it was the fat. Just like me, Irfan had struggled with his weight his entire life, reaching almost three hundred pounds at one point. He regaled me with tales of the culinary wonderland that was the greater Toronto area, and I shared weight-loss and diet hacks I was trying. Not long after he learned I was a single, divorced mother, his interest became romantic.

I thought he was out of his mind. He was twenty-three years old, never married, had just finished school to become a chaplain, had no job, and his parents would disown him for even considering marrying an older divorcee with a kid. Besides, I was enjoying my freedom too much, the last thing I wanted to do was get remarried.

While this was all true, I'd be lying if I said I wasn't flattered that he was interested, and little by little, I started to care more about how I looked.

My daughter and I had recently moved into a high-rise close to my new job, a fancier apartment building with a gym in the basement. I limited myself to 1500 calories a day and hit the gym every night. I started off on the treadmill, alternating jogging and walking for thirty minutes, and over the days and weeks increased the jogging and decreased the walking. Once I could run for thirty minutes straight, I added another five. Then another five. After six months I could run five miles without stopping.

I lost ten pounds, then fifteen. And then I hit a wall. Five miles and 1500 calories a day wasn't working anymore. So I added stairs. After my nightly run, I began walking, slowly at first, up the twenty-one flights of stairs to my apartment. A few weeks later, I was sprinting up the flights. And a few weeks after that, I was doing the twenty-one flights twice over.

Another five pounds came off, then again, the needle got stuck.

I added jumping rope. I ran, sprinted the stairwell twice, and then returned to my apartment exhausted and sweaty but didn't rest until I jumped rope five hundred times.

Another five gone.

After an excruciating year of limiting calories and working out two hours a day, I was at 170 pounds. I still outweighed my sister, and what the charts said I should weigh, by a good forty pounds, but I had gone from a size sixteen to a size twelve, a size I hadn't seen since ninth grade.

One night, a night I really needed a cheat meal, I stood in line with my daughter at Five Guys waiting to order a burger. Two young men in front of me were chatting and one turned around casually and saw me. He leaned toward the other and quietly said, "The girl behind is so pretty." The other man turned around to look, and then I turned around to look, but there was no one behind me.

I nearly melted into a puddle right there when I realized they were talking about me. A random member of the opposite sex had noticed me. The fact that I still remember the moment proves how rare and surprising such an occurrence was. It gave me the confidence to face a gauntlet I was dreading—Irfan's family.

By now I was a few years out from my divorce and ready to settle down again. This was well before smart phones and dating apps, and I had zero game myself, so I wasn't seeing anyone. But hundreds of miles north, and two years later, Irfan remained shockingly interested. I imagined he would be in for a rude awakening once he told his family about me, so I decided I wasn't going to invest too emotionally in him until he crossed that bridge.

"I will agree to marry you if your family agrees and my family agrees, that's my condition," I told him.

His family proved me wrong and agreed. They wanted to contact my parents so they could all come meet us, which meant I had to tell Ami about him.

"A younger man? A younger man who has never even been married?" Ami was perplexed.

"Why do you want to marry *yet another* man who will leave you? Younger men *never stay*. They *always stray*."

She had seen enough in her lifetime to believe this was another very bad choice I was making. I assured her that no decisions had been made. If she and Abu weren't happy after meeting Irfan and his family, I would reject his proposal.

The day they arrived, over a dozen of them in two vans, I was starving. I hadn't eaten in days, and not because I was too nervous to eat. In my entire life I have never been too nervous to eat. I hadn't eaten because I was hoping to squeeze off another few pounds before they all saw me and rejected me. I hyperventilated throughout the evening, having to escape to my parents' basement more than once to cry. While the whole system of families meeting and seeing each other's kids is supposed to be dignified and respectful, there are aspects of it that make you feel like you're being presented for inspection. Livestock at an auction.

I was certain they wouldn't be buying. But at the end of the night, all the elders seemed thrilled. Ami was particularly happy in the middle of Irfan's Urdu-speaking family. See how nice and polite they are, she whispered to me. She was beaming, and she was sold.

Everyone knew beforehand that if the families said yes, the next step was an engagement, and just in case it all went smoothly that night, the rings had already been purchased. Irfan's elder sister put a ring on my finger, and Abu put a ring on Irfan's. There, we were engaged. Now all they needed were my measurements so that, according to tradition, the groom's family could order my wedding dress.

They asked for my digits multiple times over the following months, but I kept putting them off, desperate not to give his mom and sisters the exact size of my waist and hips. Finally I told them to just use the measurements for a standard medium-size top. I was not exactly medium size, most of my tops were large, but given that I wouldn't get the wedding dress until days before the wedding, with no time to alter it, this was motivation to lose another ten pounds.

The wedding was in Canada, and my family and friends drove up in a caravan of cars. There wasn't a single detail about the wedding that mattered to me. I'd been there, done that before. Irfan and his family could arrange everything as they wished.

The night before the wedding, his mother came over to our hotel to drop off the wedding dress. When they left, I took it out to look at it. It was deep maroon with gold embroidery, a traditional lengha ankle-length skirt, blouse, and scarf, and it definitely looked like a medium size.

I had lost some more weight but my proportions weren't cooperating. I was still thick in the middle. Size ten jeans were loose in the legs, but tight in the waist. And my arms had always been like Ami's, heavier than the rest of our frames. Often times I couldn't squeeze my arms into tops that otherwise fit fine, and I ended up splitting them under the armpit.

I called Upeksha in to help me try on the wedding dress. The skirt just barely zipped up, but there was serious danger of it popping. The blouse not only didn't account for my chunky arms, it also didn't account for the breasts of a woman who had already given birth and breastfed.

I stuffed myself into the top, straining under the arms, but it wouldn't zip up.

"Suck your breath in," said Upeksha.

I put my hands on the wall and took a deep breath, and she managed to get the zipper halfway up. I couldn't fit into my wedding blouse. And it was my own stupid fault. My fault for not just telling them my measurements, and my fault for not losing enough weight to avoid this humiliation. I teared up, but we devised a solution. The zipper was in the back of the blouse. We would drape the scarf in such a way that no one could see it.

The next morning, I got married in a wedding blouse that was busted wide open in the back, but no one knew other than me, Upeksha, and the lady at the salon who did my wedding makeup. The minute I got to the hotel suite where Irfan and I were staying after the wedding, I tore off the dress, so my groom never found out, either.

In the next couple of weeks, Irfan and I picked up our lives and moved to Connecticut so Irfan could study at the Hartford Seminary. Before the wedding we had both doubled down on working out and eating right for the big day. I had gotten down to 165 pounds and felt pretty good, wedding dress fiasco notwithstanding, the lowest I'd been since college. Irfan was a buff 205 pounds, which looked great on his broad frame. I'm thankful for the pictures from those days proving that, at least for a moment, we made a lovely-looking couple.

The moment was brief. Two food addicts moving in together after over a year of discipline and deprivation could only go one way. To be fair, there are studies that prove newlyweds gain weight together, an average of up to four pounds in the first couple of months. So we weren't anomalies. But we were record breakers. In our first three months together, I gained back twenty-five pounds and Irfan gained back forty.

All the elements had gathered to create a perfect, fat-filled storm. Before the wedding we had both been working out at least two hours a day. All that came to a grinding halt; we stopped exercising completely. We had moved to Connecticut with a paltry savings and no jobs yet, meaning we were both pretty much broke and hoping we found paychecks before we ended up on the street. Being broke meant eating cheap, and the cheapest eats were the carbiest, oiliest, saltiest, and most sugar-packed.

We discovered Price Rite, a discount grocery store that sold the cheapest mass-produced, processed foods a buck could buy. Frozen pierogies, pizzas, and pastas, dozens of cookies and cheese-powder-covered snacks, juices from concentrate, and sodas filled our weekly shopping cart. Fresh fruit and vegetables, pricey proteins like fish and lamb, rarely made our budget. Mostly though, it was because we were worn down from months of dietary and fitness discipline, our willpower worn to a hangry little nub. Some people have binge meals, we had binge weeks.

We ate like no one was watching, because now that the wedding was over and we had both moved far from family and friends, no one was. We celebrated each other by feeding each other and creating new food rituals together. I never had a huge sweet tooth before, but Irfan's demons were all saccharine. So now I ate the pastries, cakes, cookies, sweetened hot and cold drinks, and ice cream that we kept stocked in our kitchen.

I never had much of a chai or coffee habit, but with Irfan, chai became *a thing*. Canadian blood, I am convinced, is laced with coffee. Irfan drank it all day, and thankfully we had been gifted a coffee maker so he could satisfy his Tim Hortons longings. But once a day, after the dinner had been cleared away, he switched from coffee to chai. The microwave turned my parents lazy decades ago, and they'd been zapping their cups in minutes most of my life. So when I made chai, I also used the microwave. A tea bag in a cup of water, two minutes on high, a splash of milk and a spoon of sugar, and chai was ready.

This troubled my husband's conscience. When his mother woke up for the predawn prayer, she put on a pot of milk to boil down, letting it simmer for thirty, forty minutes until it reduced and a film of pure malai formed on top. That's the milk she made their morning chai with, topped with that hard-earned cream. Like his mother, Irfan's chai making was laborious, an act of devotion. He cooked it low and slow: sugar, cardamom, and loose-leaf tea in mostly whole milk with a splash of water. I poked fun at it, it was chai for a child, milky and sweet. If I was going to have chai, it better be karak, strong and dark, and it better not take more than a few minutes. I could make an entire three-course meal in the time Irfan took to make two cups of chai.

He wore me down after months, though, and I finally got hooked on his chai. Every night after dinner he handed me a large mug and set down a plate of cookies and desi biscuits dotted with almonds and pistachios and cumin seeds between us. We dipped our biscuits in the chai to soften them and slurped down the soggy, hot, milky globs until we were in a stupor. Later, after my daughter went to sleep, we scooped out generous bowls of ice cream, and snuggled together in the broken-down, squeaky bed that came with our rented attic, feeding each other spoonfuls as we watched movies late into the night.

We didn't have the money for an actual honeymoon, so these indulgences were the pleasures we could afford. The indulgences became habit and for a while we ate with the recklessness of an off-the-rails boxcar. After a year or so we had finally settled into a more balanced domestic life, in which we both were working and could afford food that would be considered real food by indigenous cultures and my Dada Abu, were he alive. Food that was fresh and not frozen, processed, and preserved. By then, though, we were doughy and content.

We made friends and had a social circle, weekly potlucks just like when I was a kid in Hagerstown, and for the first time as an adult I hosted dinner parties and ladies' lunches and teas and barbeques for my own friends. Like Ami, I developed a reputation for cooking well, for having a gift in my hands. And like Ami, I basked in the praise for my stewed koftay and goat shorba and cholay and chicken pulao and kabab. Unlike Ami, though, I actually enjoyed cooking.

AK had never given me permission to be as I was, to feel like I was good enough or even fine in my own body. My size, my weight, overshadowed anything else I was or did with AK. But not with Irfan. Maybe because he knew what the struggle was like, or maybe because he loved me in a way AK didn't even know how to. Irfan and I both gave ourselves and each other quiet permission to just give in and be. Be whatever our bodies became when we lived without making any effort to constrain them.

We had spent the first year of marriage indulging every junk food whim, so of course the pounds were going to come on, but the truth was, even when we went back to eating three fairly healthy meals a day, our weight kept slowly climbing.

Whatever was the witchcraft that allowed some to stay slender without any effort, and others to maintain their weight without any diet or exercise? There was no maintenance for us. If we weren't actively fighting weight gain, working out and restricting calories, our weight climbed month after month, a pound here, a couple pounds there. The only way to stop the march of the scale was through active measures.

But we were so tired of active measures. We just wanted to be. To eat without thinking about every bite that we took. We assured each other that we could only fight our natural states for so long. We had both always been heavy, our childhood and adulthood, and the battle to get thin would always be a losing one for us. I was tired of fighting. Was it possible to be chubby and happy? The world told me no, my family told me no. Sometimes my thighs rubbing together, my labored breathing, and the rolls of my stomach popping over my waistband told me no, too.

I still thought it was possible.

I was fat. But not that fat.

That's what I had told myself years ago, when I was half a dozen sizes smaller. Now, a couple of years into the marriage, I hovered steadily around two hundred pounds.

IT WAS STILL just the three of us, and there was never any "news." It was partially expected. Irfan had survived Hodgkin's lymphoma in his early twenties and had been told the chemo and radiation could have a lasting effect on fertility. But my mother's voice from a decade ago echoed in my ears—fat women can't get pregnant—adding to the existing complication of being over thirty, the age at which I was told my eggs were practically committing suicide.

And then: miracle of miracles, I got pregnant. I was at my heaviest when it happened, proving wrong all the aunties who shook their heads at me. By the time Barack Hussein Obama was sworn in, I was cradling a new baby girl, eleven years younger than my first.

Just like the first time around, though, I steadily gained weight after the delivery. It didn't help that Irfan's mother, who came to stay with us for a few weeks, insisted on feeding me semolina and rice puddings rich with nuts, ghee, and cream and hearty kichdri—basmati and lentils cooked into a hearty porridge laced with butter.

I needed these to get my strength back, to get my milk flowing for the baby, she said, and whether or not it was true, I happily complied. As long as I was breastfeeding, I was still eating for two I figured. My size 18 clothes began tightening around my body, which had stretched further and changed shape from the pregnancy. I realized with horror that an entire fanny pack made of meat now hung above my groin. Ami was always blocky, and both she and Abu had protruding guts, but nothing like this. No one in my family was shaped like this. According to the internet, I had a FUPA. Good luck getting rid of it, the internet also told me.

I didn't step on a scale until the baby was nearly a year old, giving myself at least that much time to not worry about it. It took nine months to make a baby and I read somewhere that it took at least as many months after delivery to get your body back in shape. But I put it off much longer because I just didn't want to know. My resistance to learning how much I weighed was so strong I refused to return to the ob-gyn for all my postpregnancy checkups. Watching the nurse move the weight to the right, and farther to the right, and then just a little farther, and then write that number down in my file for all of posterity was too much to bear.

I finally built up the courage and bought a new digital scale. I spent a few days trying to eat better and just feel lighter before I did the deed. I weighed 215 pounds, a new high. I tried to fight off the rising panic in my throat with justifications that I had a baby, and I had to be gentle with myself.

"How much more gentle do you want to be, Rabia," I thought, "you spent the past four years stuffing yourself and not looking sideways at a gym."

Irfan, who was as broad as a linebacker and stood five ten, weighed 235 pounds. I weighed nearly as much as he did.

I had heard of a new workout program called CrossFit, which promised the kind of results you couldn't get from a treadmill. I found a CrossFit gym and signed up for 5-a.m. classes, figuring I'd burn more calories during the day if I exercised first thing in the morning.

The first day I arrived, still half asleep, I was slightly terrified at the brightly lit warehouse, the full front of the space opening into an industrial parking lot. This was not like any gym I'd ever seen. Women in chic athletic wear, sports bras, leggings, and crop tops, and well-toned men with massive bottles of water and gym bags streamed into the gym. They looked so prepared and so much like they belonged. Everyone was white, young, fit.

I looked like an aunty who had just arrived from the village, in my baggy sweatpants and sweatshirt, hair tied up in a scarf. I desperately wanted to stay in the car, and my eyes filled up with tears. I was intimidated and, in that moment, hated everything about myself. I despised my stomach as it rested on my thighs, cursed every roll on my back as it pressed against the seat. I hated that, once again in my life, I had so many chins that Ami would say I didn't know what I looked like anymore.

I wiped up the snot, grabbed my towel, and went inside. For the next forty minutes I did things I'd never done before, working parts of my body I didn't know had muscles. Squats, lunges, sprints, high knees, pushups, and the most accursed exercise move ever invented in the history of mankind: the burpee. Somewhere between my third and fourth attempt at falling into a pushup, then jumping back up, I felt my stomach surge. I barely made it to the bathroom before hurling whatever was left of my dinner from the night before into the toilet.

I emerged sweaty and foul, dragging myself to the instructor, thinking this would definitely merit a "get out of class early" pass. He patted me on the back and said, "Yup, that can happen when you're just starting off, drink some water, keep at it, you'll be fine," and pointed me back to my place in the circle of hell.

I returned, morning after morning, for the next four months. Up every day at 4:30 a.m., in class by five, home by six. I got stronger, had more energy, and generally just felt better. I hated myself less. Yet, I only lost five pounds. At that check-in the trainer measured me and approvingly nodded that I'd lost a couple inches here and there. But he was baffled that my weight hadn't moved much.

"Wait, what is your diet like? Did you change your food habits?"

I absolutely had not. I didn't understand why I had to. Everything else being the same, I figured the exercise should have had an impact.

"That's not how it works. Weight loss, if that's your goal, is eighty percent about diet and twenty percent about exercise."

I cussed under my breath. Why didn't he tell me that sooner, before I was up at dawn puking my guts out? If weight loss hinged 80 percent on food choices, I had no need to be suffering in a warehouse every morning.

I said thank you and canceled my membership, happy to never have to do another burpee again.

TEN

Gur Naal Ishq Mithaa: A Love Sweeter than Jaggery

I stood over a steaming pot of chai, pulling and stirring it, as a completely surreal scene unfolded behind me. Shaun T, world-famous fitness guru, sat at my dining table eating gulab jamun, while his husband, Scott Blokker, led a dozen of my friends in an impromptu dance workout class in our tiny family room.

The house was packed, and everyone was full and chatty after a homemade Pakistani meal that I'd spent all day preparing. Scott and the others kept yelling at me to come join them in the fun, but the last thing I wanted to do was shake the tires around my waist (my "waste," I thought) for everyone to see and Instagram.

I pulled my cardigan closer around me and laughed, shaking my head no. I had lately begun wearing a lot of cardigans, because my life had become nightmarish. In the past year, Adnan Syed's wrongful conviction case had taken the world, and my existence, by storm. I had been trying to help exonerate him since 1999, but it wasn't until his case became the subject of the wildly popular podcast *Serial* that it seemed like there might be some hope. That hope came with hundreds of millions of listeners, tens of thousands of letters and emails, and hundreds and hundreds of interview requests.

I gained twenty-five pounds during the three months that *Serial* aired, a combination of stress, sleep deprivation, and constant snacking as I blogged and wrote op-eds and tweeted about Adnan's case day and night. I felt sick and sluggish, but suddenly my reality demanded I be more active and dynamic and public than I'd ever been before.

I appeared in interview after interview, did magazine spreads and speaking engagements, went to podcast and true-crime conventions, and took pictures with thousands of avid fans and supporters. I said yes to as many opportunities to bring publicity to the case as possible, because I knew we might not get a second chance at this. I connected with celebrities like Shaun T, who wanted to help Adnan, and invited them into my home to meet Adnan's lawyers and growing team of advocates and supporters—and to impress them with my Pakistani home cooking.

I was on social media constantly, tweeting about the case with the hashtag #FreeAdnan, and dozens of times a week was tagged in horrible photographs of myself. I'd spent my entire life avoiding being photographed. I was the official school photographer in high school, and yet managed to keep myself out of every yearbook until my senior year. While my sister and cousins and friends posed and mugged for pictures every chance they got, I always made myself scarce whenever a camera was nearby.

The reality of what my pictures showed me was too embarrassing. Two, sometimes three chins, my torso a stack of protruding bulges, my scarf askew, my features distorted from the extra pounds. People took candids of me giving talks, then took selfies with me after events and excitedly posted them online, hoping I would repost. I wouldn't.

People magazine sent a makeup artist with their photographer, the *Washingtonian* posed me in their professional studio, and the *Baltimore Sun* did a profile with a picture of me that dominated the page. I cringed at every image. Cardigans, I came to realize, draped long and loose, helped hide some of the pounds in those pictures. Or at least hid the contours of my bulges. They also made me feel less exposed, hidden in a cocoon that I could pull tighter around me at the many public events I had to face, and the hundreds of inevitable pictures I'd appear in. I bought dozens of them.

Never before had I understood the words "It was the best of times, it was the worst of times," but now I was living it. The post-*Serial* speaking tour eventually turned into a PR tour for the book I wrote about the case two years later, which was picked up for film and TV rights before even being published. The whirlwind continued for a good three years, and multiple times a month I dragged myself onto and off airplanes, subsisting on greasy, carby airport food, eating at all hours because time no longer meant much. If I arrived at my hotel at midnight, that's when I had dinner. If the organizer for an event comped meals, I bought and ate enough food for three. My travel bag always had potato chips and M&Ms stuffed in the outer pockets, just in case I got hungry late at night in the middle of nowhere, and I drank Coca-Cola like it was going out of production.

There was a small, irrational voice in my head (or maybe it was in my stomach) that convinced me whatever I ate while traveling "didn't count," and another voice assured me it was petty and insignificant to worry about things like *how I looked* when I was on a crusade to right a monumental injustice. If the quest to free Adnan meant growing out of my size 18 jeans, it was a small price to pay for the cause.

Then came the day I sank into an airplane seat (I swore they were shrinking) and pulled on the seatbelt to latch it. It wouldn't reach across my lap. I looked down, straining to see past my tummy, and saw that the belt was extended as far as it could go. This was impossible, I thought. I absolutely could not have outgrown an airplane seatbelt. I could not be one of those passengers who needed an extender just to be secured. The passengers who people blogged about, arguing they should pay for two seats. The ones people secretly took pictures of, to post online and mock. I couldn't be one of them.

I saw the flight attendant heading down the aisle checking seatbelts and all the blood rushed to my face. It wasn't uncommon for me to be recognized on trains, planes, and in airports. If the attendant saw I needed an extender, she would have to hand it across the two passengers next to me, in full view of the rows all around me. Someone would surely think, or say, "Hey, isn't that the lawyer from the *Serial* case?"

I pulled the two halves of the seatbelt as close together as possible and tucked them under my cardigan, so it looked like they were latched. Then I leaned my head against the window and closed my eyes, pretending to be oblivious to the world. After the attendant passed by my row, I pulled my scarf around my face, so no one could see me, and for not the first time, cried.

I WEIGHED 234 pounds. A new high. There it was—all that food that didn't count. My husband kept telling me I was beautiful and attractive, as if I looked exactly the same as when we married, which could only mean he was lying. Why didn't he tell me the truth? Why didn't anyone?

Well, someone did. Someone still did after all these years, after all the publicity and kudos. Ami, who surveyed me head to toe every time I saw her, which was pretty frequently since we had moved back to Maryland a few years before *Serial* became a thing, was never at a loss for words. "They have this surgery you know," she said one day as I stood on her front stoop. "They can cut your stomach right off. Just cut it off."

I had no idea what she was talking about, but surgery, any kind of surgery, just seemed too extreme. Surely I could lose the weight without resorting to such measures. I just had to figure out what to do, and get to it. Low fat, low carb, low calorie, intermittent fasting, whole foods, raw foods, what course of action should I take? I felt completely unnerved and rattled facing the choices, like I was spinning in circles without a place to land.

A good friend shared a secret with me: she had spent her entire adult life wearing shapers like Spanx under her clothing, every day for work, and extra tight ones for special occasions. It took off inches and hid all the bulges, she swore. Didn't I wear anything to smooth out the lumps for all my events?

No, I certainly did not.

She took me shopping and together we picked out some shaping tank tops and tummy-flattening underwear. I tried them on when we got home and immediately realized there was no way I could spend the day in this stuff. I was already always hot and huffy, now I felt like I could barely breathe. How was I supposed to travel in this? Sit, stand, eat in it? Greet hundreds of people with a smile and take pics when I felt like tearing my skin off along with the nylon tubes I was stuffed in?

I agreed to give them a shot just for the next day (they get more comfortable with time, my friend insisted), so before leaving for work the next morning, I squeezed back into a tank and industrial-strength panty. I stared at myself in the mirror. My rolls weren't smoothed over, they just relocated to other areas. A muffin top hung over the top of the underwear, skin and fat spilling out wherever it could find relief. Likewise, new rolls appeared on my back, above the top of the tank, displaced from their usual position.

I threw on the most comfortable clothes I could wear and headed out for my day, hoping I would miraculously become one with the shapers. The first few hours were torment, and I could barely concentrate on work. My face glistened, sweaty and hot, from the constriction. I decided I would take them off at lunchtime, but then, suddenly, I started breathing easier. I sat back in my chair and thought, "Wow, she was right, you *do* get used to it."

The rest of the day I was back to business, mighty pleased with myself that I had conquered the shapers. When I got home and took off my blouse, though, it was apparent why they had become so tolerable. The tank top had rolled all the way up, stopping just under my bra. My stomach and waist had been scot-free all afternoon. They could not be contained, I decided. I never wore the shapers again. But I still needed a plan.

I thought back to when Shaun T had finished the two plump, brown gulab jamun in his bowl. He had then taken two more. He was the most sculpted, perfectly formed human being I'd ever seen in real life. There wasn't an extra ounce of fat on him, and I'd seen enough videos to know what his muscles looked like under his clothes. How could he eat like that?

And it wasn't just the gulab jamun. He had never tried Pakistani food before, and that night he ate very, very well. I noticed, not only because I wondered how a fitness guru eats, but also because I can't help but watch to see if guests like my cooking. He seemed to love it. He didn't fill his plate with salad or skip over the rice and naan. He hated salad, he told me, as he licked gulab jamun syrup from the back of a spoon.

"It's eighty/twenty. I eat eighty percent clean and twenty percent whatever I want, but salad? No thank you. Whatever this thing is, though, I could eat it every day," Shaun said, and grinned.

I wondered what he thought about me and if I should ask him for weight-loss advice. I decided not to. I didn't want him to think I was trying to take advantage of his friendship. And he was nice enough not to offer any tips beyond telling me how he maintained his own fitness. I imagined him moving through the world and running into dumplings like me all the time, biting his tongue and telling himself to mind his own business.

I felt pretty confident that eating 80/20 wasn't going to do anything for me, at least if my past experience was any lesson. Every time in my life I lost weight, it took Herculean amounts of control over my food, there could be no cheat meals or cheat days, otherwise the needle didn't move. It took that plus unsustainable amounts of exercise, and frankly, at forty-one years of age, I didn't know if I could do it once again.

I was tired of being trapped on the perpetual hamster wheel of weight loss and gain. Every time I lost weight, the pounds came back, and they came back with friends. All the studies confirmed that this was the fate of most overweight people who struggled to lose weight. It was a battle that over 90 percent lost, consistently. That's because fat cells you grow in childhood apparently never go away, ever. You're stuck with them. The cells themselves can get bigger or smaller, but that number is fixed forever, meaning the odds are stacked against you if you were heavy as a child.

I huddled with friends who were on the same end of the pendulum as me, at the heaviest they'd ever been in their lives, too. Between us, we had lost and gained hundreds of pounds over our lifetimes, and down the road we could see that this cycle would never end. The more I thought about it, the more I saw that my chance of losing weight and keeping it off was piddling. And if that were the case, maybe . . . maybe surgery wasn't such a bad option?

I began floating the idea with my friends, to see their reaction. At first they recoiled and I completely understood why. A decade earlier, when I weighed considerably less, my younger sister had asked me why I didn't just get a gastric bypass. "I'm not heavy enough for that, you have to be *much more overweight* than me," I snapped at her. Her words stung and stayed with me for a long time. She was trying to tell me I *was that fat*, just to hurt me, I thought. Or because it was true.

Either way, now I was much heavier and, both sadly and gladly, a good candidate for gastric surgery. I learned there was a new, less extreme technique than the bypass, called a gastric sleeve. It was an outpatient surgery and had many fewer complications than the bypass. Now, it just all clicked. Yes, this was the path for me. I was going to get off the roller coaster, the hamster wheel, the perpetual motion machine, by completely disrupting it. I wasn't going to fight a losing battle anymore. I just simply didn't have it in me.

Around this time, a woman I met, who had reached out to help support Adnan, had recently gotten gastric surgery. I watched her melt away on Facebook, in photo after photo, and thought, *Amazing. No dieting, no exercise, it's just falling off.*

I managed to convince a couple of my friends that this was the way forward and we all decided we were just going to go for it.

My insurance would pay for the surgery, but only if I spent at least four months prior in a medically supervised weight-loss program. I refused to spend another four months, and thousands of dollars, on a program when I knew damn well that I would gain back whatever I lost. It was a patronizing prerequisite, as if those of us wanting, needing, weight-loss surgery hadn't already tried a hundred different things, hadn't ever struggled to do it on our own. I'd have to pay out of pocket, without insurance, and after trawling gastric surgery message boards night after night, I found a clinic that I could afford and that had a recovery center I could stay in afterward for a few days to recuperate.

Irfan, however, was dead against it. First, he argued, I didn't need it. I was beautiful as I was, he said.

Counterpoint: I can't buckle an airplane seatbelt.

I could do it on my own, he insisted. I had done it so many times before, and so had he. We could do this together! Don't give up, he told me.

Nothing about getting gastric surgery felt like giving up, however. It felt like the best choice, knowing the facts and data on weight loss, knowing the monumental efforts I'd made over the decades, knowing that science was offering me a solution if I wasn't too proud to take it.

I was reminded of both my pregnancies, when well-meaning mothers urged me to have natural deliveries and reject the meds and epidurals.

Some even went so far as to try and convince me with religion, citing the Prophetic tradition that every prayer of a mother in the pain of labor is answered.

I was pretty sure God didn't need me to experience every labor pain to answer my prayers, and I was equally sure God had a hand in the invention of the medicine that would in fact spare me those pains. I didn't want to feel every labor pain, so I welcomed the epidurals. In the same way, I no longer wanted to feel the incessant emotional pain of feeling like I had no control of my body, as well as the very real physical pain in my knees and back, which now strained under my weight.

I made the deposit for the surgery online, and two weeks later flew across the country to the clinic alone. Irfan knew, a few of my friends knew, but I told no one else. Not my daughters or my parents or my siblings, and I certainly didn't announce it online, like I did many other things. I knew the response from too many would be like Irfan's, that the surgery meant I was giving up. I didn't need to hear it, because I knew that I was instead, finally, taking control.

Early on the morning of the surgery, I was picked up, along with three other gastric sleeve patients from our hotel, and whisked off to the clinic in a minibus. We were excited and nervous, and also starving, since we hadn't been able to eat or drink anything for the past twelve hours, but today was going to be the day that changed the rest of our lives. In anticipation of the fact that, postsurgery, I could only have liquids for a few weeks, I had eaten ravenously in the days before we had to fast. I treated every meal like my last meal before execution, for a good dozen meals. This was explicitly against the advice we were given—to eat smaller portions, and eat clean, before the procedure—but I figured I'd have the rest of my life for that.

A few hours after checking in, getting weighed, and watching the anesthesiologist adjust my IV, I woke up fuzzy and disoriented, cajoled by a nurse calling my name.

"Ms. Chaudry, Ms. Chaudry, how are you doing, honey? Let's get up and see if you can stand yet."

I wobbled out of bed and onto my feet. I was groggy but alive, hallelujah. I leaned on the nurse and went for a short walk, then returned to my room, where she offered me some water.

"Sip it, slowly. Just a tiny sip."

I was so parched I wanted to guzzle it, but instead I took only a swallow and suddenly, immediately, I felt the cold liquid fill up my stomach and reach up into my throat.

"Too much, don't take so much," the nurse said.

Was my stomach now really so small that a bit of water would fill it up? Could I never gulp down a drink again, I wondered frantically?

Two days later I was home, and the following few weeks I alternated between mild and extreme regret. My stomach was indeed so small, it turned out, that it could only take a few tiny sips of liquid at a time. I felt physically full after a few mouthfuls of a smoothie, but mentally I ached with hunger. I experienced hunger the way I assume an amputee misses a phantom limb: not there, yet there still, persistent and unsatisfied.

I had read that gastric surgery patients often suffered emotional hunger from lack of satiation, but nothing could describe the actual experience of it. I truly felt like I was starving even when my stomach was unquestionably full. Starving while surrounded by food, most of which I couldn't eat because my new insides weren't ready to move on to solids yet. One night, as I cleared the dinner plates, I stared long and hard at a leftover shaami kabab. It sat, golden brown and plump, smelling of onions and cilantro and cumin.

My brain knew there was absolutely no way in the world I could eat the kabab. It wouldn't fit in the sleeve. But in that moment every intellectual faculty left the building and I shoved the kabab in my face, the entire thing, heart racing, breath heaving. I chewed fast, afraid someone would see me, and gulped it down, not even enjoying the flavors that I had missed for weeks.

I immediately felt like I had been punched in the stomach. The pain was instant and intense, because the masticated glob of kabab had nowhere to go. It came up as fast as I had tried to force it down. This was the first of many dozens, maybe hundreds, of times that I would vomit up my food after eating too fast, or too much.

I had wild mood swings, crying one moment out of anger at not being able to eat, happy the next that my knees hurt less already, and depressed the next, convinced I'd made a mistake undergoing an irreversible procedure. It took an inordinate amount of mental discipline to learn to nibble and not gobble. Before surgery, I was advised, by the doctor and every message board I read, not to drink at the same time as I ate—there would only be room for one or the other. I hadn't given it too much thought, not truly understanding that there wouldn't even be space for much water in my stomach. Water should just pass through, right?

Wrong. Very, very wrong. I didn't anticipate how bitter this issue would make me. I loved ice water, and I loved to chug it. I loved soda and juice, too, and I never ate a meal without a drink accompanying it. Did this mean I would never again savor the satisfaction of a cold draw of Coca-Cola after a mouthful of fries? I rebelled against this rule, and ate and drank at the same time, though in the smallest of bits. And I didn't rebel alone.

Not long after the surgery I met up at a movie theater with one of the friends who'd had the gastric sleeve procedure a week before me. We hadn't seen each other since, and both of us had already dropped over ten pounds. We were both in the phase where solid food was not yet recommended.

We bought sodas and popcorn and candy anyway and took tiny

bites, bites we hoped wouldn't perforate our newly stitched tummies, a risk that didn't prevent us from indulging. That moment defined the entire year following the surgery. I saw the pounds come off, a few every week, despite the fact that I didn't change my diet. Yes, I ate much less than what I could before, but I still ate complete crap.

I was lying to myself that since I could only eat petite portions, it could be petite portions of terrible foods, and I'd still lose weight. *What I ate* didn't matter so much anymore, I decided, since it was so limited anyway. I also found, strangely enough, that real food was much harder to get down my gullet than junk food. Starches like rice and bread, even homemade roti, turned into gluttonous blobs that stuck in the middle of my chest. Meat was impossible to digest, and fruits and vegetables had to be completely mashed to swallow.

Magically, potato chips and cookies gave me no trouble. I never, not once, vomited up the things I shouldn't have been eating in the first place. After a while I started avoiding real food altogether and stuck to the empty calories that were kindest to my new system.

Every night, just as had happened in college, and then again as I stayed up late studying for law school, and pretty much my whole life, the munchies hit me at almost exactly 10 p.m. The sleeve hadn't changed that. I could go without eating much of the day, but between 10 p.m. and 2 a.m., I roamed the pantry, made repeated rounds past the kitchen counters, bent over to find something in the back of the fridge to nosh on.

I had hoped to lose 70 or 80 pounds from the surgery, which was the weight loss estimated by my doctor before the procedure. But a year later I was only down 32 pounds, half of where I should have been at that point, and this most likely had everything to do with the fact that I didn't follow the recommended dietary plan at all.

At all.

There is, however, a possibility I would have lost more, but for the fact that my forty-two-year-old body sprung a surprise on me that I didn't see coming from any direction.

I got pregnant.

I HAD MY first child when I was twenty-two, my second when I was thirty-four, and my third baby at forty-three. I would be lying if I said I was full of excitement when I realized I was pregnant. For the first five months, I told no one other than my husband, and I forbade him from telling anyone, as well. The doctor suggested an obstetrician who specialized in geriatric pregnancies, pregnancies in which the mother is over thirty-five. I thought the label was ridiculous and sexist, given how commonly women were having children later in life, but I couldn't deny I felt too old to have another one.

I cried, because I didn't have the energy for this now, and because there had not been a single time in my adult life that I wasn't juggling small children and work, which meant no time for myself. I thought my forties were when, finally, I would have the time and freedom to make impromptu plans with friends, take bubble baths and go for hikes when I wanted, prioritize my health and my body, or just spend a day in bed reading if I felt like it.

I was also embarrassed. My eldest was nineteen, we all expected her to get married and make me a young grandmother in the next stage of my life; I did not expect to go through pregnancy, labor, diapers, breast-feeding, and the sheer exhaustion of a baby all over again myself. How mortifying was it going to be to tell her she was going to have a sibling twenty years younger than her? Though, to be fair, her father had gone on to remarry three more times after our divorce, each time with succes-sively younger women, having babies consistently as he headed toward fifty. I guess he won on the embarrassment front.

I lay in bed, night after night, remembering the searing physical and emotional pain I'd experienced breastfeeding my second and the long nights awake with her as she wailed with colic, and worrying about the tons of baby stuff we would have to buy because, of course, I had long ago given away what we had. Highchair, crib, carriers, bigger carriers, car seats, potty training seats, bibs, a million diapers.

I did the calculation. I would be doing elementary school projects well into my fifties.

It was a blessing that for much of the pregnancy I barely had time to think about it. We were buying a new house, I was still doing speaking engagements around the country about my book and Adnan's case, and I was in the middle of running a project for a think tank that required multiple trips to Pakistan and Sri Lanka. I made one of those trips at the beginning of my second trimester. I had been to Pakistan more frequently in the past few years but hadn't returned since the gastric sleeve. I spent most of the week at Dada Abu's old home, with Taya Abu's son, Rehman, and his full brood. His twin sons were now grown, and themselves married with children, all of them living together as God, and Pakistani culture, intended it. He had two daughters as well, the eldest of whom was married and living with her in-laws.

Their hospitality was, as always, incredible, every meal a spread despite my begging them not to go to the trouble. I didn't tell them I could barely eat because of the sleeve and because of horrendous pregnancy-induced acid reflux.

"Eat! Why aren't you eating?" My cousin's wife hovered over me as I dabbed small pieces of roti into the array of goat and chicken saalan and fried fish and chutneys on my plate. I wanted to eat, I desperately did, because it was absolutely delicious and I felt famished, but the food had nowhere to go. "Okay, you don't like this food? What do you like? What should I make instead? You look so good because you have obviously been dieting, I think you aren't eating this because of dieting!" she declared as the whole family looked at me, worried and earnest.

"No, no it's not that. Everything is so tasty, it's just too much food, please don't go to such trouble every single day," I pleaded. "I will eat anything I swear, I'm not dieting, I just have some heartburn right now."

"Well, you look very, very good, but keep going, don't stop dieting now! Just maybe lose twenty more kilograms and then you'll be perfect!"

I nodded silently, not telling them I wouldn't be thinking about dieting or weight loss for another six months at least. I still wasn't ready to reveal the pregnancy to anyone.

At five months I learned we were having a boy, which only increased my anxiety. Girls I was an old pro at, and after the first year or so both my daughters were sweet and easy to manage. But boys terrified me. My friends with boys, no matter their age, seemed perpetually exhausted, and anytime I saw boys playing together it was chaotic. Wrestling, sword fighting, jumping off furniture. My daughters, on the other hand, would have a group of girlfriends over and play so quietly I would forget they were there.

I also had an aversion to boys because so many of the male relatives in my own family were not good to their families. Girls grew up and cared for family. They gave back, while too many of the men I was related to mostly just took and took. All the violence in the world, I connected to men. Cheating, domestic violence, rape, war, all of it. How would I raise one to be good, kind, and gentle and loving?

Existential fears aside, there was also the very real frustration at having taken a step as drastic as gastric sleeve surgery only to be thwarted by this pregnancy. I had finally seen the light at the end of the weight-loss tunnel, and now I was going to be run over by a steam engine barreling back through the tunnel at me. I wagged my finger at the heavens. This was not cool, God, this was not cool.

When I hit month six, and was starting to show, I finally told everyone. My sister was overjoyed, my father surprised, my daughters had trouble believing it, but I have to hand it to Ami for reacting in a way I never saw coming, and yet completely on brand.

"That's good," she nodded, "you need a son to shoulder your funeral procession one day."

I hadn't thought of that but thanks, Mom.

As my tummy grew, life became even more hectic because HBO was making a documentary series based on my book, and the production was underway. Amy Berg, an Oscar-nominated director who had already created an incredible investigative documentary about the notorious West Memphis Three wrongful convictions, was tapped for the project. Her team had begun popping up every so often at my house to take footage, which filled me with more trepidation than all my pictures floating around on social media.

It would have been bad enough had the camera crew just followed me around videotaping. But Amy also needed dozens of B-roll takes, which required me to stare longingly out of windows, or carefully adjust my scarf in a mirror, or get out of my car and walk into the house three or four times until they had it right.

I knew they were there to work, but I had nowhere to stow my natural aunty inclinations, so every time they came, I had a pot of chai brewing and a table laid out with biscuits and nuts and chai-appropriate snacks. They *loved* the chai. Every camera- and sound-person who rotated through the crew had chai with me, and Amy was ready for her chai the minute she stepped in the house. They taped me making and serving chai multiple times.

The chai-making wasn't just to be hospitable; it also helped calm my nerves. I was cringing, anguished, on the inside every time the film crew showed up. I took deep breaths and I tried to focus on the purpose of it all—to help exonerate Adnan. I tried to push away needling thoughts of how I would look across high-definition screens everywhere, broadcast on the biggest premier network in existence, but it was hard when there were already trolls online circulating the worst pictures of me imaginable, making fun of how I looked. When you're a female public personality and people don't like your ideas, it's often your looks that get targeted, low-hanging fruit for the trolls.

When I hit my third trimester and was really showing, I discovered two old wives' tales to be completely accurate. First, I'd always been told that mothers gain more weight when carrying girls and that baby girls sit low and broad in their mother's womb. Boys, it was said, ride narrow and high, and don't pile the pounds on their mothers as much. With both of my daughters, I looked like I was having twins by the time of my due date, that was how broad my tummy expanded and how much weight I gained. This time, my stomach was indeed narrower and higher, and I only gained twenty pounds. That was further surprising, because the second old wives' tale also was on point for me: Mothers pregnant with girls crave tart, while mothers carrying boys, they say, crave sweets.

I am not a baker. It isn't just that desserts are not my weakness, it's that they are also kind of a pain to make. Cooking is easy. A sprinkle of this, a dash of that, change things up as needed. But desserts, especially baked ones, require measuring and proportions and proper ingredient temperatures. It's art versus science. Get something wrong in a dessert recipe, and it just doesn't turn out right. You get cakes that are too crumbly, or brownies that are too hard, or cheesecake that won't set.

Pakistani desserts required so many steps that I refused to even try. Hours of stirring pots of thickening milk or caramelizing halwa, cooking separate syrups, making and hanging homemade cheese curds overnight, deep-frying doughs and batters. It wasn't that I couldn't make them, I just didn't want them badly enough to want to.

But when I hit those last few months of pregnancy, the sweet tooth I had always been missing sprouted from nowhere and I craved sugar all day, and in the middle of the nights. I didn't want just any kind of sweets though, not candy or cookies or even pie or cake. I specifically wanted Pakistani desserts.

I wanted gulab jamun, kalakand, jalebi, kheer, gajar halwa, falooda, ras gulla. I wanted mithai, the confections my mother swore drove her own father into an early grave. I wanted them injected directly into my bloodstream. I couldn't get enough.

Some nights I couldn't sleep, I so badly wanted falooda, a dessert I'm almost afraid to explain to the uninitiated, because of how odd it sounds. Usually served individually in tall sundae glasses, falooda is part drink, part dessert, made with layers of kulfi ice cream, noodles, basil seeds, jello, and ruh afza, a fragrant, sweet syrup made from fruits, flowers, and herbs. If you've never slurped sweet noodles through a straw, don't knock it till you've tried it.

I developed a craving for falooda once a week, but also for barfi, a thickened milk fudge, which I discovered I could eat by the pound, all day, every day. I'll never forget the harsh lesson I learned as a child the first time I took barfi to school in my lunch. There was no explaining what I was eating after telling kids the chewy, melty little square in my hand was called barfi.

"BARFeeeeeee!! Ew I'm going to BARF!"

I should have seen that coming.

Almond barfi, cashew barfi, pistachio barfi—as my pregnancy progressed, I ate cube after cube of the fatty, rich, creamy stuff, which Irfan dutifully hauled home week after week. I still wasn't hungry for real food, and also couldn't eat much of it anyway, so at least 90 percent of calories that grew my son those last few gestational months came from barfi.

My surprise baby was born in March of 2017, and he came a couple of weeks early, smaller than he should have been, but his labor took longer than my two girls combined. Every time I pushed, his heart rate dropped, and I would have to stop. It took nearly two days of trying and stopping, trying and stopping, before we both were finally freed from that terrifying dance.

He was perfect, and I again fell completely and immediately in love. He was the first child I had who looked just like me. My girls both looked like their fathers. But this little man, this baby-man, his ears, nose, eyes, even the shape of his head were my spitting image, and I've always looked just like Abu. And so his middle name would be my father's name, and I hoped and prayed that he would turn out like my father, one of the good ones.

Throughout my pregnancy I refused to believe in the fabled special connection between mamas and boys, hating the male privilege in Punjabi culture and, well, everywhere. Within weeks of his coming into my life, though, I became the Punjabi mother who looked at him and murmured, "Raaj dulara, jaan say pyara, maa sadqay, meda chotu gabbru jawaan." My little prince, dearer than my life, my life be sacrificed, my tiny strong little man.

Positively nauseating, I know.

On both sides of the American–Canadian border, the grandparents ordered hundreds of laddus to distribute to family and friends, celebrating the birth of this miracle grandson of a geriatric pregnancy. My father-in-law had boxes and boxes delivered to our home, and I was reminded of my mother's laddu-making marathon thirty years prior, when our townhouse in Chambersburg smelled of cardamom syrup for months. All these years later, I understood the obsession.

My weight after delivery went right back to what it was before delivery, a small mercy given how much sugar I'd consumed for the past few months. It was 198 pounds, and for the next year, it stayed. My sleeve had quit her job, given up the ghost. The needle wouldn't budge.

I followed the journey of another woman online who had gastric surgery around the same time and watched her daily uploads on Facebook and Instagram from the gym, head tied in a bandana, looking strong and fierce in her leggings. I reached out to her to ask how she was doing it. Simple. She worked out every day, ate the high-protein, low-carb diet that was recommended, and with the help of the surgery was headed toward a hundred-pound weight loss.

I thought once I got the sleeve, I wouldn't actually have to work to lose weight anymore. If I still had to control my diet and exercise, what was the damn point of it all? The point, she patiently explained to me, is that the sleeve was just a tool to help weight loss, not the magic pill for weight loss itself. If I wasn't careful, I could even expand the sleeve and then gain back the thirty-odd pounds I'd lost.

"Drink lots of water and start every meal with protein and salad. Trick yourself into thinking you'll get pasta or rice after you finish it. You'll be so full because of the sleeve you won't be able to eat the carbs."

Maybe, I thought to myself. But I could definitely still eat dessert. No matter how full I was, I could still eat dessert. Was there a second stomach somewhere, an overflow room for sweets? Because it definitely felt like it.

The friends who had gotten the sleeve along with me were experiencing similar plateaus, but both had lost twice the weight I'd lost, though they had started off at a higher weight than me as well. Maybe my sleeve wasn't working, I worried. Maybe I'd stretched it already, or the doctor didn't make it small enough.

Reset the sleeve, the internet advised. A three-day liquid diet would shrink the sleeve back to its original size and I'd again start shedding pounds. After a day of liquids only, I caved. I hadn't exercised any dietary discipline in years, *years*, and it was a muscle that was now pretty much dead. The self-loathing I felt at this point was some of the worst of my life. I thought I was taking control by getting the sleeve. I underwent an irreversible surgery to forever alter how I ate, and still failed. The sleeve didn't fail me, I failed it. All I had to do was follow the guidelines, but I didn't. I was over two years out from the surgery and still stuck a good fifty pounds from my goal weight, from the weight that was deemed "almost" acceptable for a five-foot, four-inch frame.

It was the fall of 2018, I had a sweet, energetic toddler running circles around me at home, and the HBO series had been in production for over two years. It would air in the spring of 2019, and that meant premiere events, in LA, in New York, in London. Events with media, interviews I'd have to sit for, photo shoots the producers expected. Two years earlier, Adnan's conviction had been overturned, but the State of Maryland kept appealing it to higher courts. A second court overturned it again, and the State appealed once more. Now we were in a holding pattern waiting to see what the highest court in Maryland would do.

If everything went the way we believed it would, the way I dreamt it, the HBO series would come out around the same time Adnan was finally released from prison. It would be a lot to celebrate, and I wanted to feel like celebrating when it happened.

That's when I met comedian Mona Aburmishan at, of all places, a conference in a creaky old castle in Switzerland. If there's one thing I've learned, it's that no matter how idyllic a conference setting, conference food is starchy and tasteless the world over. Mona was there to perform one evening, and during the performance she shared the story of how she lost 150 pounds. She was flitting around in a completely unforgiving silk jumpsuit that would ordinarily enhance every extra fold of skin or fat. But she didn't have any. She didn't look like she'd been heavy a day in her life.

Trainers, she said. She had hired a personal trainer and it changed her life. I had never used a personal trainer, ever, because I knew they didn't come cheap and I didn't see what added benefit could come from paying someone to do what I already knew how to do—work out. At this point though, given Mona's results and my lack of options, I decided to give it a try. I called around locally and found Compel Fitness, a personal training program that rented and ran a space right inside the local gym, a gym with childcare, which sealed the deal. I signed up for an evaluation and went in a few days later, desperately not wanting to get weighed and measured.

An incredibly fit young woman greeted me with a big smile and asked me why I decided to join up.

"I . . . am an executive producer on this documentary and have a number of big premiere events coming up in six months and I need to lose at least forty pounds." I decided to skip the other forty years of my weight-loss history and struggles, so the conversation didn't turn into a therapy session.

"Okay, that's completely doable," she said, "first let's get these numbers out of the way."

She pulled out a tape measure and a fat-measuring doodad. I sighed and stood up, staring off into space as she wrapped the tape around my thighs, arms, neck, waist, and hips. I held the fat-measuring meter ("body composition monitor," she corrected me) at arm's length, and it reported that I was 39 percent fat. This may as well have been 40 percent, which wasn't far from 50 percent. Nearly *half my body* was fat.

I removed my shoes and got weighed, and thankfully weighed the same as I had that morning at home. After she entered every numerical measure for my body possible into a computer program, she said, "Tell me about your exercise history."

I explained I'd exercised on and off in my life, never consistently. I spent a few months doing CrossFit, I told her, didn't amount to much. And long ago, I used to run as much as five miles a day.

"How well did running work for you?" she asked.

"Uh. I enjoyed it, but I guess not great. I was eating healthy, running, doing stairs, jumping rope, but the weight loss was pretty slow and hard, and then it stopped."

She leaned forward in her seat. "No more running for you. No stairs. No jumping rope. Really, we aren't going to spend much time on cardio. But if you do what we tell you, you'll lose forty pounds a lot sooner than you think."

She printed out a sheet with some nutritional guidelines that seemed . . . reasonable. I could eat carbs, but complex ones, and only before 3 p.m. I needed to prioritize water, protein, and fiber in my diet, I could snack on cheese and nuts and fruit, no processed food, and once a week I could have a cheat meal.

"These are guidelines. You can create your own meals around them with the kinds of foods you love, and I promise you won't feel hungry or deprived." Then she walked me around the corner to a mirrored room where two perfectly sculpted young men were yelling "HOLD THAT POSE" at a group of sweaty, red victims on the floor. They sat in a circle, their legs lifted off the ground, holding their bodies in a V shape, arms extended. I had apparently interrupted a medieval torture session.

One by one they gave up, until a victor emerged. I could have sworn she was the eldest of the group, at least in her sixties, but clearly had the muscles of a twenty-year-old sprinter. Then I was introduced to the two trainers, Darius and Eric, and talked with them briefly about what I wanted to achieve.

"What is your dream physique? If you could have a body like anyone, who would it be?" asked Darius.

I stopped for a beat and then spit out, "Beyoncé."

Eric snorted. Darius smiled and looked at me kindly, as if he was about to break some devastating news.

"Okay, well, we are going to work our hardest to get you to your goals. As long as you promise to work your hardest, too. Six days a week is what we are asking of you."

Yes, I nodded, I will, I will, I will.

"Good, see you tomorrow."

THE ONLY WAY this would all work, given the schedule I was already juggling, was if I organized my day around my workouts. Thankfully, there was an app for that. I could plan my training sessions and group classes, three of each a week. Every Sunday I booked my classes and then worked my days around them.

When I began I had the muscle tone of processed cheese. But it didn't take long, just a few weeks really, to be able to do more pushups, squats, and lunges than I thought possible, and I could hold a plank longer and longer each week. The dreaded burpee returned to my life, but I turned off my mind and did whatever they told me, like a programmed robot. In fact, I spent most of the workouts like that—brain shut off, plugged into a podcast, no anguished thoughts of not wanting to be there, no letting excuses fester. Maybe it was the amount I was paying for the sessions that motivated me, or my semi-failed sleeve surgery, but day after day I showed up on time, spent nearly an hour busting my ass, and rarely complained. Which was highly unlike me.

By the end of the first month, I looked forward to my workouts every day, to the burst of adrenaline that left me elated and the fifteen minutes in the steam room afterward that left me even further drenched. Even though most days I took my two younger ones along with me and they hung out in childcare while I exercised, it still felt like *me time.* The only time in my entire day that what I was doing was *only for me.* I hadn't had this kind of luxury since my single-mother weekends, when my eldest was with her father and I had breaks that felt like a gift.

No one puts you first, it finally hit me. You have to put yourself first. No one will carve out time for your self-care. You have to do that. Everyone else will figure it out.

If the family got dinner a little late or early, they'd be fine. If the kids had to entertain themselves for thirty minutes a few times a week because I was finally soaking in the tub with jets that is literally in my bathroom yet had gone unused for years, they'd be fine. If I wanted to spend ten extra minutes in the sauna at the gym, they would survive ten more minutes of playing with other children in the childcare area.

Nearly every week Abu visited us—okay, actually he visited the baby, his namesake, his Mini-Me—and saw me transform before his eyes. "Beta, daughter, what are you doing at the gym every day? Can I go with you to watch?"

Abu tagged along a few times and watched from a seat in the corner as people of all ages ran around him, jumped, heaved, pumped, and worked their butts off. He had never been to a gym before, certainly never joined one, and now, at seventy-seven, felt inspired to give it a shot.

Some of his senior friends went to the gym, he said. He would ask them to take him, too. A few weeks later I swung by my parents' house as he was returning from the gym, wearing dress pants, button-down shirt, suit vest, and sneakers. He reported that he was going to the gym a few times a week now, doing some light rowing and weights, and feeling stronger. I looked him up and down and asked what he wore to work out.

"This is what I wear. What's the problem, I have sneakers on." Given he had only ever mowed the lawn and painted the deck and put up drywall in dress pants and a button-down, I should have expected it. The next day I went and bought him some jogging pants and long-sleeved T-shirts, since he didn't own a single T-shirt, long- or short-sleeved. He never had in his entire life.

I was excited to have influenced Abu, remembering the toe touches he advised me on decades earlier. The student had become the master, I giggled to myself. The truth is, both of us were surprised at what our bodies were capable of at our ages. The stronger I got, the better I felt. The better I felt, the better I ate. The better I ate, again the better I felt.

And for the first time in a lifetime of trying to lose weight, my focus shifted to wanting to be *fit*. I wanted to do what I saw other people in the gym doing with their bodies, things that I thought I could never do.

Then one weekend Eric told me I could. "Your first set," he said, "is box jumps and tire flips."

Oh no, I thought. I couldn't handle either. I would break my knees and my ankles, all in one go, if I tried to jump onto the boxes he pointed at. And I had seen grown men, whose muscles had muscles, grunt when they worked with the tire that Eric thought I could flip.

Eric stacked up two boxes until they reached about as high as the top of my thighs. Thighs that were considerably more toned than six weeks before, but still not thighs that could jump that high.

"I can't do it, Eric. I know my body. I have bad knees and my ankles twist really easily."

"Has a doctor told you not to jump?"

"Ah, well no, I haven't been told . . ."

"Then get your ass over here, because you are doing this."

Eric turned around and addressed a few other women in our corner of the gym.

"Ladies, Rabia doesn't think she can do this. I know she can do this because I've been training her for weeks and I know she's stronger than she thinks she is. So let's all watch Rabia do what she thinks she can't."

I wanted to punch Eric.

A handful of women gathered around the box and began offering encouragement. Eric reached out to me. "Come on now, hold my hand, Rabia. Focus on the spot on the box where you want both feet to land. Plant your feet shoulder-width apart, squat, and then leap like a spring."

I was going to be humiliated. I was going to face-plant on the top of the boxes in front of an actual audience. I might break my teeth. I hoped that would satisfy Eric.

I took Eric's hand, stared at the top of the box, squatted, then stood back up. Squatted, then stood back up.

"Okay, no I'll do it this time. Promise." I steadied my feet, squatted, and sprang with all the force I could muster. I landed on the box, clean and hard, on both feet, knees still bent.

I stood up and looked down, amazed, as Eric and the others clapped.

"See? I *told you* you could do it," Eric guffawed.

After that, when he told me I could absolutely flip the three-hundred-pound tire by simply using my legs for leverage, I believed him. And I flipped it. Eric pushed me and pushed me to use heavier weights, pick up bigger kettlebells, jump higher, hold a plank longer. This, I realized, was the value of a trainer, and I felt lucky to be able to afford one.

Soon, even when I worked out alone, I pushed myself, because you simply don't know what you can do until you actually try it. More reps, an extra set, a thicker resistance band, small incremental increases in the intensity of my workouts, were literally changing my body faster than any other exercise regimen in my entire life. Of course, I was eating pretty clean, but I remembered back years ago when I was calorie-restricting along with running five miles, climbing forty-two flights of stairs, and jumping rope every night and still didn't see results like I was getting with forty-five minutes of resistance training a day. The secret to this program was building muscle through circuit and interval training. Build muscle, which burns fat and burns calories, and leans you out.

I steadily lost two to three pounds a week, amounting to an average of ten pounds a month. At the end of four months, I had lost nearly forty pounds.

I could not believe it. I had never lost this amount of weight before, ever. Not on any soul-crushing diet, not while running miles and miles a day, not even with the sleeve. And none of the work, and yes it took work, felt like drudgery. My eating habits had aligned with less effort than I could have imagined, to support the workouts. I wanted to kick ass in the gym, so I ate the things I knew would help my body do so—protein smoothies and nuts and eggs and tons of fruit and salads. I still nibbled on sweets and chips once in a while, had a couple spoons of ice cream or a piece of naan when the craving hit, so I didn't actually feel deprived.

I discovered small joys that I had completely excised from my life. One weekend, as I sauntered with friends through an area full of clothing boutiques and jewelry shops, they stooped to peek into windows, pointing at different pieces. My hand suddenly went to my throat. I wanted a necklace.

Except at my weddings, I hadn't worn a necklace my entire adult life. Ami's rule about not calling attention to your problem areas had taken root in my psyche, and I fastidiously avoided anything that would make my heavy parts even more noticeable. The day a teenage me wore a choker and Ami told me it made my neck look fat was the last day I wore anything around my neck. Now I froze in the street when I realized that I hadn't allowed myself the simple pleasure of a necklace, ever.

I made it my mission to find a simple gold chain that I would keep on at all times, an affirmation that I deserved to wear what I wanted, what I found appealing. Irfan bought me the chain, slender and delicate, and it has been around my pleasantly soft neck ever since.

As the weeks went by, I posted pictures of my progress online. People were as surprised as I was, watching my body morph in real time. I hadn't, however, ever publicly divulged that I'd gotten the gastric sleeve. While a part of me felt a bit duplicitous about that, I wasn't emotionally ready to share it. I still hadn't told friends outside a handful, or any family other than my husband. Besides, I rationalized, I couldn't credit the sleeve for these forty pounds lost. It took six days a week in the gym and better eating habits to get to this point. That experience changed a lot about what I had believed for years—that after a certain age, the body just couldn't change, that I couldn't be physically strong at forty-five with three kids, that I lacked the discipline to follow through on such a regimen, and that the work was a punishment instead of being a gift to myself, from me.

Ami wasn't so sure the changes she saw were a result of my own efforts, though. She was convinced something was very wrong with me and I wasn't telling her. Every time I saw her over the course of those first few months, she stopped me and carefully looked me over. "Do you have cancer?" she asked seriously.

The first time she asked me, I thought I'd heard her wrong. The fifth or sixth time, not so much.

Each time, I took a deep breath before reiterating, "No. I do not have cancer. I told you, I joined a personal training program and have been working out almost every day. I'm finally losing weight, I'm finally how you wanted me *my entire life*."

"Stop. That's enough. No more weight loss, you are starting to look sick. So sick."

Most others were thrilled and supportive, of course, but there was a negative reaction on social media that surprised me. It existed on two levels, though they were basically the same thing: why was I advocating weight loss? The less aggressive of these reactions was something like, "I'm so happy you feel great, but you were always lovely and didn't need to lose weight, and everyone should feel wonderful and love themselves as they are."

Okay, fine. Maybe everyone should. But not everyone does. It feels as oppressive to me when someone insists I feel good about myself as I am as it has felt in the past when others insisted I feel *bad* about myself as I am. Don't make me feel terrible now, yet another failure, for not being able to feel great no matter what. Every person, I'd argue, has the right to pursue what feeling good means to them.

Then there were the other, less gentle, admonitions: "Why are you undermining body positivity and making others feel bad about themselves? As a public figure you should support fat positivity instead of further demonizing fat people. You've internalized fat hatred."

This one stumped me. As a lifelong fat person, disparaging overweight people wasn't ever my intention, but was my desire to share my weight-loss progress in and of itself a demonization of those who didn't? I didn't think so, but these were untested grounds for me. I did a little digging into the world of fat advocacy and the body positivity movement and came away impressed. Impressed in the same way I am with anyone who has achieved contentment in their life, that thing that some even call nirvana.

I took the question of whether I'd internalized fat hatred to my friends and to my therapist. There's no doubt that self-loathing was real, in many moments in my life and in the lives of most of my friends who found themselves struggling to lose weight. But when I dug deeper, I realized the self-loathing was less about what I looked like on the outside, and more about feeling out of control and helpless.

Being in control, regardless of what the scale said, was what made me finally, now, content with myself. The truth was, I still wasn't close to what anyone would call skinny. My weight hovered around 160 pounds, which was still a good 30 to 40 pounds heavier than what the BMI calculator told me I should weigh. I was still in the "overweight" category according to it, but I was fitting into small and medium tops and size 8 pants. That's when I realized the BMI calculator could fuck right off. It didn't account for muscle weight, bone density, genetics, physical fitness, or even general health. The BMI calculator is a complete lie, and complete trash.

And in many ways, so is the scale. All you have to do is google images of people at any given weight. You'll see how the same exact weight looks different on everyone, even people of the same height. Yes, that number tells you something. But it doesn't tell you everything.

•••

AS THE DATE for the documentary launch approached, the premiere events began. New York was first. I wore a snug-fitting dress with a blazer, leggings, and high boots, and thought, Okay, I can face a camera in this. I was ready for the media, but not so ready to watch the first episode in a theater full of strangers.

I knew the story, had been living it for decades, but seeing these first episodes was like being stripped raw to the bone. Reliving the story is trauma and watching myself on a ten-foot screen when I was fifty pounds heavier was also trauma. It threw me off emotionally, and there was a part of me that was afraid to watch the rest of the episodes when they aired on HBO.

Two days before they did, though, we all got the wind knocked out of us. The highest court in Maryland granted the State's appeal and reinstated Adnan's conviction. The panel of seven judges ruled four to three against us. Adnan would not be getting a new trial, and he certainly wouldn't be coming home this year.

The blow was heavy. I knew we had to regroup and strategize our next legal moves, organize new appeals that could take years and years more, but more than anything I knew I had to be kind to myself. I had finally learned that. I knew if that required time off, time away from it all, that was okay. In the long run, winning meant simply not giving up. Not giving up on Adnan. Not giving up on myself.

I couldn't bring myself to work out or stay away from barfi in the days following the ruling, but that was okay, too. I didn't feel like I was spinning anymore. I knew, finally, after four decades, what my body responded to and what it needed. It needed my time, my attention, and my love.

And I needed my body's forgiveness for never recognizing these things before.

I watched the remainder of the three episodes of the documentary with my family, including the chubby little boy who looked just like me, on the following Sunday evenings. I made myself a steaming mug of chai before settling in, and I monitored the chatter on social media as people talked about the series in real time. They raged against the State of Maryland, hated on the prosecutor, were astonished by the new evidence, were surprised to see the new baby in our selfies, adored Adnan, cheered me and his legal team on, and promised to keep following the story until Adnan was finally free.

But the most overwhelming reaction, after seeing the footage of me standing in my kitchen above a gently bubbling pot, was dozens and dozens of people tweeting me the same question: What's your recipe for chai?

EPILOGUE: GOAL WEIGHT

I come to you live, ensconced in a faja. I have been wearing one for over a month and will be in it for a few more. If you don't know what a faja is, I pray you never need to find out. A faja is what the Colombians created when they looked at shapewear and thought, how can we make this more painful?

A faja is an incredibly high-compression garment used by some to look more shapely and by others, like me right now, to reduce inflammation after plastic surgery. It took two nurses to squeeze me into this one as I leaned on my hands, braced against a wall.

After over a year with Eric and Darius at Compel Fitness, I had hit a stumbling block. One that was attached to my body. My lower tummy, the FUPA I'd nourished for years, had essentially . . . deflated. I was seventy pounds lighter than I had been at my heaviest, but now had a sack of empty skin hanging above my pelvis.

It flapped *thwack thwack thwack* between my abdomen and thighs when I did mountain climbers, made an embarrassing slapping sound when I jumped on a box, and generally stood apart from the rest of my much-better-toned body like an alien growth.

"Eric, what do I *do* about this thing?" I held the pouch in my hands, squishing it sadly.

Eric gave me a knowing look.

"It's hard to get skin to bounce back with big weight loss. And harder when you're . . . older."

I nodded, acknowledging I was not a spring chicken.

"You can't really 'work off' skin. The only option might be a tummy tuck." He shrugged.

No, I thought. That can't be right. But then I asked Darius. He agreed. And I reached back out to Mona, the comedian. She said, *Of course* massive weight loss requires surgery to remove skin.

I spent another six months thinking about it, and a million crunches later decided they were right. This was not something I could exercise away. I visited three plastic surgeons for consultations and to further convince myself to do it. The first one held up my FUPA and let it fall. *Thwack*, it sounded against my groin. Then he did the same with my breasts.

"Look, I've breastfed three kids over the span of twenty years, don't judge them," I told him. And he told me he could make my tummy and boobs look like I was twenty again and I thought, *I definitely don't want that*. Then he tried to convince me I needed a chin implant, too, so I knew he was not the one.

The second one advised me to get a tummy tuck and breast reduction. "Ideally you want them to fit in a champagne glass," he said. Nope, not him.

The third surgeon asked me what I wanted, and when I told him, said, "Let's do it." He was the right one.

To ensure that I wouldn't back out, I told a few friends about my decision, and one of them asked, "Are you okay with having that line across your pelvis forever?"

"You mean the part of my body no one can see, where the sun don't shine because it's covered by a skin pouch? Yeah, I'm fine with it," I responded.

A tummy tuck will leave you feeling like a truck ran you down, backed up, and then drove over your midsection one more time to ensure maximum pain and swelling. Like being tied down and kicked in the midriff by a team of angry donkeys. Like stretching will split you right in two. The doctor showed me a picture of the skin sack he removed, almost *nine pounds of skin*, sitting by its lonesome in a surgical tray. I felt almost wistful about losing it, we had been together so long.

I've taken actions in the past few years to reach my goal weight that I never thought I would, and I still have moments of regret about the sleeve, especially when sitting in front of an incredible meal that I wish I could gobble up. My eyes remain bigger than my stomach. Irfan, who still constantly struggles with his weight, though he looks absolutely perfect to me, sees my predicament and says no, he would never consign himself to such a fate. Not worth it.

I could have done it all with just discipline and exercise, he still believes. Maybe I could have, but how do I know for sure that personal training alone would have gotten me here without the sleeve? And where is *here*? I still don't love my body, I'm not happy with it, just as most people aren't perfectly happy with their bodies. I don't have a single friend, of any size or shape, who is content with her body. Most of the men I know aren't, either. Almost everyone wants to eat a little better, work out more, take up hiking, lose a few inches, lower their blood sugar, build stamina. As far as I'm concerned, there's nothing wrong with that. It's no less normal than having career goals or wanting progress and success in any other area of your life. (I won't get into the caveats about food disorders and body dysmorphia, because I hope it's clear that these are diseases that need treatment, and not lifestyle choices to improve your quality of life.)

So, yes, it's normal not to love your body. It is also healthy not to hate your body, and for me it is a big relief, finally, to not hate mine. It took a journey of decades, and some years of therapy and introspection, to get to a place where I don't feel defeated by my body, where it's no longer my enemy. Which I was always told it was. I was told it was the enemy of my dreams, my prospects, my happiness. That it masked who I really was, didn't allow me to shine, was a big, ugly fat suit that hid the real me from the world.

In truth, though, the misery I've felt around my weight as an adult was less about how I looked than it was about how helpless it made me feel. I swung between food deprivation and food depravity, miserable on both ends of that pendulum, feeling out of control, crushed by not being able to just get my shit under control. I have been able to manage most of my life. When I put my mind to something, I did it. Over and over again I accomplished things I never imagined, but this issue kept me defeated.

That is the feeling that I've now finally shaken.

It turns out my body was never the enemy. It has been waiting for me to treat it with patience, and attention, and kindness. It has been waiting for me to learn what nourishes it, and what it can achieve. We are friends now, my body and I. I know what she needs and what she wants.

Sometimes, she just wants mutton pulao and a cold Coke. And she will get them.

I will never deprive myself of the joy of food, especially of good, wholesome, home-cooked Pakistani food, where I am the master of every ingredient, where the dishes flood me with memories of places I love and loved ones I've lost. I drink a lot of water, I can even guzzle it again, and I don't drink as much juice or soda as I used to, but there will never be a time in my life I don't have a cup of chai with whole milk and real sugar. It is a daily gift I give to myself, along with a zeera biscuit, crumbly and dotted with cumin, sweet and salty, perfect for soaking up chai.

I've put back on ten pounds in the past year, and Ami no longer thinks I have cancer but also is no longer urging me to lose weight, which means maybe I'm in the sweet spot. She is, however, highly concerned that my hair is thinning, a sure sign of early menopause, she says.

Abu stopped working out after a few months, having decided that, at his age, he had done enough.

I think I've done enough, too. No more depravity and no more deprivation. I've spent years of my life wildly gluttonous, and other years not touching rice or bread. I've taken Shaun T's 80/20 advice to heart now, because you simply can't sustain any extreme. And because I deserve the joy of food, and I also deserve not to harm myself with it.

I will be back in the gym when I get out of this faja. I miss the exhilaration of sweating and huffing and feeling powerful. I've lived with a mythical goal weight in my head for thirty years, a magical number that I thought I had to reach to be happy, fulfilled, successful, accepted. I don't have a goal weight anymore. I have goals for taking care of myself, for the time, energy, and love I invest in myself, whatever the results may be. But I am and will likely remain, by the standards of many, fat.

But that's okay, because I'm not *that fat*.

RECIPES

ABOUT THE RECIPES

In this book, I write about Pakistani food, not Indian food. True, plenty of the cuisines of India and Pakistan overlap. But many don't. You won't find dosa and idli in a Pakistani restaurant, and you are unlikely to find nihari and goat karhai and haleem in an Indian one. Believe me, we Pakistanis know that our cuisine is much less known than Indian cuisine. I hope to help change that with this book.

My disclaimer: To be absolutely as specific as possible and to avoid offending anyone, I'm writing about the Pakistani food *I grew up eating* and that I now cook, which, given regional and familial differences and preferences, could be totally different from the food other Pakistanis eat in their homes. The way I cook the dishes I love is simply the way I have been taught or have learned through trial and error on my own. My recipes and techniques aren't the only way, or even the best way. They're just the way I do it, the way I like it. The last thing I want is a flood of messages from readers telling me your grandmother didn't make pakoray the way I make them. God bless all your grandmothers, I'm sure their pakoray are delicious and perfect.

So why recipes, even some rich ones, in a book in which I've written pages and pages about struggling with weight? First, because everyone has to eat, yes, even fat people. Because, as my story shows, so many of the best memories of my family revolve around food. Because I was loved as a child through food, and because my parents and I discovered America through her food.

Most important, however, it's because I have learned to center home-cooked, Pakistani food in my adult life as I've found balance in my approach to eating. There is a widespread misconception that South Asian dishes are unhealthy, and that's because what is served in restaurants has been changed to suit American palettes and also because they're what you could call "special occasion" dishes. The dishes are often rich and heavy, full of oil and cream, not the kind of food you can eat every day. At home we cook with fresh, whole ingredients, temper the addition of too much oil, use healthy fats, and cook a much simpler, albeit broader, variety of daals, legumes, and vegetables than you'll find on a restaurant menu.

Having said that, of course not all Pakistani food is healthy, but then again, this is neither a health food nor weight-loss book.

Don't be daunted by the many spices you find in the recipes. One trip to a local Pakistani or Indian grocer, and for twenty bucks you can stock up on everything you need for months of cooking. Here's a handy list to take with you, and don't be shy to ask someone there to help you (pro tip: I generally only buy National- or Shaan-brand boxed spice powders and small bags of the whole spices):

Garam masala powder
Red chili powder
Kashmiri chili powder
Cumin seeds
Cardamom seeds
Fennel seeds
Ajwain (carom) seeds
Green cardamom pods
Black cardamom pods

Garlic-ginger paste

Curry leaves (often sold fresh in bags, you can freeze what you don't use)

While you're at the desi store, you can also grab the few nonspice ingredients found in these recipes: besan (chickpea) flour, basmati rice (Tilda is my preferred brand), whole wheat chapatti (durum atta) flour, and ghee (I include a recipe for it, but you can always buy it, too).

And if it still feels too daunting to cook these Pakistani foods, I hope you seek out a local Pakistani restaurant and try some of the dishes you won't find on an Indian menu.

Ghee

"Ghee shakkar tere muun main"
(May your mouth always be full of ghee and sugar)
—traditional South Asian blessing

Butter is fine, but you see, ghee is divine. I'm not just saying that, I mean it literally. Vedic worship can't be fulfilled without ghee, used in both offerings and to light the sacred fires through which the deities are invoked. Hindu lore includes accounts of demigods being created from it, and its Ayurvedic properties have been recognized for thousands of years. Believe it or not, this delicious, sacred food is also good for you.

Now, I'm not Hindu, but generations ago my ancestors on the subcontinent likely were, and regardless of your religion, it's not hard to see why ghee is considered a food of the gods. The best fudgy, sticky sweets begin with roasting nuts and flour in ghee. No daal is complete without a glistening layer of the melted gold swimming on top, and no self-respecting flaky, layered paratha is made with vegetable oil instead of ghee. For the record though, ghee is not clarified butter. It goes beyond clarified butter, because it's cooked longer to develop an entirely different layer of flavor. It's the creamiest, most aromatic, nuttiest, carameliest, butteriest incarnation of butter, deeply flavored and sumptuous. It feels like a caress in your mouth.

If that's not enough to sell you, ghee has an incredibly high smoke point, can be stored without refrigeration for a few months, and is ridiculously easy to make. There is no excuse, none, for you not to make your own ghee. Run as fast as you can from the charlatans selling "gourmet" or "artisanal" ghee, because believe it or not, making ghee is so simple that you can do it on your stove in less time than it takes to watch a sitcom.

HERE'S HOW I MAKE IT:

Melt two pounds of good-quality unsalted organic butter in a heavy-bottomed saucepan, and keep the butter at a gentle simmer, as gentle as possible. You'll see foam forming at the top, the milk solids separating from the water in the butter, water that we want to evaporate completely. The milk solids will settle near the bottom and begin to lightly brown up. Don't stir it too much—you don't want the milk solids to come back up—but keep an eye on it to make sure they don't burn. Keep the simmer going for about 20 minutes until much of the foam has disappeared, and until you can see caramel-colored milk solids on the bottom of the pan through amber-colored liquid ghee. Strain into an airtight container, keep next to your stove, and the next time you fry some eggs, fry them in ghee.

Classic Onion Pakoray

"Ramzaan kya pakoray bina?"
(What's Ramadan without pakoray?)
—Abu

Somewhere between the falafel and the tempura and the fritter, you find the pakora. Like a falafel, its basic component is the chickpea. Like a tempura, various veggies can be dipped in a pakora batter and deep-fried. And like a fritter, the batter is usually mixed with a variety of vegetables and dropped in fat spoonfuls into hot oil, producing crispy, savory dumplings eaten right out of the oil, dipped into chili sauce and chutney. My parents would explain the pakora to neighbors as "salty donuts," which is such a distant approximation that it likely put them off, but it was the best description Ami and Abu could come up with.

Pakoray* are a quick, easy, cheap, and tasty snack to make for kids after school, for teatime—which was traditionally a must in Lahori

---

* "Pakoray" is the Urdu plural of *pakora*, and while I might say "pakoras" while talking to an English-speaking person, it just doesn't sit right, because it isn't right. Also, important to note for those of you seeking recipes online or looking to order from a restaurant: many also call pakoray "bhaaji."

homes, for a time when guests often unexpectedly popped by—and when it rains.

Don't ask, I don't know why. But when it rains, my people sentimentally make pakoray.

Ami was never sentimental, so the only time during the entire year she ever made pakoray was during Ramadan—every single night, without fail. For years as an adult I did the same every Ramadan, until I realized that every passing year made it harder and harder to digest and metabolize the greasy little lumps of joy. Now, they get made only on rare occasions in my kitchen, but still not a Ramadan night goes by in my mother or sister's house where they aren't made.

I make pakoray three different ways. Surely there are hundreds more, but they all break down into these three basic types: a doughy, puffy variety that are more batter and less vegetable; the opposite, which is mostly copious amounts of thinly sliced and chopped vegetables barely held together with a batter (sometimes called a "bhaaji"); and a third variety, which is various vegetables dipped individually, tempura style, into the batter and then deep-fried.

The variety of vegetables used in pakoray is pretty wide open, and every household has their own tradition and preference. While I was growing up, my mother was most fond of dipping large, flat slices of eggplant and whole mushrooms (completely nontraditional) in batter to fry, or mixing handfuls of chopped, drained frozen spinach in batter to plop by the dollop into the oil. My kids and husband love allu pakoras, thin large slices of potato, dipped and fried, eaten with ketchup. I've never been fond of the tempura style, so my favorite is the classic onion pakora, bursting with thinly sliced onion and green chilies, crispy but still fluffy and soft, studded with whole cumin and coriander seeds.

HERE'S HOW I MAKE THEM:
2 large white onions, thinly sliced
4 green chilies, finely chopped

1 cup besan (chickpea) flour (found at every Indian/Pakistani/
Bangladeshi grocer)
½ teaspoon baking soda
1½ teaspoons cumin seeds
1 teaspoon coriander seeds
1 teaspoon ajwain (carom) seeds
1 teaspoon dried pomegranate powder
½ bunch cilantro
Handful of curry leaves, fresh or frozen (I freeze mine fresh so I can
use them for a long time.)

Mix the onions, chopped green chilies, cilantro, curry leaves, and all
spices and seasonings together in a bowl. Let this all sit for 10 minutes,
then add the besan and baking soda and mix everything by hand. Add
¼ cup of water and continue to mix by hand until the mixture just
comes together. You can fry the batter at this sticky stage, which will
give you crispy, textured, strikingly abstract-looking fritters, or you can
add another half cup of water and mix until you have a thick batter similar to a brownie batter, which when fried will give you chubby, fluffy
dumplinglike results. They're both delicious, and I'm all for frying half
the batch at the first stage, adding more water, and then frying the rest,
so you get to taste the difference.

The mix at the second stage, when it's more batterlike than sticky, is
the perfect consistency to dip thinly sliced potatoes or eggplant, whole
mushrooms, or cauliflower florets in, to then deep-fry, tempura style.

Let the mix rest, whichever stage you choose to fry it in, as you heat
up oil for frying. I use canola or vegetable oil, and you want the oil at
least three inches deep. Heat up the oil on a medium high flame, until
it sputters when you add a drop of batter to it. Then turn the heat down
to a medium and begin adding your mix, a full teaspoon at a time. Pros
will often use their hands to drop the pakoray, scooping up the mix with

their fingers and plopping it into the oil. You can add as many of the pakoray as will fit into the pan. They should rise to the surface as they hit the oil and expand a bit because of the baking soda. Turn them once after a couple of minutes—they should be a dark golden color on the side that's cooked—and then fry them two more minutes on the other side. Use a slotted spoon to remove the batch to a plate or tray lined with paper towels, sprinkle with a pinch of salt and chaat masala while hot, and eat with chutney as soon as they are cool enough to handle!

Parathay*

In some homes, the morning paratha is eaten simply, torn by hand and dipped in chai. In others, it's spread with butter and marmalade or sprinkled with sugar, then rolled up and handed off to a kid running out the door for school. When Abu visits, I make a spicy omelette studded with green chilies, onions, and cilantro to serve with a fresh paratha. But my favorite way to eat paratha is on a lazy weekend morning with fried eggs, yolks still runny, with a side of vegetable bhujiya—any vegetable or combination thereof—stewed together with browned onions and spices, low and slow so it caramelizes as it breaks down. Few things are as good as bhujiya scooped up in a little paratha funnel, then dipped in golden, buttery egg yolk.

The perfect paratha is soft and flaky enough to fold and scoop, but still crispy, and well browned around the edges. And ideally, it should be eaten hot off the tawa.

It took me a long time to finally get my paratha right, but in all my years of making rotis and parathay,* I have never been able to master the technique my mother uses. She's never owned a rolling pin in her life, and I've never been able to make roti or paratha or naan without

---

* Just like pakoray, "parathay" is the plural of the singular *paratha*. The desi aunty in me won't allow myself to write "parathas." Likewise, "samosay" is the plural of *samosa* and "tukray" the plural of *tukra*.

one. My mother blames the size of my hands, which are on the smaller side, like Abu's. If I had her boatlike hands, she believes, I'd be able to do it, too.

I've seen countless YouTube videos of real pros, the men who work at neighborhood tandoors all across the subcontinent, doing what she does, slapping the dough back and forth between their palms as it grows and grows in a perfectly shaped circle. I've tried to mimic them, and Ami, but never seem to be able to build up the requisite velocity and pressure. Instead I end up passing the flat disk of dough back and forth so gently that it stays exactly the same size and shape, and that shape is nearly never circular.

Even now, with the rolling pin, they are rarely perfectly circular. They are more often just approximately so.

The thing about parathay, however, is that they don't have to be round. There are a number of different ways to achieve the layered flakiness that makes a paratha so delightful, and you can end up with different shapes. For example, the dough, once rolled out about half as big as your final paratha size, can be slathered with oil, ghee, or butter, and then folded in half, slathered again, and folded once more, giving you a triangle. My mother-in-law makes almost exclusively triangle-shaped parathay.

You can fold the disk into a square, giving you a square paratha. And even if you opt for a circle, you can achieve the layers the way I described earlier, rolling the disk into a cigar shape and then twisting it into a spiral, or layering small circles of dough on top of one another with pats of grease in between, or using any one of a hundred pastry-layering techniques found online.

The point is to get some fat, any fat of your choosing, into layers inside each paratha, and then roll it out to its fullest size without the dough breaking, and without using too much flour to dust—otherwise you'll end up with a thick, tough paratha.

Your first paratha each time will suck. Trust me on this. To this day,

I know my first paratha will be fed to the birds, and that's okay, because they deserve parathay, too. This happens because every time I make the dough there are slight variations in it, in the room temperature, in the different fats I might use, depending on what I feel like or what I have on hand. The first paratha gives you a feel for all the variables, so you can adjust by the second one, adding a little less butter to the layers, grabbing a bigger handful of dough for the paratha, or lowering or increasing the temperature of the stove. Sometimes the second one won't work either, but keep at it. It takes time to get right, but it's worth every minute.

HERE'S HOW I MAKE THEM:
2 cups whole wheat chappati flour

1 teaspoon salt

1⅓ cups water, at room temperature

ghee (you can also use vegetable oil or butter, but really,
parathay are best made with ghee)

In a bowl, bring together the flour, salt, and 1 tablespoon ghee, giving it a coarse mix by hand. Make a well in the middle of the flour and add half the water. Work the water into the flour with your fingers and knead well, adding the remaining water in bits until it forms a ball and you have a smooth, pliable dough. The dough shouldn't stick to your fingers and should be a bit on the stiffer side. Let the dough rest for 10 minutes, give it second knead for 5 minutes, and let it rest again another 10 minutes.

Some people can work with fresh dough, but I find it easier to roll out if it's been refrigerated, so I will either make my dough the night before a morning meal, or I'll pop it in the fridge for at least an hour beforehand, to chill. If you do decide to refrigerate it, wrap or cover it in a piece of plastic wrap coated with a thin film of oil, to prevent a hard layer from forming. If you're not refrigerating, you still want to cover it with a warm, damp cloth as it rests.

When you're ready to make your parathay, heat up your skillet or tawa on a medium flame. Divide your dough into 8 equal parts and roll each into a smooth ball. Dust your countertop with a sprinkle of flour and, using a rolling pin, flatten out one of the dough balls into a disk, flipping it over every so often and giving it another dusting if it starts to stick. When your disk is about 5 inches across, spread a light layer of ghee across the top. Roll the disk into a cigar shape so that the ghee is spiraled inside the cigar, then twist the cigar into a disk, tucking the end underneath.

Dust both sides of this new disk again and roll it out gently as far as possible without tearing it, flipping and rotating it, making sure the paratha is an even thickness all around. Once it's rolled fully out, pick up the paratha in one hand and lay it on the dry skillet or tawa. Flip the paratha after 30 seconds and then dot the surface with ghee and add a little ghee around the edges of the paratha with a spoon. You don't want a pool of ghee or oil! Just a teaspoon or so, per paratha.

Press the paratha with a spatula as it cooks, to make sure it cooks all the way through, flipping it as needed so both sides get browned in the ghee. As this paratha is cooking, you can begin rolling out the next one and repeating the process.

To keep the parathay warm and soft, stack them as you go into any tea-towel-lined container that has a lid—it can be a big Tupperware container, a tortilla warmer, a glass bowl with a lid, whatever. The point is, you want to add your parathay to the stack as soon as it's cooked, then cover them all back up with the towel and container lid.

Serve any way you like them, there is no wrong way to eat a paratha!

Lahori Fried Fish

"Jinnay Lahore ni vaikya, oh jamiya ney"
(If you haven't seen Lahore, you haven't even been born)
—traditional Punjabi adage

I admit my bias toward the foods of Lahore, but believe me, there's a reason Lahori-style fried fish is the gold standard of fried fishes of the region. Karachi, the coastal city that is the largest in Pakistan, has its own style, however, which is usually a whole fish, marinated and fried without any kind of batter or crumb coating. It's likely loads healthier, but if you're going to fry fish, you've already abandoned any pretext that *healthy* matters.

Also, a mea culpa: my seafood repertoire is severely limited. I can make exactly one fish curry, one kind of tandoori-flavored salmon, and Lahori fried fish, which is the one I make nine times out of ten.

You might be wondering where on earth you'll find rohu, the monster fish that roams the rivers of South Asia, but rest assured you don't need it. There are likely South Asian grocers that carry it, but I've never made this dish with it. Like red meat and chicken, there's an argument to be made that a fish cooked with bones and thorns intact is tastier than a deboned fillet. I accept that argument, but counter with my lazy American preference for not having to make the effort of finding and pulling out bones as I eat. That would just slow me down.

And so you can pretty much use any fish you like here, but I'm partial to cod, flounder, and catfish fillets.

You don't have to wait until a cold, wintery day to eat Lahori fried fish. But for some reason, it tastes better when you do.

HERE'S HOW I MAKE IT:

1 pound fish, cut in preferred piece sizes

1 lemon

1 teaspoon garlic and ginger paste

1 teaspoon cumin seeds

1 teaspoon coriander seeds

1 teaspoon carom (also known as ajwain or caraway) seeds

1 teaspoon red chili flakes

1 teaspoon dried fenugreek

½ teaspoon turmeric powder

½ teaspoon red chili powder

1½ teaspoons salt

6 tablespoons besan (gram) flour

½ teaspoon orange food coloring (optional)

Oil for frying

Rinse your fish pieces, then pat them dry. Give the lemon a good roll to soften it up, then cut in half and squeeze the juice onto the fish in a bowl, making sure to remove any seeds. Add the ginger and garlic pastes to the fish and give it a mix so it's well coated. Lightly crush the fenugreek with your hand and sprinkle it on the fish. Dry-roast the cumin and coriander seeds, and then give them a coarse crush with a mortar and pestle or, wrapped in some paper towels, with a rolling pin. Mix the cumin, coriander, and carom seeds, red chili flakes, chili powder, turmeric, salt, and half of the gram flour together in a separate bowl, then massage it onto the fish gently by hand, turning the pieces over so all sides get coated. If the besan is too dry, add a few splashes of water to moisten it up. The coating should be on the thick, dry side. Cover and refrigerate for at least an hour, but you can also leave it overnight.

When you're ready to fry, heat oil, on a medium high flame, 2 inches deep in pan (or you can use an electric deep fryer). As the oil comes to temperature, mix the remaining half of the gram flour with the food coloring and three tablespoons of water. This should give you a fairly thin batter. Pour the batter over the fish and coat well, using your hands. The oil is ready if a little batter flicked into it starts bubbling and frying and rises to the top. Turn the flame down to medium low and carefully lower the fish into the pan, making sure not to crowd it: there should be at least an inch of space around each piece.

Let the fish fry for 5 minutes before turning once and frying on the other side for 5 more minutes. (Thinner fillets like flounder will need only 3 minutes on each side.) When done, the color should be very deep golden (or almost orange, like tandoori chicken, if you use the food coloring). Remove and drain on paper towels. Serve with any chutney, and a slaw of chopped or finely julienned radish, red onion, and seeded cucumber dressed with just salt and vinegar.

Everyday Daal

I once answered a Twitter question, "What food could you eat every day, without ever getting tired of it," in a matter of seconds with this response: "Daal chawal." I have never been on an extended trip in my entire life without making a pot of daal and a pan of steamed basmati rice as soon as I returned. In the lowest times of my life, I didn't crave chocolate to lift my spirits, I longed for daal.

And there is nothing like the sizzle of the tarka—hot oil tempered with some combination of garlic, onions, whole spices, dried chilies, chopped green onions, or curry leaves—to take me back to the years of impatiently waiting for Ami to finish making dinner. It was the best sound in the world, the *ssshhhh* of oil hitting water. There was something mystical about when she tilted the skillet into the pot of daal and a rush of steam flew into the air, like gusts from a witch's cauldron. In those moments, I was in awe of Ami, the alchemist in our kitchen turning humble dried pulses into a creamy, buttery, garlicky, cuminy, luscious pool of comfort.

Daal also brings back a rare early memory of helping Ami cook, because generally speaking she didn't like anyone in her kitchen. But there were a few things she let us do—chop salad, pick cilantro from the garden and pluck the leaves from their stems, and clean the daal. A common first task young kids will learn in a desi kitchen is cleaning the daal by removing any black stones found among the dried pulses, the "daal may kuch kaala." God forbid someone crack a tooth on a stone still left in the daal, though it's rare for that to happen here because the daal that is imported to the US is already cleaned and ready to go. They know this market doesn't have the patience to clean daal.

Daal can be confusing, for lots of different reasons. First, because the word *daal* refers to the actual split, dried pulses, and it also refers to the dishes that are made with them. Many folks also get confused between daals, beans, pulses, lentils, and legumes, and really there is every reason to be. To try and make it as simple as possible, *legume* is the umbrella term for the many species of plants that include lentils, beans, and pulses, and the like. The dried seeds of legumes are pulses, and the split version of many dried pulses, like chickpeas or lentils or mung beans, is called daal.

But wait, there's more. The different varieties of daal can come in three different forms: split with the skin still on, and split without the skin, or even not split at all, which means you end up with lots of different kinds of daal to choose from when you hit the desi store. There are, at any given moment, at least six varieties of daal in my pantry, mixed between whole daal, skinless split daal, and skin-on split daal. Even so, when I visit the local desi grocer, I'll find another half dozen that I've never cooked with before.

Which takes me to the final layer of this matrix. There as many ways to cook and temper daal as there are kinds of daal, and any one kind of daal can be cooked numerous different ways depending on the region you're from or, frankly, the mood you're in.

There are a few daals that are most commonly cooked in Punjab. There's masr, the black flat lentils that are easily found in most grocery stores here, cooked creamy and buttery. The same lentils, when split, are called masoor daal; these are tiny and orange, and are also usually cooked in a thinner preparation. Then there's chana daal, which come from split black chickpeas called desi chana, which we often cook either with red meat or alone in a tomato-based brothy base. Finally there's sookhi maash, which means "dry maash." Maash daal, also called urad daal just to confuse you further, is split, dried black gram. I love cooking maash daal in a creamy preparation because it has, similar to okra, a naturally viscous quality. But the more popular way to cook it is "dry," meaning the daal is stewed in a base of onions and tomatoes with whole spices, and then steamed to cook through. You don't end up with a gravy per se with this preparation; instead, the daal has a bit of a bite, and each grain stands apart, coated in fiery masala and usually eaten with parathay.

There is no wrong way to eat daal. It's wonderful with roti, paratha, naan, or rice. But I wouldn't advise you to eat it with any rice other than plain, steamed basmati. Don't make the mistake of pairing it with biryani or other heavily seasoned rice. The rice is there to be a warm, carby blank canvas that soaks up the daal. Traditionally, there are a few elements you want on your plate to complement the daal and rice. First, a crispy, cool kachumber salad of cucumber, onion, seeded tomato, and cilantro dressed with lemon juice. Then, a good, spicy, tangy achaar, the desi pickle in which lemon, mango, chilies, carrots, garlic cloves, and a host of any combination of these things are preserved in mustard oil with lots and lots of spices. Every South Asian grocer will carry at least half a dozen varieties, and just a teaspoon on the side of your plate will suffice for you to pick from with each bite of your daal chawal. Finally, something crispy. Papad, or papadum—which you may recognize as those crunchy little disks served as appetizers at fine desi restaurants— are often eaten with daal chawal. But to be honest, my husband is happy with a handful of potato chips crumbled on top of his plate.

This combination of tangy, spicy, fresh, crunchy, soft, and warm is the simplest, unbeatable, pleasure.

But there's one more way to heighten the pleasure and bring another sense into the experience—eat with your hands. Eating with your hands is an ancient practice in the subcontinent, with roots in Ayurveda, and is also the traditional, and recommended, Muslim method of eating. It is believed that there are enzymes on our (washed) fingers that help digest the food better, and maybe there are or aren't, but there's no question that eating with your hands elevates the entire experience. The deliberateness required to move small amounts of food from different parts of the plate, to shape it into a single bite, slows down the experience delightfully. There is a sensuousness to eating with your hands that cold, hard, sterile, weaponlike utensils can't replicate. The sensory experience of feeling the food on your fingers, of licking savory drips of curry and masala from them, can turn an ordinary meal into an extraordinary one.

Yes, it can be messy. But not if you're a pro. If you're a pro, only the first two joints of three fingers and a thumb will get any food on them. Your pinky and palms should remain completely clean, and at the end of the meal, you lick what remains on your fingers, getting every last bit of those enzymes, and then wash your hands with soap and water.

If I ever have my own restaurant, you won't get any utensils there.

Now there are so, so many more types and ways to make daal, and the internet is a treasure trove of daal recipes, but I urge you to stick with recipes from . . . well, the folks who know best. I've seen daal recipes concocted by non-desis with all sorts of nontraditional ingredients that may taste just fine but aren't authentic. The recipe I'm going to share is the one I make the most, the one I close my eyes and think about on a plane ride after having suffered days of conference food, and it's a mix of two of my favorite daals (yes, you can mix them, too!). It's the daal that, no matter how many times I make it (okay, at least thrice a month), leaves my family licking their fingers.

HERE'S HOW I MAKE IT:
1 cup split urad (maash) daal
1 cup split masoor daal (the tiny, orange daal)
1 teaspoon red chili powder
1 teaspoon Kashmiri chili powder (or unsmoked paprika powder)

1 teaspoon cumin seeds

2 teaspoons garam masala

2 teaspoons salt

2 whole green chilis

1 tablespoon garlic and ginger paste

1 large black cardamom (optional)

2 tablespoons butter

FOR THE TEMPERED OIL:

3 tablespoons ghee (or vegetable oil if you must,

but ghee is just so much better)

3 cloves garlic

1 teaspoon mustard seeds (optional)

1 teaspoon cumin seeds (optional)

6-8 curry leaves (dried or fresh, optional)

2 dried red chilies (optional)

Mix the two daals in a bowl, fill with water, swish it around a bit, and drain just by tipping the bowl into the sink carefully. You don't need a strainer and you don't have to get all the water out, just most of it. Do this three times so the water isn't so cloudy anymore.

The daal will "grow" when you cook it, so make sure to use a good-size pot. Bring the daal to a boil in 6 cups of water. If any white foam rises to the top, skim it off, and then lower the flame to a simmer. Add all the spices and salt, the whole green chilies, garlic and ginger paste, and black cardamom, then partially cover, simmering it for 20 minutes or until it has turned creamy and homogenized. Add the butter, cover it, and let it steam with the flame off while you prepare the tempered oil.

I'll be honest, I can't eat daal without a tarka, it doesn't taste finished and lacks richness. Paper-thin-sliced garlic was always the most common component of the tarka Ami made for most daal, except for channa (split gram) daal, which needs a browned onion tarka. Thin-sliced garlic is the most basic, and mandatory, tarka for my everyday daal, and you can add the other optional items if you have them. Each one will add another layer of flavor and depth.

To make the tarka, add your garlic and any of the other optional additions (see p. 309) to the ghee in a small saucepan, and heat low and slow on the lowest flame possible. You want the ghee to slowly become infused with all the flavors swimming in it, and you don't want anything to burn. Once the garlic has turned a deep golden brown, quickly pour the tarka into the daal, but do so from an arm's-length distance.

Garnish your finished daal with chopped fresh cilantro and serve with hot, steamed basmati rice.

Seekh Kabab

"Kabab is the king of the plate," Abu has always firmly believed. An event, a function, or even an invitation to a home where kabab is not served is a veritable insult to guests as far as he's concerned.

But if you're offered a kabab made without meat, any kind of meat, you are being offered a lie. A kabab must be made of meat—grilled, fried, or cooked in a tandoor; minced or whole—standing alone in its glory, not cooked in any sauce or gravy. That's not to say that if you search for "vegetarian kabab" recipes online, you won't find hundreds of Indian vegetarian recipes, but in any average Pakistani household or restaurant it can't be a kabab without meat.

While kababs didn't originate in Punjab by any stretch of the imagination, the subcontinent happily adopted them almost a millennia ago, from the Muslims who descended from Persia and Afghanistan. These were hearty, chunky, simply seasoned kababs that the famous fourteenth-century Moroccan world traveler Ibn Battuta noted were eaten in India hundreds of years before the Mughal conquerors ever got there. The Mughals refined the kabab by tenderizing it and adding aromatics and seasonings, and over time, desis turned these delicacies into fiery staples of our diets, swimming in garlic and ginger and red chili and cumin, doused in mint and cilantro and plum chutneys for good measure. That's why, when my parents first encountered the humble

American burger, its meat largely unseasoned and confusingly bland despite whatever secret sauce it came slathered in, they sighed at this very sad, neglected kabab.

I remember the first time I made seekh kabab for a Persian-American friend: they said, "Oh, they're like sausages," to which I took great offense. But it was a learning moment, in that in some cultures only chunks of grilled meat are called kabab, while in Pakistan a kabab is most commonly made of minced meat, and whole hunks of meat are usually called tikka . . . but can also be called kabab.

Yes, it's a confusing, but delicious, world to get lost in. There are so, so many kinds of kabab in the Pakistani stratosphere, many that you won't find at traditional Indian restaurants.

One of my favorites is chappli kabab, hailing from northern regions of Pakistan and Afghanistan. Chappli means "sandal," a strange name for a kabab it might seem, but this minced meat patty is shaped flat and oblong, sort of like the bottom of a flip-flop. Chappli kabab is deep-fried, and it has a distinctive flavor and texture, with whole, tangy spices, and the addition of besan give the kabab an extremely soft interior and a terrifically crunchy exterior.

There's bihari kabab, a barbecue favorite from Karachi: thin-sliced, tenderized filets of beef grilled over charcoals. These kababs are called bihari because migrants from the state of Bihar brought this dish to Pakistan during the Partition, and now they've become a familiar part of Pakistani cuisine. They're marinated with papaya paste and heavily seasoned before being threaded in S shapes onto flat skewers and then smoked over coals. If made right, they will literally melt in your mouth.

Reshmi kabab is yet another popular grilled kabab, this time made of chicken. Reshmi means "silky," and that's because the minced chicken is marinated in both cream and curd to tenderize it, leaving it moist and silken after being grilled. Marinating and cooking with cream is often a hallmark of Mughal cuisine, a luxury afforded only to the select few.

Shaami kabab, some will argue, isn't a kabab at all, it's a cutlet. But there's no point in arguing about it because they're called kababs. Shaami are made by combining finely shredded cooked beef or mutton with mashed chana daal, and then mixing in chopped or thinly sliced onions, cilantro, green chilies, and seasonings. The mixture is then shaped into patties, dipped in beaten egg, and shallow-fried. The legend goes that they were created by Syrian chefs in a royal kitchen, hence the name *shaami*, from the Arabic name for the Levant, Al-Shaam. Once, as I was making them, I explained the origins to our Syrian nanny, who didn't believe for a second that Syrian chefs would have created a kabab so spicy and so different from any Syrian kabab she had ever had. Shaami kababs are smooth and velvety, and for good reason. They're time-consuming to make, as is befitting a royal palate, and in the homes of commoners like us, Ami made them by the dozens to freeze, so they could be quickly fried when we had last-minute guests.

A similarly silken kabab is the tunday kabab, named after the chef who created them. His name wasn't tunday, it was Haji Murad Ali, but he was disabled in one hand, earning him and his kababs the unfortunate moniker tunday, meaning "cripple." A famous elderly nobleman who had lost his teeth held a contest to see what chef could create a succulent kabab that could be eaten without being chewed, without compromising any flavor. Haji Ali mixed together finely pounded meat with a hundred and sixty spices, tenderized it with papaya, and then mixed it with besan. The meat was then smoked with coals, shaped into patties, and fried, resulting in decadently soft, savory meat cutlets still popular hundreds of years later. It goes without saying that Haji Ali won the contest.

Dhaga kabab gets the name dhaga, meaning "thread," for the thread that is wrapped around a skewer of minced meat that's been so tenderized that it can't stay on the skewer without it. This kabab is also a Karachi specialty, and not really found in Punjab, or at least I've never seen it there. After being grilled over coals, the kabab is slid off the skewer, breaking down into what amounts to a mound of soft mince-meat. The thread is fished out and the smoky, spicy, tender meat is eaten with another Karachi specialty, the puri paratha, a chewy, crispy deep-fried flatbread that is puffed up like a balloon. Another great kabab for the tooth-challenged.

Because I still have teeth, I am more partial to kababs with a bit of bite, and the first kabab that I ever fell in love with, I ate late one night with Pummy Mamu in the exclusive gated community of Model Town, Lahore. One night, he told me to ask him no questions but to just hop onto his motorcycle. I did as requested, and after half an hour we pulled up to a street-side restaurant where they were grilling kababs on metal skewers over open coals. This, he said, was the famous Bhaiya Kabab, established in 1970, and I wouldn't find anything like it anywhere else in Pakistan.

He ordered three dozen beef seekh kababs, which seemed excessive until I saw them. They were like little caramelized mincemeat fingers, thin and just a few inches long. I couldn't see any discernible cilantro or onions or even whole spices in the meat. Smoky, spicy, and savory, they were both succulent and chewy, served with fresh, hot tandoori naan, salad, and a couple of chutneys. I didn't even bother with any of the accoutrements, going straight for the tiny, sizzling kababs and downing at least a dozen of them successively.

They were the best kababs I had ever tasted in my life, and yes, they're still being served there today.

Over the years, though, I grew partial to seekh kabab with more texture, with thinly sliced onions and lots of fresh cilantro, and developed my own recipe, which has been a hit with family and friends for decades now. They are simple, fresh-tasting, and don't even need to be grilled.

HERE'S HOW I MAKE THEM:

1 pound ground beef or chicken (or lamb, if you're a heathen)

1 medium white onion

1 tablespoon coarsely chopped fresh ginger

1 tablespoon coarsely chopped fresh garlic

1 tablespoon coarsely chopped fresh green chilies

1 bunch cilantro, chopped

1 tablespoon cumin seeds

1 tablespoon coriander seeds

1 teaspoon coriander powder

1 teaspoon cumin powder

1 tablespoon fresh cracked black pepper

1 teaspoon red chili flakes

½ teaspoon red chili powder

1 teaspoon coarsely crushed cubeb pepper (aka tailed pepper or kabab chini) (optional)

2 teaspoons salt

½ cup melted ghee

Run the meat through a food processor for a minute to get a finer mince, which helps to bind the kabab without using any egg or starch. Slice the onion very, very thinly, break apart the slices into thin threads of onion, and sprinkle a bit of salt onto it. The salt will soften the onions, but if they release water, make sure to squeeze them dry before adding to the meat. Mix meat and onions together well, and set aside.

Crack the coriander seeds between your palms slightly, then dry roast them along with the cumin seeds in a dry pan over medium heat for a few minutes, until they release their aromas. Add these along with all other spices, onions, chopped cilantro, garlic, and ginger, and mix well.

Let the mixture marinate, covered, in the fridge for at least an hour, up to overnight. Divide the meat into 8 equal parts, for 8 kababs.

There are a few ways you can cook the kababs: grilled, baked, or fried.

To grill your kababs over coals or an electric or gas grill, shape each portion of the meat onto flat skewers. Either refrigerate the skewered kabab until ready to cook, or grill them immediately; if they sit in room temperature too long, the meat will start to fall off the skewer. Place the skewers above the grill, but not directly on it. You don't want the meat to touch the metal grill, or it may stick and never come off. We place bricks on our grill so the ends of the skewers can sit atop them, the kababs suspended over the heat source. Brush with ghee and rotate frequently for 6 to 8 minutes, until all sides are a deep, even golden brown.

To bake the kababs, preheat your oven to 400 degrees. Shape the meat by hand onto a skewer and then slide off, so you have a hole in the middle of the cigar-shaped kabab. Place them on a baking dish lined with heavy foil, pour the ghee on top, and bake uncovered for 8 minutes, then turn and bake 3 more minutes.

To fry the kababs, shape them as you would to bake them. Heat the ghee in a large skillet on a medium flame and add the kababs side by side. Sear the kababs on each side for a few mintues. Lower the flame and cover the skillet and cook the kababs for 5 minutes, then turn the kababs over, cover, and cook 5 more minutes, covered.

Serve with naan, roti, or rice; green chutney; and thinly sliced onions that are lightly dressed with salt and lemon juice.

Sarson da Saag
(Mustard Greens Saag)

Before you decide to skip this recipe altogether, because really does anyone like greens?, you need to understand that sarson da saag is not just any greens. If made right, you will crave this dish every few weeks. Buttery, earthy, tangy, fiery, and just slightly bitter: that's what a good saag tastes like. I have few addictions these days, but saag is definitely one of them. If there's saag in my fridge, I will eat it for breakfast, lunch, and dinner until it's gone.

Now, to be clear, not all South Asian dishes made of greens are saag, and it kind of kills me when people call any old curried or stewed greens "saag." Maybe that's because saag is a very specifically Punjabi dish and I take it a bit personally, or maybe because it's like saying creamed spinach is the same as sautéed spinach, and we all know that is false on every level.

You can think of saag as a specific preparation of greens, creamy, thick, and buttery. It may be a village food, but it has a luxurious mouth feel. People may use different greens to make saag, but traditional Punjabi saag is made with *sarson*, mustard greens, and you'll find this rich, filling dish, topped with tarka (tempered ghee), cooking on every corner of the region during the winter.

It's no surprise, given that Punjab is lush with legendary mustard fields that look like seas of gold right before harvest. The greens can be tough and pungent, with an unmistakable bitterness that is a hallmark, so often something else is added to temper the bitterness—turnip greens or actual turnips, radish or fenugreek greens, or spinach.

Preparing sarson da saag is no easy task, especially if you're working with fresh greens. First, they'll cook down into a fraction of what you started with, like any green, which means you need to prep what will feel like bushels of them for a single pot. The tough part of the stems must be removed, and the greens have to be washed in batches, repeatedly, to make sure any dirt or debris or little critters are cleaned out. Then—whether fresh or frozen—they have to be chopped very fine to make it easier to cook and to get the consistency of perfect saag.

That's not all though. The traditional way takes some muscle to get its signature texture, which means pounding and mashing it with a wooden masher as it cooks. Of course most of us nowadays just pop the greens into a blender, but authentic saag isn't a complete paste. It does retain just a slight texture, and that's not easy to get when you run it through a blender.

You're also going to miss something of its authentic taste unless you cook it over a wood- or coal-fired stove in a handi, a traditional clay pot. These pots aren't found much today either in Pakistani cities or the homes of Pakistanis abroad, but they are still omnipresent in villages in Pakistan, and sometimes in trendy restaurants that are trying to capture the traditional essence.

There is something to be said for food cooked in a handi, as the minerals in the clay—calcium, phosphorous, iron, magnesium, and sulfur—have Ayurvedic health qualities and add a flavor that can't be replicated in our everyday pots and pans. It's an earthy flavor, je ne sais quoi. But before you go buying a clay cooking pot, buyer beware: don't get one that's glazed or polished, as the glaze could have chemicals such as lead or mercury. You'll have to find a pure, unglazed cooking vessel to make sure the food cooked in it is safe to eat and healthy, but it will be worth the work to do so.

Sarson da saag is traditionally eaten with makkai di roti, a roti made of maize. You don't have to be Punjabi to know greens and cornbread go great together, but making cornbread is a lot easier than making makkai di roti. Believe me, I've made both, I know. The dough isn't like regular roti dough, it's crumbly and breaks easily, and I deeply admire the masterful cooks who are able to roll them out without a crack. If you want to try your hand at them, there are hundreds of recipes online, but you can also use the shortcut Zuby Aunty uses—store-bought corn tortillas, or "sopes." Toasted and buttered, they are an easy, great substitute for makkai di roti, even if the flavor isn't exact.

Ami didn't grow up in a household that cooked saag, but being married into a Punjabi family meant she had better learn. She not only learned, but saag became one of the dishes that she is known for. Hers is creamy, slightly tangy, the bitterness perfectly balanced out. Over the years she developed her own recipe with an unexpected ingredient, which she finally divulged to me about a decade ago even though I grew up eating this saag a few times a month. Now that I've learned her secret, it's become one of the dishes I'm known for, too, and I've worked in a couple more shortcuts so it's easier to make when you're raising a family and working a full-time job.

HERE'S HOW I MAKE IT:

4 cups chopped mustard greens

4 cups chopped spinach

4 cups chopped broccoli (the unexpected ingredient!)*

2 large jalapenos, stems removed

2 tablespoons roasted cumin seeds

2 tablespoons salt

1 tablespoon red chili powder

1 tablespoon grated fresh ginger
8 cloves peeled garlic
4 tablespoons maize or besan
4 tablespoons butter
3 dried red chilies (optional)
1 tablespoon Kashmiri red chili powder or unsmoked paprika
(optional)
4 tablespoons ghee
1 bunch fresh cilantro

Add the mustard greens, spinach, broccoli, jalapenos, ginger, half of the garlic, and all the seasonings to a large pot with six cups of water; cover, and set to simmer on a medium low heat.

Check your pot and give it a stir every 15 minutes, until the water has almost but not quite cooked out and the greens have nearly disintegrated. Lower the heat and add the maize or besan and cook for 5 to 7 minutes, continuously stirring, until the starch has been absorbed, making sure there are no clumps. Add the butter and mash the mixture as well as possible with a potato masher or the back of a large cooking spoon or, if you happen to have one, a wooden masher. Here is where your own personal preference comes into play. Some people like their saag completely smooth. Others prefer it with some texture. I've found the perfect consistency by blending half of the saag with an electric blender and adding it back to the pot with the other half that was mashed by hand. You can also use a hand blender and stop blending when you get it how you like it.

I don't like my saag too runny, it should be thick enough to scoop with roti, and there should be no extraneous water floating on the surface. If there is, cook it further on a medium low flame, stirring every couple of minutes, until it begins sputtering. That's the sweet spot.

Give the saag a taste and add salt if needed. Thinly slice the remaining four cloves of garlic as you heat the ghee on a low flame in a small pan. Add the garlic to the ghee, slowly browning it. Once it gets lightly golden, add your dried red chilies. Once the garlic gets a deep golden color, turn off the heat and stir in the Kashmiri red chili powder.

Add the tempered ghee into the saag and give it a good stir. Top the pot with chopped cilantro and top each individual serving with an additional pat of butter, and serve with toasted and buttered naan, roti, makkai di roti, or corn tortillas.

* I know there will be those who say it's blasphemous, a travesty, to make saag with anything but fresh greens, but I'm not one of those people. I make this recipe with fresh or frozen greens, or a combination of the two, and either way, it turns out fine. Fresh greens may have a slight leg up on frozen ones, but not enough of one to deter me from using frozen when I need to.

Chicken Salaan

"Ghar ki murghi daal barabar"
(A chicken at home is the same as daal)
—Urdu proverb

I t is strangely rare to find a true homestyle chicken salaan at a Pakistani or Indian restaurant. You'll find plenty of other chicken preparations: chicken karhai, chicken korma, chicken with spinach or with chickpeas. But a basic, simple chicken salaan with a rich, brothy shorba is something I never see on a Pakistani menu.

Before I go any further, and to clear up any confusion, shorba literally means "soup," and "salaan" refers to what you may call a curry. Not all shorba is a salaan and not all salaan is a shorba. This entire section, however, is about shorba salaan, which kind of looks like deep-reddish-brown soup, thanks to a base of browned onions and tomatoes.

I've never been sure why you don't find it much in restaurants, but Ami's theory posits that not everyone knows how (or wants to take the time) to coax the goodness out of bones while simultaneously killing the hamak, the unpleasant meaty smell of meat. This is completely anti-thetical to the Western priority of retaining the flavor of meat so that when you eat beef or lamb or goat, you can actually taste the animal. So much so that, over here, it's often eaten as rare as possible with as little seasoning as possible. In other words, the stuff of Pakistani nightmares.

The desi concern with hamak is even stronger with poultry, which, if not prepared right, will ruin your entire dish with a lingering, unpleasant, raw-chicken-y smell.

The horror of this possibility is a great issue in our family. When my sister got married to a doctor from the UK, we all flew to Birmingham for the wedding. It was an emotional affair because we knew that, after the festivities were over, we would be leaving her behind, far away, across the ocean. After the wedding we were gathered in the groom's parents' house. My sister—resplendent in bridal red, jewels hanging from her forehead, ears, fingers, and nose—was seated next to her husband in the living room. Dozens of family members were spread throughout the house, and others sat in a circle of chairs placed around the living room, making awkward small talk while the bride and groom sat quietly, as they were meant to.

Abu suddenly and ceremoniously cleared his throat, ready to make an announcement. "There is a word of advice I want to give you, my daughter, as you begin this new life."

Everyone waited expectantly for the fatherly wisdom he was about to impart, certain it would bring us to tears.

"When you cook chicken, make sure to cook all the hamak out, give it a good bhoon, otherwise it can ruin a perfectly good dish."

My sister will never forget his unexpected words.

As you can see, in our family getting the stink out is the most important step in preparing any kind of meat, and the way to do it is to "bhoon" it. A bhoon is best described as a high-temperature sauté that renders excess blood and juices from the meat and bones, the liquids that hold the smell, until this liquid is all gone and the meat is well seared. In most preparations, meat is bhooned in onions that have already been browned, so the onions further kill any unpleasant flavors and scents, help brown the meat, and infuse it with rich onion flavor.

Here is where things can go wrong and the reason why some home cooks avoid making saalan with shorba. Instead of going the brothy route, they opt for throwing in a lot of tomatoes and spices to stew the meat with. If your meat has not been properly bhooned, you can still get away with masking the hamak with a heavy, tomatoey base. But if instead you add cups of water to cook a broth, letting the bones soften and release their flavor, there's no way to mask a failed bhoon. You'll end up with a pot of stinky broth.

This is always more likely to happen with chicken than red meat, and it's always more likely with chicken that has not been skinned. Chicken used in Pakistani dishes, whether in rice, or grilled, or in a saalan, is always, *always* skinned.

A light, savory chicken or goat shorba salaan is one of the dishes I remember my Nani Amma most by. In her elderly years, eating heavy foods became impossible for her, so almost every day she would make a small, fresh batch of shorba to eat like children often do, with bits of roti torn up in it to soak up the broth. If this sounds like tearing up crusty bread into a bowl of soup, that's because it's pretty much exactly what it is. Shorba is, ultimately, a soup, with whole pieces of meat and sometimes vegetables. In our home, if there was anything Ami made more often than chicken shorba, it was allu gosht, goat and potato shorba, another classic home staple that's not always easy to find in Pakistani restaurants.

Rest assured, though, once you master the technique of making a shorba saalan, you can pretty much use any meat with bones for it. Yes, the bones are important, and I'm not budging on that.

HERE'S HOW I MAKE IT:

1 whole chicken *or* 2 pounds chicken legs and thighs;
skinned and cut into small pieces
1 large white onion, thinly sliced
2 medium tomatoes, chopped

2 tablespoons garlic and ginger paste
1 tablespoon garam masala
1 tablespoon salt
½ tablespoon turmeric powder
1 teaspoon red chili powder
2 teaspoons Kashmiri red chili powder or unsmoked paprika
2 black cardamom pods (optional but highly recommended)
¼ teaspoon ground cloves (optional)
2 green chilies, sliced lengthwise
½ cup ghee
5 cups water
1 large bunch fresh cilantro

Use a good, heavy-bottomed pot for this dish, one wider than it is tall. Rinse and pat the chicken dry. Add the ghee to the pot and heat on a medium flame. Thinly slice the onion and sauté in the oil until a deep brown, then immediately add the chicken, garlic, and ginger. Bhoon the chicken uncovered, stirring frequently, until the meat renders its juices and fat, and keep on the flame until all liquid dries up. Add tomatoes, red chili powder, Kashmiri red chili, turmeric, salt, garam masala, cloves, and black cardamom, and lower flame. Cover the pot, but give it an occasional stir every few minutes, until the tomatoes have broken down and their water has been released and then dried up; you'll know you're at the right point when the oil begins to separate in the pot. Slice the green chilies lengthwise and add to the pot along with the water. Increase the heat so the broth reaches a low simmer, then cover and cook until the chicken is very tender, 30 to 40 minutes. That means the bones have also softened and cooked, giving you a rich stock. Turn off heat and top with chopped cilantro. Serve with naan, roti, or steamed white basmati rice.

Chicken Yakhni Pulao

My favorite comfort meal is daal chawal, but if I am honest, the comfort part really comes from the chawal, the rice. Simple, hot, white steamed rice. The perfect steamed rice will be basmati, its grains long and delicate, each kernel fluffy and separate—the sign of a talented hand at the helm.

I don't have to make the argument that rice may be the ultimate global comfort food; we all know this to be true. In our own cuisine, rice is always about comfort, whether eaten simply steamed, or cooked, porridgelike, into kichdri, or turned into savory dishes like biryani or pulao, or even eaten as dessert, cooked into puddings called kheer or with saffron-tinted sugar syrup into zarda, sweet rice. We even eat it like a cereal, sprinkling sugar and pouring hot milk over leftover white rice for breakfast, a favorite of children.

We may eat rice a dozen different ways, but the most well-known rice dish from the subcontinent, found on every desi restaurant menu, is unequivocally biryani.

Abu's harshest culinary judgment has always been reserved for this most famous dish. "Just a bunch of gich mich mixed up with rice" is his take on biryani, but "pulao," he says, "a good pulao, that leaves your fingers lightly glistening with ghee, that is rice worth eating."

His disdain notwithstanding, biryani has a fairly distinguished pedigree. Whether or not it originated in Persia is up for debate, but it was certainly refined and ubiquitous in royal Mughal kitchens. Versions of biryani are found all over the subcontinent, in Sri Lanka, North Africa, and the Middle East, and probably other places, too, but the basic concept is the same: white rice, usually basmati, is parboiled with aromatics, then layered and steamed with either marinated and spiced raw meat or a spicy, cooked meat. In some places, potatoes and boiled eggs are added to the layers. Saffron mixed with rose water or yogurt is drizzled on top, coloring a layer of the rice as it steams, so when it's given a final mix, you end up with the signature orange and white colors. The rice is fragrant, the meat is fiery, and with a little salad or yogurt raita on the side, it makes for a complete meal.

Pulao looks, if anything, like the subdued, neglected middle child of biryani. No fiery colors punctuate it; instead it comes in a range of tan. Not very exciting. Neither is it spicy like biryani, as it is lacking green and red chili, and it's not even fancy enough to merit saffron.

Yet, YET! It is the superior rice dish, the queen of rice dishes, in my humble estimation.

And like biryani, it boasts an admirable lineage.

Pulao, pulow, pilav—it's called by different names in different regions and in its various incarnations. The earliest known mention of the dish actually comes from Alexander the Great, who writes of it being served to him when he conquered Samarkand in 329 BC. But like much of civilization, historians believe the origins of pulao can be traced to Persia, from where it traveled in every direction possible. I'm no expert on all the different versions, I'm just here to talk about Punjabi pulao.

A true Punjabi pulao requires the rice itself be cooked in yakhni, a meat broth simmered with aromatics and whole spices. Abu's favorite is goat pulao, but it can be made with chicken, mutton, beef—really anything you can get a bone broth out of. Unlike biryani, you can't parboil the rice and then drain it. Having to cook the rice in broth means there's no room to mess up your rice-to-liquid ratio. There has to be exactly enough broth for the rice to absorb while staying fluffy and separate. Too much broth, and you'll end up with mushy rice. Too little, your rice will be raw.

Biryani may be spicy but pulao is sumptuous. It is elegant. It won't set your mouth on fire, but when made right, it is deeply savory and aromatic, with an umami that biryani lacks. Each grain soaks up the rich goodness of bone broth.

An authentic pulao should be made with bone broth, but that doesn't mean you can't make vegetarian versions, and I do. I make chana pulao with chickpeas, and one of my favorites is mattar pulao, made with sweet green peas. Abu loves kala chana ("black chana") pulao, made with a smaller variety of chickpea, the Bengal gram, that is unpeeled.

Abu loves pulao so much that he does something with it I've never seen anyone else do, which I still refuse to try. He pours whole milk over a bowl of warm chana or mattar pulao and eats it like a bowl of cereal. I chalk it up to some childhood memory he holds dear, and anytime he asks for it, I happily comply.

My ex-mother-in-law did a lot to make my life difficult, but she made a very fine Punjabi pulao, well on par with Savour Foods in Rawalpindi, if not better. She taught me exactly how much water to use to get perfectly fluffy rice, what seasonings to simmer the meat with, and how to steam it at the end so every grain is tender. I sopped up all of my former mother-in-law's cooking secrets before fleeing the marriage.

When we have guests, I offer pulao. When my children or I need comfort, I make pulao. When I die, serve Punjabi yakhni pulao.

HERE'S HOW I MAKE IT:

2 cups basmati rice

1 whole chicken, bone in; skinned and cut into small parts

1 large white onion
1 tablespoon minced garlic
1 tablespoon minced ginger
2 tablespoons salt
2 sticks cinnamon
6 whole cloves
4 green cardamom pods, slightly crushed
¼ teaspoon black peppercorn
2 black cardamom pods
1 whole green chili
1 teaspoon black pepper
1 teaspoon garam masala
1 tablespoon roasted cumin seeds
1 teaspoon fennel seeds (optional)
1 teaspoon roasted coriander seeds, slightly crushed
⅓ cup whole milk yogurt
½ cup plus extra 2 tablespoons ghee
½ cup cooking oil
3 cups of water

Rinse the chicken and pat dry. Heat ½ cup of ghee and ½ cup oil together in a heavy-bottomed pot. One of the things my ex-mother-in-law taught me was that rice is best cooked in a pot that is wide as opposed to high. You want to give the rice space to "grow" and fluff, and it's more prone to get sticky and gummy in a narrow pot. Basmati has a remarkable ability to grow, so using a large, wide pot will give the rice kernels room to expand, and you'll get the best result.

Add thinly sliced onion to the ghee and sauté on medium low flame until the onions are deeply caramelized. The darker the onions, the browner the pulao will be. You want it colored like rich dark caramel, but be careful with the onions—a few extra seconds could end up burning them. Add chicken, garlic, and ginger and bhoon the chicken on a medium flame in the onions, stirring frequently, until the meat releases juices and the juices dry up.

Here is where AK's mother's water formula comes in. The perfect ratio of water to rice is one-to-one, *unless* you soak the rice first. You don't have to soak the rice, but basmati will fluff up better if it is soaked. For soaked rice, the perfect proportion of water is double the amount of rice, minus a cup. For example, if you have 2 cups of soaked rice, double that (4 cups), then subtract 1, and this gives you 3 cups of water.

Soak the rice in lukewarm water and add 3 cups of water to the chicken, along with the yogurt and all the aromatics and seasonings, like this: tie up the green and black cardamom, cinnamon, and cloves into a small square of cheesecloth, but add the cumin, coriander, green chili, fennel seeds, garam masala, black pepper, and the remaining salt directly into the broth. You don't have to use a cheesecloth for the bigger whole spices, but it can be a pain to eat around them if you don't.

Cover and simmer the chicken on a medium flame for 20 minutes, periodically skimming off any foam that rises to the top. Remove the spice sachet and discard.

Drain the rice and add to the broth, give it a stir to evenly distribute it, cover and continue to simmer on medium for about another 10 minutes, until the water is nearly absorbed and small air holes appear on the surface of the rice. That's the right time to turn off the stove.

Dip a spoon in and taste how salty the water is. It should be slightly saltier than the final result you want. If it tastes bland, sprinkle another teaspoon of salt over the top and give the rice a gentle stir. The rice can break at this stage and we don't want that. Drizzle the remaining 2 tablespoons of ghee on top of the rice, cover with a towel and the lid, and turn on the flame as low as possible to steam the rice, for 10 minutes or until the broth completely dries up and the rice is fluffy. The flame on my stove is rather high, even at its lowest setting, so to be safe, I put a tawa or skillet under the rice pot to further dissipate the heat.

Then gently fold the rice to fluff it.

Garnish with caramelized onions (optional), and serve with a chutney or yogurt raita of your choice.

Shahi Tukray

Pakistani desserts, which are basically the same as many Indian desserts, aren't as well known to Western palates as are more commonplace dishes such as tandoori chicken, daal makhni, and naan. I've never been sure why but have chalked it up to their being an acquired taste; maybe the flavors don't quite suit mouths used to chocolate and vanilla and cinnamon.

Shaun T, however, dispelled me of that assumption. He and his husband, Scott, loved the gulab jamun I served so much that I had more shipped to their house later that same year. Other non-desis I've hosted also seemed to enjoy the desi desserts I served in my home. So maybe it was the way the desserts were described in restaurant menus that put people off from ordering them? For example, these are some common desserts and their descriptions:

Gulab jamun: fried balls of milk solids in syrup
Ras malai: cottage cheese disks in sweetened milk
Barfi: condensed sweetened milk solids cooked in ghee

I admit none of that sounds very appetizing, and that may have something to do with the phrase "milk solids," which leaves most people confused. Milk solids are simply dried milk, i.e., what you're left with after the water in milk evaporates. Milk is unquestionably the foundational ingredient in dozens and dozens of desi sweets, and I happen to think the way in which South Asian dessert chefs turned something as simple as milk, without any flour or rising agent, into so many kinds of sweets is rather genius.

With age I've grown to love desi desserts, but did I mention I hate making desserts? I *can* make them; I just don't want to. But of all the desserts I am loath to make, this is the one I am *least* loath to make, and also it is one of my favorites to eat. It's not easy to find in Pakistani or Indian restaurants and is rarely even found at weddings or dinner parties, and I don't know why, because it is exceedingly delicious and rich and simple.

You could call this the desi version of bread pudding crossed with French toast, but it's truly so much better than either of those things. The name is fitting: shahi, meaning "royal," and tukray, meaning "morsels." They are indeed royal morsels: ghee-fried slices of bread doused in thickened, aromatic, sweetened cream, topped with chopped pistachios. It can be eaten warm on a cold night or cold on a hot night, and either way you'll need a nap afterward.

Ami rarely ever served elaborate desserts when we were growing up. Usually she dispensed with the protocol by making a pot of zarda, the sweetened rice laced with nuts and sultanas. A one-pot dessert, if you will. When she made shahi tukray, though, it meant we were having extra special guests.

Making shahi tukray is pretty straightforward but has two basic steps: frying slices of bread and thickening milk into rabri, the second of which takes the most time. Rabri is made by literally cooking down sweetened, cardamom-flavored whole fat milk until it is half its original volume and then preserving the film of cream that forms on the top to fold back in at the end. There is more than one way to skin the rabri cat, however; you can find at least a dozen recipes for the delicious, thickened milk product online, including some shortcuts. My method requires patience, but the result is well worth the effort.

And every desi dessert, or any and every dessert irrespective of origin, is enhanced by a hot cup of chai.

HERE'S HOW I MAKE SHAHI TUKRAY:

½ gallon of whole milk

1 cup sugar

8 whole cardamom pods or 2 teaspoons cardamom powder

1 teaspoon saffron strands (optional)

½ cup ghee

8 slices of white bread

2 tablespoons Kewra (pandan flower) essence

Chopped pistachios

Getting the rabri started is the first priority; do so by combining the milk, sugar, cardamom, and saffron strands together in a heavy-bottomed nonstick pot. Bring the milk to a boil as you continuously stir, and then lower the heat so it remains at barely a simmer. Every time a film of cream forms on top of the milk, gently push it to the sides of the pot. Pushing the film to the sides allows for a new film to form after the milk condenses further. Repeat this process every time a film forms, ideally as many times as possible, building up layers of the cream on the sides of the pot, until the milk is approximately half its original quantity. Then gently fold all the cream gathered on the sides into the thickened milk and set aside.

The bread slices in shahi tukray are cut in triangular pieces, as if a regular piece of packaged white bread had been halved. And you can certainly use basic sliced white bread for this recipe. It will turn out delicious. But I've found that if you can use thicker white bread, like

Texas Toast, the tukray are plumper and richer. Either way you decide to go, trim the crusts from the bread slices and cut them in half diagonally so you have sixteen triangles. Melt the ghee in a large nonstick sauté or frying pan on medium heat and shallow-fry the bread on both sides for a few minutes each, so they are an even, golden-brown color.

Arrange the triangles in two rows in a shallow dish. Mix the Kewra (pandan flower) essence into the rabri once it is at room temperature, and then spoon or pour it over the bread.

The bread needs an hour or so to soak up the rabri properly; it can then be garnished with chopped pistachios and served at room temperature, chilled and served cold (my preference), or heated in a microwave or oven and served warm (my husband's preference).

Chai

I know there are chains across American that now sell "chai tea," which is a redundancy that literally means "tea tea" but I suppose is the Western way of distinguishing it from teas like chamomile, jasmine, or Earl Grey. Whatever this chai tea may be, it is not the chai I make at home. The "chai tea" I've had at establishments that shouldn't be serving chai tastes heavily of cinnamon, cloves, and other seasonings, but doesn't actually taste of chai.

Yes, chai itself has a taste, which comes from the dried tea leaves. Black tea is traditionally used to make it, and my favorite brands use orange pekoe. Distinct from any added flavorings, the leaves themselves should yield a rich, deep flavor. That's the flavor that makes you sigh after taking the first sip.

Chai can be as simple as tea, milk, water, and sugar, or you can add the flavorings that turn it into masala chai. My everyday chai only gets a couple of green cardamom pods. But when I'm feeling under the weather, I'll boil a piece of ginger in the water before adding the tea. If my digestive system needs a little help, a dash of cinnamon in my chai does the trick.

I'm going to confess something that will horrify chai enthusiasts and that is this: I usually make my daily mug of chai in the microwave. I've learned how to make a great cup of chai by lowering the power and zapping it long enough after adding the milk. But when there is more than one cup to be made, I pull out a heavy-bottomed nonstick pot to brew it in.

The proportion of tea-infused water to milk is also important, and that varies among people. I like a spot of milk in my tea so that it stays strong, the color a deep caramel. My husband would dispense with water altogether if he could and just cook the tea leaves directly in milk, that's how milky he likes it.

When Irfan and I first married, chai became a point of contention between us. When I made chai for us, he hated it because he thought it was bitter and inauthentic out of the microwave. When he made chai, he cooked the milky concoction in a pot for twenty to thirty minutes, low and slow. Who had time for that? And who wanted to drink a chai so milky that you could give it to a kid in a bottle?

Our battle was silly because there are plenty of ways to make chai. The way I like it is called karak, meaning "sharp," and the way he likes it is doodh patti, which literally translates to "milk tea." Over the years we've come to appreciate each other's chais, with the tacit agreement that mine is a better morning chai, and his is a perfect bedtime chai.

When we have guests, we make something in between.

If we ever grill over coals, Irfan takes advantage of the dying embers to "smoke" chai. He puts a pot with everything already in it—water, milk, tea, sugar, cardamom—over the smoking coals and closes the lid of the grill. The chai cooks as you enjoy your dinner, and the smoke adds a rich layer of flavor to it.

Abu hates the habit Irfan and I have developed of drinking chai from monstrous mugs, though that is how much chai my body demands every day. He prefers the beauty and delicacy of chai in a proper teacup with a fine, curved handle, served on a saucer. He insists the chai tastes better that way, but my guess is the experience itself makes the chai feel more special. And certainly, if anyone deserves that, it's Abu.

HERE'S HOW I MAKE CHAI (MAKES TWO LARGE MUGS):
2 full teaspoons loose-leaf orange pekoe black tea, or 4 tea bags
2 cups water
2 cups whole milk
4 green cardamom pods

I only buy my tea from Pakistani or Indian grocers, because nothing in a general supermarket tastes as rich and flavorful as teas imported from back home, though Tetley comes close. My favorite brand is called Vital Tea, but Tea India and Tapal Danedar are also pretty damn good.

Combine the water, milk, and cardamom and bring to a boil. Reduce heat to a low simmer, add sugar and tea and any other flavorings you're in the mood for (ginger, clove, cinnamon), and let simmer for 10 to 15 minutes.

Strain and serve piping hot, preferably Abu's way, in lovely teacups with delicate saucers.

ACKNOWLEDGMENTS

This is a story I've long avoided telling. Years ago a friend asked if I would write about my weight issues for her online magazine, and I outright refused. I couldn't bring myself to bare my soul like that. I was neck deep in the struggle and the self-loathing that so many of us on this journey feel. I knew it would hurt too much to write about it, and I couldn't imagine opening myself up to ridicule and attacks, for not being in control of my weight and also for not being content as an overweight woman. I don't know if I feared the "you fat slob" attacks or the "why don't you love yourself as you are" shaming more. But all these years later, and after many conversations with friends and my amazing agent, I realized I wasn't worried anymore. I knew pretty firmly what my journey had taught me, and where I stood.

For that, I begin by thanking my agent, Lauren Abramo, who virtually held my hand through Covid and self-doubt to convince me this story was worth telling and that I wasn't alone in my experience. Lauren first reached out to me seven years ago after reading my blog and asked, "Hey, have you ever thought about writing a book?" Thank you, Lauren, for that email; it changed my life. And for your kindness and patience through all my ups and downs, and for entertaining every crazy idea I have in the middle of the night for future book projects.

I want to thank Amy Gash, the editor of this book, for her keen and discerning eye, and for always meeting me where my sentiments and emotions are. Amy, I appreciate so much your gentility and graciousness throughout the process of bringing this book to life. Thank you for believing in me and in the value of my story.

Then there's my family. Why would I thank the people who focused on my weight and body most of my life? Because I know they did it out of love, out of concern for how the world would treat me, wanting to protect me from judgment, knowing others wouldn't see any part of me but my size. There is an Islamic belief that God rewards actions by their intentions, which is a good thing because actions themselves don't always give us the results we hope for. That's the grace with which I think about my family's many attempts at getting me to lose weight. Their intention was fueled by love, even though their attempts often ended up landing badly.

Thank you, Ami and Abu, for wanting the best for me, for incentivizing me in every way you could think of to lose a few pounds, and throughout it all, still demanding that I feast along with everyone else lest I starve. You loved me through food because you loved food yourself, and I cherish the hundreds of memories I have tied to the food we discovered and shared together. Thank you for doing all you did for me and my siblings. For leaving behind everything you knew to start a new life for our sake. For working multiple jobs to keep a roof over our heads and food—delicious, abundant food—on the table. Ami, all the determination I have for anything I do comes from you. You taught me not to fear and not to cower, ever. Abu, your support and love has been the foundational rock of my life. There has never been a time that I couldn't turn to you and in return receive your gentle guidance and support. You are the best father a girl could ever ask for.

Thank you, Zuby Aunty, for always sharing your cooking secrets, for feeding and feeding and feeding us (and everyone) every opportunity you get, for loving me and my siblings as your own children.

Every woman in my life who has taught me to cook and fed me—my sister Lilly, my mother-in-law, my friends—thank you for nourishing me through your hands and always making me feel like I deserve goodness and abundance.

The support and companionship of friends is what has sustained me for decades in my struggle with weight and self-worth. Irfana, Rana, thank you for sharing years of fat-related moans and groans together, for spending countless nights commiserating with me, for starting and stopping too many weight-loss schemes with me to count, and for always being down for saying "screw it" and going out for a splendid meal instead.

To my childhood friends, Shubnum, Anu, Veena, and Upeksha, thank you for always being there to lift me up when I'm at my lowest, for being the voices that have always told me not to believe what others say about me. You are the friends who, my entire life, made me feel worthy of acceptance and friendship, who saw me for me, who literally grew up with me and stood by me through it all. I don't have sufficient words to express how much I truly love you.

Finally, to my husband and children. You've put up with me in my most insufferable moments, when my own misery spilled out and over you, and as I've worked through unraveling and rebuilding myself. Sana, you are the very first light of my life, the hope and love that got me through the hardest years, my quiet little best friend on the nights that I wept, and there is no measure of how proud I am of you; of the young woman, beautiful inside and out, loving and kind, you have turned out to be. Haneefah, you are my spitfire, you with the energy of a thousand stars, with such steely determination and discipline that I am left in awe. Yaseen, my surprise little man, my Babyman, who loves with such fierceness and tenderness at the same time, it leaves me in a puddle. Thank you for making me a boy-mom, for giving me the gift I didn't know I needed. I see my sweet Abu in your chubby cheeks, your blocky head, your Bollywood hair, your sparkling dark eyes, and I know you are God's gentle elbow-to-the-ribs for always being a daddy's girl.

To Irfan, my big beefy husband who has never gone more than a few days without telling me I'm beautiful, regardless of the number on the scale, you are the best foodie and fatty life partner I could ask for. Our shared love of feasting brings me immense joy, and our shared lifelong struggle with weight will always unite us. Thank you for sticking with it through the hard times, and for the love you shower me with every single day.